DAILY LIFE SERIES NO. 6

DAILY LIFE IN FRANCE

JEAN ROBIQUET

DAILY LIFE
IN FRANCE

Under Napoleon

TRANSLATED FROM THE FRENCH BY
VIOLET M. MACDONALD

THE MACMILLAN COMPANY

NEW YORK

1963

FIRST AMERICAN EDITION

*This translation © George Allen & Unwin Ltd
1962*

Translated from
LA VIE QUOTIDIENNE AU TEMPS
DE NAPOLEON
© Librairie Hachette, Paris, 1942

PRINTED IN GREAT BRITAIN
in 11 on 12 point Caledonia type
BY THE PITMAN PRESS
BATH

FOREWORD

THOSE epochs most crowded with history are not always the best understood: much of their intimate life is lost to us. During the almost uninterrupted wars of the Consulate and the Empire the great events obscure the little ones; the soldier outshines the civilian as the epic does the chronicle of manners.

What do we find most often in the memoirs of the time? Political anecdotes or purely military recollections. We are taken at a gallop to the four corners of Europe, but with things of so much greater moment to be shown to us, we are not given a glimpse of what is going on in the houses of the Rue Saint-Denis, under the red umbrellas of the Halles or the elms of the Mall in the provinces.

Tiny matters these, no doubt, compared with the immense game being played elsewhere, but details worthy of attention none the less, since everything in history is interconnected, the infinitely small with the infinitely great, the former complementing the latter, reducing it to our scale, making it seem less improbable and more human.

Even at a time when the fate of armies outweighed all other considerations, it is not a matter of indifference to know how the misfits of fame, the *Incroyables* of Carle Vernet or the placid bourgeois of Boilly, spent their days and nights, to learn how they dressed, gossiped, amused themselves, tied their cravats and wove their intrigues, enjoyed their ices at Frascati and the novels of Mme Cottin, made fortunes at the Bourse or ruined themselves at *biribi*. It is instructive to follow the housewife to market, glance at the artisan at his bench and the merchant in his counting-house, to view, in a word, the spectacle of a new society springing from the ruins of the old one, order replacing anarchy, towns recovering their quietude, the countryside its natural wealth and the churches the voices of their belfries.

Defined in these terms, the chronicle of everyday life is far removed from the historical indiscretion concerned only with the person of Napoleon and a minute account of the way in which he spent his time. In the case of such an exceptional man everything is food for reportage – his habits, his mannerisms, the ceremonial of his toilet, the menu of his meals, the intimate side of his conjugal life and the brief *intermezzi* of his amorous adventures. Our curiosity may be tickled by investigations of this sort, but we have a right to enlarge its sphere and explore a less official world.

We are therefore proposing to seek the acquaintance of a modest character, to be met with by the thousand – the average Frenchman. Parisian or provincial, strolling on the boulevard or looking out, morning after morning, for the arrival of the stagecoach in some distant sub-prefecture, there is nothing exceptional about him. But this is precisely his chief merit: because he lives in the same way as everybody else, we have only to observe him to know how everybody lives.

In his person the spectacular drama of the First Empire inevitably loses much of its splendour, and in such an epoch a painting of the modest pleasures, the humble cares, the trivial daily happenings forming the woof of everybody's life, will look like a conversation piece hung by mistake in the Galerie des Batailles at Versailles. But after all, where is the harm? Can one be sure that minor and major history have distinct frontiers between them? Even in the study of current manners many a detail will come to light that concerns them both.

Of course any mention of the Napoleonic era brings to mind first of all the prodigious military adventure that lasted fifteen years. But behind the armies of the Empire lay the country from which they drew their sustenance, and the physical and moral condition of those thirty-seven million Frenchmen who were made to pay so dearly for the *Te Deums* at Notre-Dame and the salvos of the Invalides is worth some attention.

It is all the more worth it because from the beginning of the Consulate the evolution of taste, ideas and customs appears closely linked with the development and the fortunes of the regime. Domestic comfort, public safety, gaiety of the street, luxury of the drawing-room, all these issued from the hands of the Master, everything appeared to have been prepared, thought out and directed by him.

Every bulletin of the *Grande Armée* elicited a response from the rate of exchange. The price of glory regulated the price of bread. And on the walls of domestic life the shadow of the little cocked hat seemed to fall throughout the reign.

Such is the purpose, then, of the following pages. Unfolding in the midst of famous events, the everyday life of France, from 1800 to 1815, bore their imprint at every turn. To evoke it is to illustrate by domestic pictures the most astonishing chapter of our history.

J. R.

CONTENTS

CONTENTS

ILLUSTRATIONS

CHAPTER I

THE HERITAGE OF THE REVOLUTION

*The last months of the Directory – Distress of the State and
of individuals – Poverty and usury in Paris – The provinces –
The countryside – Epidemic of brigandage – Bankruptcy of
liberty*

THE last months of the Directory were a sad epilogue
to the Revolution. Just as some women do not know
how to grow old, some centuries have not the good
fortune to die a beautiful death. This was the case with the
eighteenth, which, after enjoying the last rays of the reign of
Louis XIV, then the age of *douceur de vivre*, and then the
dawn of liberty, was preparing to finish up in the mud, along
with Barras.

Maledictions on the Government of the Luxembourg
echoed from every quarter – from the armies claiming their
pay, from the towns crying famine, from the countryside
infested with brigands. An endless civil war was spreading
from province to province, like a badly extinguished fire
creeping among dry grass.

To describe the general state of public feeling on the eve
of the 18th Brumaire, Albert Vandal coined this aphorism:
'France, which was no longer revolutionary, was still revolu-
tionized.' Nothing could more aptly express the reigning disorder of daily life. We are very far from the comic-opera Directory, popularized later on by the theatre and by the works of
the engravers, and suggested to the fancy by the fol-de-rols of
Madame Angot. It is true that Paris, in the year VIII, was still
full of low dancing-halls and public ballrooms, and of pleasure
gardens where dandies came to ogle fair ladies in the semi-
nude; it was full, too, of restaurants where the *nouveaux-
riches* could gorge themselves, and of gambling-houses where
the Queen of Spades lightened their purses; but this was only
a little world apart, the domain of a handful of rakes dividing
their leisure between the avenues of Frascati and the arcades
of the Palais Égalité.

To the other classes, that is to say to the immense majority of Frenchmen, life wore less attractive colours. For some time now money had been so scarce, and prices had risen so fast, that many householders were hard put to it to boil the pot. Nobody could feel sure of the morrow, and as the instinct of self-preservation never loses its rights, many patriots, grown wiser, were beginning to take less interest in politics than in two questions of a more personal character: the leanness of their purse and the emptiness of their larder.

Imagine these small stockholders, ruined already by the official robbery of 1797, the *Tiers consolidé*, threatened by a fresh tax more severe even than the earlier ones, the Forced Loan. How could they stand up to it, receiving their income as they now did, only in the form of dividend bonds, that is to say in worthless paper? Shopkeepers were suffering in the same way; many of them, having no goods to sell, were shooting the moon, and so were most industrialists, who had been forced to disband their workers. In 1791 Paris still had seven thousand factory hands, in 1799 there remained only seventeen hundred. For a city of that size such a figure is astounding.

Even the civil servant class and the state pensioners were not spared this disaster, for in the last few months the Exchequer had suffered strange blanks of memory.

Even in the highest official circles people were beginning to feel worried on the subject, especially at the Institute, whose president, Creuzé-Latouche, had just drawn up a report informing the Government of the cruel difficulties in which several of his colleagues, deprived of their 'salary' – or as we should say today, 'attendance tokens' – were going to find themselves involved. And the perturbation of the Immortals was shared by far humbler mortals: government quill-drivers wondering when they would get their pay, civil service assistants waiting in vain for their monthly wages, all sorts of humble workers necessary to the life of others, but with a right to earn their own – registry-office hacks, Customs personnel, lamplighters, firemen, policemen. . . . Yes, even the pay of the police was being held over! Was this not a sure sign of the times? When a government neglects to feed the flower of its personnel, it can be reproached with want of

Although since Fructidor election had been done away with as regards a certain number of posts, most public offices were still obtained by means of local suffrage. Nothing could be more natural in the case of the municipal body itself. But to employ the same procedure in the appointment of all those wielding a tittle of public authority, from the commanding officer of the national guard to the assessor of taxes, was obviously more dangerous, and it is easy to imagine the result.

Any citizen provided with a post is bound to serve those that appoint him. The Justice of the Peace will favour the plaintiff that canvassed for him, the revenue official will lighten the contributions due from the ground landlord whose vote he obtained; politics, in short, will be reduced to an exchange of services between elector and elect, and an exchange of countersigns between elect and elector. This, after all, is the eternal rule, the rule which, a century later, was to find expression in this heartfelt cry of one of our great men, 'Remember your constituencies!' The municipal officers of the year VIII had begun to think of theirs, and France was none the healthier for it.

Behaviour of this kind did not tend to increase the prestige of the communal Bench; the honest residue, towards the end of the Directory, shunned it more and more. In many regions candidates went on strike, and if they were appointed without having been notified, they hastened to resign. This was what happened, for instance, in 1797, in the pleasant town of Laval, where we learn from an official report that of eight municipal officers nominated by the electors only one accepted. 'Moreover,' complains the author of the note, 'he was the least capable of the lot!'

The least capable was perhaps also the least honest, for everybody knows that appointments of this sort are only theoretically unpaid, and often bring those who know how to make use of them quite substantial advantages.

Bonaparte was soon to give a striking description of this game of grab developing in the country. In a note dictated to his brother Lucien he showed the 36,000 *communes* of France pillaged for the last six years by their municipal wardens. 'In changing their mayors, deputy mayors and

heart; but when it no longer pays its police it can be said to be ruined.

Poverty of the State, poverty of the individual – such was the double bankruptcy marking this turning-point of history. The first was a godsend to the gang of army contractors and high financiers, the second to the rabble of usurers lending money at every street corner, at two and a half or three per cent *per month*. Everybody needed them, but everybody hated them, and their origin had not a little to do with this. No matter whether they came from Frankfort or Lombardy, they were always found to have an air of resemblance to a certain Shylock of unblessed memory. . . . For the first time a wave of anti-semitism, worthy of note, swept through the French press.

'Ever since the Revolution,' wrote a journalist of the year VIII, 'the Frenchman has been daily obliged to deal with a Jew for his business or his domestic affairs, without a chance of discovering that he is dealing, not with a man but an enemy, whose sense of honour is invariably *circumscribed* within the circle of his religious community.'

A rather mediocre pun, the author of which had at least the excuse of having made it involuntarily.

*   *   *   *

After a revolution, the wounds suffered by the towns are always somewhat slow to heal, far more so than those of the country, where Nature at once sets to work to repair the follies of man. At the end of the Directory one has only to turn to one or other of our large provincial centres to see the consequences of the late troubles: life asleep everywhere, or at best re-awakening in hesitant fashion.

Export trade having come to an end, Brittany was no longer manufacturing linen, nor the Languedoc its textiles, nor Thiers its cutlery, nor Valenciennes its lace. Of the 15,000 workshops formerly busy in Lyons, 13,000 had closed down. Business was so bad in Havre that tradesmen no longer bothered to open their shops. With no oil for its street lamps, Bordeaux spent the night in darkness. There were no more carriages in Marseilles, where the streets had turned to quagmires for want of repair. As for its glorious harbour, the less said the better: it was now a mere cemetery of ships.

Rural France presented a less depressing picture. There, except for the regions directly affected by the war, prosperity seemed on the point of recovery. Not everybody was of that opinion, it is true; certain writers of the time even exaggerated the desolation of the countryside, but their evidence is suspect. When Chateaubriand, returning from emigration early in 1800, tells us that all along the road from Calais to Paris he saw nothing but felled woodlands, demolished villages, and women with 'faces tanned and hardened, barefoot, heads bare or wrapped in a handkerchief, tilling the fields', when he keeps pointing out 'mud and dust, dung and ruins', he is speaking as an exile who for the last seven years had been piling pessimism on pessimism. And when the first English tourists crossed the Channel a little later, and John Dean Paul or Redhead Yorke, driving along our roads, tells us that all he could see was sparsely populated land and poor harvests[1]; when they declare that 'nothing can exceed the wretched condition of the farming implements except that of the livestock and of the labourers in charge of it'[2] we are not bound to believe them. These so-called witnesses must have looked at France with English eyes, as Chateaubriand did with the eyes of an *émigré*.

Far more reliable is the information furnished by some of the great landed proprietors in direct contact with the countryside. Even if they had suffered personally from the Revolution, they could not help recognizing that the condition of the peasants had been improved by it. 'They are richer', wrote La Fayette of the people of the Limagne, 'the fields are better cultivated, the women better dressed. Estates fetch a third more in the market, and sometimes twice as much as before the Revolution.'

Life was easier, too, for the communities around Blois, according to Dufort de Cheverny, whose veracity is not to be doubted. 'Day-labourers get wine for three sols, bread for two, and their daily wage amounts to thirty or forty, the inevitable result being that the taverns are much frequented,

[1] Sir John Dean Paul, *Diary of a Journey to Paris in 1802*.
[2] Henry Redhead Yorke, *Paris and France under the Consulate*.

and the people themselves dictate the conditions of their work.'

But another inevitable result was that they produced a great many children, for 'conscription having spared married people, all the young men got married from the age of sixteen upwards, and the number of births, in all the *communes*, is double or treble what it used to be.'

The great changes just brought about should really have completely ensured the independence and welfare of the peasants. They had been freed from most of the burdens that had weighed them down for centuries, and the liquidation of feudal domains and property in mortmain allowed them to acquire, under excellent conditions, lands they had so far cultivated for the benefit of others. But there was another side to the medal. Hardly had the countryside had time to feel emancipated when it underwent a strange crisis, a sort of disease manifesting itself in innumerable ways: a reawakening of old hatreds between proscribers and proscribed, executioners and victims of yesterday, robbers and robbed of today, quarrels between house and house, persistence of religious struggles, danger in travelling the roads, in inhabiting an isolated farm, in possessing the goods of an *émigré*, and still more those of the Church, lack of security for everybody. So many signs of the heavy mortgage encumbering the heritage of the Revolution.

The average Frenchman was beginning to be aware of it. In his efforts to repair the old clock of the Monarchy, which was grievously slow, but had contrived for centuries to show more or less the right time, he had broken its mainspring, so that now nothing functioned any more, neither the Government, nor justice, nor finance. There was a sort of masked anarchy paralysing work, poisoning social relations, sowing fear and discouragement. People still talked of liberty, and many honest souls were still proud of having attained to it complete with Phrygian cap and symbolic attributes – but they were sorry to have lost it in a more modest form, when it meant simply liberty to live in peace.

At the bottom of all this disorder, in almost every *commune*, is to be found the less than mediocre standard of the local authorities and the method of their recruitment heart; but when it no longer pays its police it can be said to be ruined.

Poverty of the State, poverty of the individual – such was the double bankruptcy marking this turning-point of history. The first was a godsend to the gang of army contractors and high financiers, the second to the rabble of usurers lending money at every street corner, at two and a half or three per cent *per month*. Everybody needed them, but everybody hated them, and their origin had not a little to do with this. No matter whether they came from Frankfort or Lombardy, they were always found to have an air of resemblance to a certain Shylock of unblessed memory. . . . For the first time a wave of anti-semitism, worthy of note, swept through the French press.

'Ever since the Revolution,' wrote a journalist of the year VIII, 'the Frenchman has been daily obliged to deal with a Jew for his business or his domestic affairs, without a chance of discovering that he is dealing, not with a man but an enemy, whose sense of honour is invariably *circumscribed* within the circle of his religious community.'

A rather mediocre pun, the author of which had at least the excuse of having made it involuntarily.

* * * *

After a revolution, the wounds suffered by the towns are always somewhat slow to heal, far more so than those of the country, where Nature at once sets to work to repair the follies of man. At the end of the Directory one has only to turn to one or other of our large provincial centres to see the consequences of the late troubles: life asleep everywhere, or at best re-awakening in hesitant fashion.

Export trade having come to an end, Brittany was no longer manufacturing linen, nor the Languedoc its textiles, nor Thiers its cutlery, nor Valenciennes its lace. Of the 15,000 workshops formerly busy in Lyons, 13,000 had closed down. Business was so bad in Havre that tradesmen no longer bothered to open their shops. With no oil for its street lamps, Bordeaux spent the night in darkness. There were no more carriages in Marseilles, where the streets had turned to quagmires for want of repair. As for its glorious harbour, the less said the better: it was now a mere cemetery of ships.

Rural France presented a less depressing picture. There, except for the regions directly affected by the war, prosperity seemed on the point of recovery. Not everybody was of that opinion, it is true; certain writers of the time even exaggerated the desolation of the countryside, but their evidence is suspect. When Chateaubriand, returning from emigration early in 1800, tells us that all along the road from Calais to Paris he saw nothing but felled woodlands, demolished villages, and women with 'faces tanned and hardened, barefoot, heads bare or wrapped in a handkerchief, tilling the fields', when he keeps pointing out 'mud and dust, dung and ruins', he is speaking as an exile who for the last seven years had been piling pessimism on pessimism. And when the first English tourists crossed the Channel a little later, and John Dean Paul or Redhead Yorke, driving along our roads, tells us that all he could see was sparsely populated land and poor harvests[1]; when they declare that 'nothing can exceed the wretched condition of the farming implements except that of the livestock and of the labourers in charge of it'[2] we are not bound to believe them. These so-called witnesses must have looked at France with English eyes, as Chateaubriand did with the eyes of an *émigré*.

Far more reliable is the information furnished by some of the great landed proprietors in direct contact with the countryside. Even if they had suffered personally from the Revolution, they could not help recognizing that the condition of the peasants had been improved by it. 'They are richer', wrote La Fayette of the people of the Limagne, 'the fields are better cultivated, the women better dressed. Estates fetch a third more in the market, and sometimes twice as much as before the Revolution.'

Life was easier, too, for the communities around Blois, according to Dufort de Cheverny, whose veracity is not to be doubted. 'Day-labourers get wine for three sols, bread for two, and their daily wage amounts to thirty or forty, the inevitable result being that the taverns are much frequented,

[1] Sir John Dean Paul, *Diary of a Journey to Paris in 1802.*
[2] Henry Redhead Yorke, *Paris and France under the Consulate.*

and the people themselves dictate the conditions of their work.'

But another inevitable result was that they produced a great many children, for 'conscription having spared married people, all the young men got married from the age of sixteen upwards, and the number of births, in all the *communes*, is double or treble what it used to be.'

The great changes just brought about should really have completely ensured the independence and welfare of the peasants. They had been freed from most of the burdens that had weighed them down for centuries, and the liquidation of feudal domains and property in mortmain allowed them to acquire, under excellent conditions, lands they had so far cultivated for the benefit of others. But there was another side to the medal. Hardly had the countryside had time to feel emancipated when it underwent a strange crisis, a sort of disease manifesting itself in innumerable ways: a re-awakening of old hatreds between proscribers and proscribed, executioners and victims of yesterday, robbers and robbed of today, quarrels between house and house, persistence of religious struggles, danger in travelling the roads, in inhabiting an isolated farm, in possessing the goods of an *émigré*, and still more those of the Church, lack of security for everybody. So many signs of the heavy mortgage encumbering the heritage of the Revolution.

The average Frenchman was beginning to be aware of it. In his efforts to repair the old clock of the Monarchy, which was grievously slow, but had contrived for centuries to show more or less the right time, he had broken its mainspring, so that now nothing functioned any more, neither the Government, nor justice, nor finance. There was a sort of masked anarchy paralysing work, poisoning social relations, sowing fear and discouragement. People still talked of liberty, and many honest souls were still proud of having attained to it, complete with Phrygian cap and symbolic attributes – but they were sorry to have lost it in a more modest form, when it meant simply liberty to live in peace.

At the bottom of all this disorder, in almost every *commune*, is to be found the less than mediocre standard of the local authorities and the method of their recruitment.

B

Although since Fructidor election had been done away with as regards a certain number of posts, most public offices were still obtained by means of local suffrage. Nothing could be more natural in the case of the municipal body itself. But to employ the same procedure in the appointment of all those wielding a tittle of public authority, from the commanding officer of the national guard to the assessor of taxes, was obviously more dangerous, and it is easy to imagine the result.

Any citizen provided with a post is bound to serve those that appoint him. The Justice of the Peace will favour the plaintiff that canvassed for him, the revenue official will lighten the contributions due from the ground landlord whose vote he obtained; politics, in short, will be reduced to an exchange of services between elector and elect, and an exchange of countersigns between elect and elector. This, after all, is the eternal rule, the rule which, a century later, was to find expression in this heartfelt cry of one of our great men, 'Remember your constituencies!' The municipal officers of the year VIII had begun to think of theirs, and France was none the healthier for it.

Behaviour of this kind did not tend to increase the prestige of the communal Bench; the honest residue, towards the end of the Directory, shunned it more and more. In many regions candidates went on strike, and if they were appointed without having been notified, they hastened to resign. This was what happened, for instance, in 1797, in the pleasant town of Laval, where we learn from an official report that of eight municipal officers nominated by the electors only one accepted. 'Moreover,' complains the author of the note, 'he was the least capable of the lot!'

The least capable was perhaps also the least honest, for everybody knows that appointments of this sort are only theoretically unpaid, and often bring those who know how to make use of them quite substantial advantages.

Bonaparte was soon to give a striking description of this game of grab developing in the country. In a note dictated to his brother Lucien he showed the 36,000 *communes* of France pillaged for the last six years by their municipal wardens. 'In changing their mayors, deputy mayors and councillors', he said, 'they have mostly merely changed the method of brigandage; they have robbed the parish road, they have robbed the footpaths, they have robbed the trees, they have robbed the Church, they have robbed the chattels of the *commune*, and they are still robbing under the lax municipal regime of the year VIII.'

❋   ❋   ❋   ❋

The more we consider this epoch, the more we see what a number of great and little plagues were tormenting the French. There were not only the collective misfortunes attacking a whole class of the nation, the reprisals inflicted on 140,000 *émigrés* guilty of having crossed the frontier, or on other thousands of nobles guilty of having remained at home, and seized upon as scapegoats;[1] there were the dangers lying in wait for the ordinary individual, citizen or countryman, who took no part in politics, did nobody any harm, and was trying only to live in peace and avoid trouble, apparently without success.

He awoke every morning with a more or less heavy sword of Damocles hanging over his bed. Hadn't he paid his taxes? He saw the bailiff's man arriving and settling himself in the house, robbing his hen-roost, drinking his wine, stripping him of all he possessed by way of stimulating his zeal. Did he need to go to market in the neighbouring town? The roads had become so bad that it was ten to one he would be upset, the remaining chance being that he would have to leave the cart stuck in a rut. Was he thinking of starting on a longer journey? Beware of risks in the *diligence*! Even if it was escorted by a military picket, this precaution might not always prevent attack. At the first turning the coach might be held up by bandits wearing masks or with faces blackened with soot, pointing pistols at the occupants and extracting from their pockets what the *Gueux* of the Nord, the *Barbets* of the Cévennes and the *Chauffeurs* of the Midi called in all honesty the King's share.

And the adventure wore still darker colours when these

---

[1] The 'Law of Hostages' sanctioned the imprisonment of the relations of *émigrés*, and of all ci-devant nobles in general. Their heads must answer for any crimes committed against the Republic.

gentlemen came to carry out operations in the victim's house, as they had formed the habit of doing ever since the country had become transformed into an immense Forêt de Bondy.[1] The scum of every party – deserting soldiers, aristocrats driven to extremes by fury and poverty, non-juring priests saying mass in the open fields, with two pistols in their belts and a musket laid across the altar,[2] all these pinchbeck ruffians parading as genuine bandits were sowing real terror in every part of the country. In the Var and in the Rousillon, on the Central Plateau and in Normandy, even in the Île de France itself, almost at the gates of the capital, they were engaged in ransacking the public coffers, intercepting couriers, murdering those unfortunates whose opinions displeased them, forcing their way into the homes of the purchasers of national property, holding them to ransom, and if the victims refused to say where their money was hidden, roasting their feet before the fire until a perfect understanding had been reached between roasters and roasted.

Was it worth while having made the Revolution to arrive at this state of affairs? With the behaviour of savages prevailing, what was left of the Rights of Man and the fine promises of yesterday? One of the last *commissaires* sent by the Directory to carry the Good Word to the provinces towards the end of the year VII had drawn attention, even then, to the general disillusionment. 'There is no disguising the fact', he wrote, 'that the French people today are a long way from the noble enthusiasm for their liberty and independence that helped them at the outset to accomplish so many miracles.'

This amounted to an acknowledgement of the regime's bankruptcy. Dragging on for years, it resembled those religions whose temples are still standing, but whose cult has been reduced to purely external manifestations. The republican ideal still held sway by virtue of its rather puerile formalism, by the more or less severe rules to which it submitted the life of the period – special regalia, periodic festivals, an

---

[1] A notorious haunt of robbers in the department of the Seine. [Translator.]

[2] On the 7th Prairial, year VIII, the prefect of the Gard announced the arrest of one of the fiercest chiefs of the brigands of the Midi, a former prior, nicknamed 'Sans-Peur', who officiated surrounded by a veritable arsenal.

individual language, singular fashions – but if it still lingered in people's minds it no longer dwelt in their hearts.

To outward view nothing had changed. Beautiful vignettes and grandiloquent mottoes still headed official documents, there were still trees of liberty in the middle of the squares, men garbed in Roman togas on the benches of the Five Hundred. To avoid suspicion, one still had to address a man as *Citoyen*, not *Monsieur*, knock off work every tenth day unless it fell on a Sunday, and allow one's doorkeeper to address one with 'thee' and 'thou'.

But if the heritage of the Revolution was reduced to these advantages, could people be reproached for thinking them a trifle meagre? Some went further: they began to regret their old habits, the old calendar with its festivals and popular saints, the old money, less mendacious than the abominable *assignat*, permission to talk in the old way, to rest once a week, and to be called by other names than Lycurgus or Epaminondas.

To these disillusioned souls the conquests of the new era appeared somewhat negative; to a great many citizens they had merely brought a supplementary servitude. But no one dared to say this aloud, because of all confessions the hardest for a nation to make is that of having been 'duped by its principles'. The majority of Frenchmen went on proclaiming themselves, and even believing themselves to be, republicans, thanks to which the Directory still existed. But its days were numbered, none the less, and an accident was to prove enough to shorten its death rattle.

Bonaparte has been reproached with having murdered liberty. The historians of the nineteenth century and the romantic poets united in cursing the smooth-haired Corsican. Far be it from us to plead Not Guilty. All the same we must not overlook the fact that the damsel tanned by the sun of Messidor was already in very bad condition on the eve of the 18th Brumaire. Mathieu Dumas, a man who had served the Republic by bringing Louis XVI back to Varennes, hit on this ingenious argument to justify the *coup d'état*: 'Bonaparte was not attacking liberty, for it no longer existed.'

CHAPTER II

RETURN TO OLD HABITS

Tumult at the theatre – The day after the coup d'état *– Old friends reappear – New Year's Day, the Carnival – The new 'Messieurs' – Conversion of a musician*

O N THE evening of the 19th Brumaire, year VIII, there was a crowded audience at the Théâtre Feydeau. In spite of the strange rumours afloat since the day before, and the movements of troops to be seen that very morning on the boulevards, politics had not prevented the devotees of comic opera from coming to see a new play, *L'Auteur dans son ménage*.

It was progressing very peaceably when suddenly the actors stopped. The one playing the principal part, that of the author himself in his home, advanced to the footlights without so much as throwing off his dressing-gown or his nightcap, and shouted in a loud voice:

'Citizens! General Bonaparte has escaped being assassinated at Saint-Cloud by traitors to the country!'

It is easy to imagine the panic that seized the audience. Amid the tumult one scream overpowered the others, coming from Box No. Two with its gilded grating, where Pauline Bonaparte was having a fit of hysterics. Beside her, Madame Laetitia, equally horrified but more mistress of herself, leaned for support on Mme Permon and her daughter, the future Duchesse d'Abrantès. These ladies had dined together; they knew, of course, that there was thunder in the air, but they were so little alarmed that they had come to end their evening at the theatre. And now chance, in its brusque fashion, had acquainted them with the *coup d'état*.

Fortunately the announcement was merely a fanciful communiqué issued by order of Fouché for the purpose of exciting public opinion. At the moment when the *canard* took wing, Bonaparte had already secured his victory, and if the Feydeau audience had been able to transport itself to Saint-Cloud it would have witnessed, not a drama but a far more

comical scene than in any opera of that description – the
hair-raising nocturnal sitting thought up by Lucien and his
brother in the attempt to 'legalize' the somewhat brutal
operation of that afternoon.

The picture is worthy of Roman history. Some dozens of
deputies, recruited as best they could be in the avenues of the
park and the suburban restaurants – the same who, only two
hours before, had escaped from the Orangery by jumping out
of a window – now re-entered it docilely by the door, resumed
their seats by candle-light and signed without demur the
death certificate of the Directory. Still hardly recovered from
their fright, they voted for everything they were asked to:
the appointment of the Consuls, the adjournment of the
Assembly. . . . They carried the pardoning of insults so far as
to decree that the soldiers, 'and especially the Grenadiers',
had deserved well of their country, and listened without a
smile to their president Lucien singing the praises of this
memorable day: 'Citizens, Liberty, born in the Tennis Court
at Versailles, had dragged itself towards you, a prey by turns
to inconsequence, weakness, the convulsive ailments of childhood. Today it has donned its *toga virilis*.'

Finely said, indeed . . . and as it was growing late and
everybody was dead sleepy, victors and vanquished took
leave of one another, shouting 'Vive la République!'

❋ ❋ ❋ ❋

We may pass over the political side of this conjuring trick,
which was to remain the model of its kind, and take note only
of the climatic change it produced in France at the time. We
must beware of imagining that life changed suddenly merely
because new men had settled into the Luxembourg. Brumaire
had been well received by the capital, but without excessive
rejoicing. The rebirth of confidence was marked only by
certain symptoms: the bankers found a little money with
which to set public finances going again;[1] the rate of exchange
was doubled in a week and, incredible phenomenon, *louis*,
real *louis d'or*, began to chink again at the bottom of certain
pockets.

[1] The day after Brumaire Gaudin, Minister of Finance, had nothing left in
the Treasury but the miserable sum of 77,000 frs., the entire fortune of France.

Other no less favourable signs were noted by the press. In the *Gazette de France* of 1st Frimaire, for instance, exactly twelve days after the *coup d'état*, there appeared the following paragraph: 'Landed properties in the neighbourhood of Paris, which had so far failed to find either buyers or lenders, are now finding both ... dismantled apartments are being refurnished, carriages are coming out of the livery stables. ... And yet there is not an écu more than before; none has come from abroad by *diligence*, no Potosi mine has been discovered in France since the 18th Brumaire.'

But this was something of a flash in the pan. After the surgical operation it had just undergone – an operation in which the sword had taken the place of the surgeon's knife – the country continued to be a patient so seriously ill that its convalescence would call for all sorts of precautions. So many events could not have been brought about in the last ten years without upsetting a number of things to which the mass of Frenchmen clung. In this matter as in others, Bonaparte intended to make reparation. But whereas he had gone straight to the mark in politics, he preferred to temporize in the realm of manners.

Although he still proclaimed his fidelity to the Revolution, he was not blind to the fact that by making a clean sweep of the past it had singularly complicated the present. Certain customs it had suppressed by a stroke of the pen were worth re-establishing. But it was better to do nothing in a hurry. Let the public revert of its own accord to its old habits, and the Government would turn a blind eye, however much this might annoy the little Jacobin rags, the *Citoyen Français* and the rest.

The first thing to be restored to favour was that old friend of the old regime: New Year's Day. Treated as suspect by the Convention, vaguely tolerated by the Directory, it was handed back to the Parisians two and a half months after Brumaire. Imagine their joy at recovering the traditional hamper, to be filled with the traditional offerings at Berthelot's, the famous confectioner of the Palais-Royal! There, at number fifty-three in the Stone Gallery, the gapers swarmed in front of a shop window crowded with *marrons glacés*, pistachio nuts and mushrooms made of sugar, multicoloured

sugared almonds and, of course, bonbons *à la Bonaparte*. The
young lady assistants were thrilled by a visit of the Second
Consul of the Republic, the solemn, big-bellied Cambacérès.
They were astonished, too, at the number of carriages drawing up at the door of their shop. The same thing was happening in the Rue des Lombards, the headquarters of the other
confectioners. In front of one of their shops, according to a
police report, 137 carriages were counted in one day. From
which we may conclude that Paris, so long deprived of means
of transport, was by now rather better supplied.

This reappearance of coaches would permit many people
to get through the onerous duty calls and card-leaving without fatigue. The German tourist Reichardt was amused to see
seven or eight young gentlemen crowding into a single carriage with all sorts of provisions – bottles, pies and so forth –
'While a hired servant left the visiting-cards at the doors
of the patrons, masters and colleagues of these slaves of
etiquette, they themselves were gaily consuming their provisions in defiance of cold and boredom.' No better way of
digesting Berthelot's sweetmeats could be imagined.

New Year's Day having recovered its rights, other traditions thought to be forgotten were not long in following suit;
first and foremost the Carnival, another Lazarus recalled to
life from among the masks. But before putting such a turbu-
lent lad back into circulation the police were seized with mis-
givings. As the feast days of the year VIII drew near, Dubois,
the new Prefect of Police, began by issuing a total ban on
masks and masked balls. Thanks to God, and no doubt to the
First Consul, these severities were soon modified, and in the
end it was decided that five balls, four of them masked,
should take place at the Théâtre de la République, i.e. the
Opéra.

The first, which coincided with the old mid-Lent, attracted
an unbelievable crowd. As tickets only cost six francs, the
whole of the Faubourg Saint-Denis arranged to meet there,
which somewhat diminished the elegance of the attendance.
All the same, people were able to point out to one another
a number of celebrities in the boxes, whom they thought they
could recognize under their disguise. Here a pretty woman
very like Joséphine, there another who must be Mme

Récamier, allowing the Prince of Wurtemberg to snatch one
of her rings as a souvenir; further on an Oriental in a turban
with a strong likeness to Barras – a post-*coup d'état* Barras,
cut out for the role of 'Turk's head'.[1]

Another year of patience, and the Carnival would be
allowed to descend from the Opéra into the street, where it
would soon recover the wealth of its old attractions. Decorated carts, sumptuous or comic, would be seen proceeding
along the boulevards: the gods of Olympus surrounded by
cupids, the Three Estates of 1789 in caricature, or a little
later, the famous Doctor Gall astride a donkey, above a sea
of cardboard skulls.

By way of varying these processions and restoring that of
mid-Lent, there would be the Apotheosis of the Laundresses,
or the March of the Fatted Ox, the triumph of the butcher-
boys;[2] Paris would never lack invention. Carnivals would
succeed one another, each contributing some novelty, but all
ending with the same ceremony: the funeral, by candle-light,
of the god of the festival, a tragi-comic farce taken so seriously by the actors that one of them, after playing the part of
the defunct Carnival forty-five times, was to play it the forty-
sixth time on his own account, and leave one bier only to lie
down for good on another.[3]

The popular amusements which the feast days would bring
back to the streets of Paris usually had a gayer conclusion,
but at the sight of all these pirouetting Harlequins and
Pierrots, foreigners on a visit to the capital took it now and
then for 'the country of the mad'. The expression was that of
a Swiss lady, Mme Cazenove d'Arlen; and Reichardt, the
German already mentioned, had the same feeling when he
saw the street urchins of the Rue Saint-Honoré whirling a
life-size scullion at the end of a rope, or thirty pseudo-
Spaniards amusing themselves by tossing a lay figure in a
blanket up to the third story.

Our tourist was particularly struck by the traffic jam on the
main boulevards. Amid the crowd of onlookers and masked

[1] Scapegoat. [Translator.]
[2] This was not re-established until 1805.
[3] This was a certain Ricord, a bill-poster of the Rue de la Huchette, who,
after appearing in the Carnival in the classic ceremony of the funeral, was
found dead at his home next morning.

figures, the confusion of gigs, barouches and delivery vans, he was astounded to see diligences and even hearses. But lost in this crowd, with two women to look after, he was surprised to have suffered no insult or ill treatment. 'So long as you adopt the tone of good humour the French are accustomed to,' he says, 'you can always get on with the Parisian populace.'

* * * *

Twelve years earlier this same populace – no doubt because it had not been approached in that 'tone of good humour' – had made the Revolution. Now, without quite realizing it, it was in the act of unmaking it, putting, every day, a little more of the past into the present. While the old festivals had now come back into fashion, certain anniversaries dear to the Jacobins were no longer celebrated; neither the lugubrious 21st January, nor the 10th August, nor the 9th Thermidor, given up for opposite reasons: it was a reminder of the proscriptions, and people preferred to forget all that.

Another imposition people longed to be rid of was the *Décadi*. For the moment it was the only day of rest allowed by republican law, the only day marking officially the cessation of work, the idleness of government offices, the closing of shops. To plant a bed of lettuce or sell two sous worth of string on that day was to behave as a bad citizen, and those who chose a Sunday to go and drink new wine in the armours of Suresnes were committing a still more serious crime. The Décadi possessed, moreover, the monopoly of marriage ceremonies; one could only be married on that day – married for good that is.

Everybody knew by experience the hardships inflicted by these little tyrannies, and they remembered that the good old Sunday had the advantage of returning every week, fifty-two times a year, that is, instead of thirty-six. A gain of so many days for the workers in town and country, for the humble mass of the lower class, whose Sunday programme consisted of a twin delight: a shave and a white shirt.

It would have been pleasant to give them satisfaction, but the Government was afraid of forsaking revolutionary principles too soon. For this reason, during the first months of the

Consulate, the police registers still record a number of prose-
cutions against Paris shopkeepers who had not observed the
tenth as a rest day. It took seven months for the Council of
State to solve the difficulty by a decree. In future the official
day of rest would be obligatory only for civil servants, the rest
of the citizens would be free to fold their arms on Sunday.

The game now half won was soon to be wholly so. Finally
supplanted by its rival, the Décadi was not long in retiring
to sleep in the firmament of old moons. And from one end of
France to the other the refrain would be sung:

> *Nous supprimons le décadi,*
> *Avec sa kyrielle en i . . .*
> *Le dimanche l'on fêtera,*
> *Alléluia!*

One reform brings another in its train. Now that Sunday
had returned, the old calendar dividing the year into twelve
months had of necessity to be re-established. But the contest
threatened to be a fierce one, for there were two opposing
doctrines on the subject:

'The revolutionary calendar', said those in favour of it, 'has
reason and the metric system on its side.'

'Its predecessor', said those against, 'is based on the usage
of centuries and almost universal custom.'

'It has been the calendar of French history,' adds a correspondent of the *Journal des Débats*, 'it is therefore the one
best suited to an epoch such as ours. The man that has
restored to our country its happiness and its glory, its old
festivals and its old virtues, would like the people of all
countries to connect recognized dates with the victories, the
great feats of arms marking the course of a life so precious to
the French. . . . And I myself, Mr. Editor, would like the
Spanish and the Germans to know that I had the honour of
writing this letter to you on September 25, 1803.'

The author of this note was ahead of events, for the
Gregorian calendar, the 'dear old man', as people called it,
had not yet recovered its legal existence.[1]

It was used more and more, however, in everyday conver-

[1] It became official on January 1, 1806, for the New Year's Day of
Austerlitz.

sation. The Church employed it to announce its ceremonies, and the *Gazette de France* to advertise theatrical performances. It was beginning to reappear, too, in the almanacs. The old familiar saints it brought with it found themselves in the company of a rather unexpected colleague, mentioned by Julie Talma:

'The *National Almanac* sends our Parisians into fits of laughter,' she writes to her friend Benjamin Constant, 'they see that the poor devil Saint Roch has been struck out of the calendar and Saint Napoleon has been put in his place – a younger, happier, more amiable saint, no doubt, and more to be recommended. But the old saint's disgrace seems the funniest thing in the world. I didn't specially care for him, but I regret his dog. You know how I love them.'[1]

*   *   *   *

During the same period another, no less burning, question was to divide opinion: should the revolutionary formulas be preserved in the language, especially 'Citizen' as a mode of address.

This was a legacy of the Paris Commune, which in 1792 made the word obligatory. In theory it still was so, the measure never having been rescinded. But in the new century, with the change of regime, this mass distribution of citizenship was beginning to appear a bit ridiculous. Ever since the First Consul had taken up his abode in the Tuileries and begun to form a little Court there, it had become evident that changes would have to be made in the official vocabulary.

To make the transition easier, it was first decided to reserve the title of citizen for Frenchmen possessing civic rights. At once the women began to be called madame or mademoiselle, titles that had the advantage of distinguishing between them. Foreign diplomats were baptized Excellences, and the dead, who were doubtless no longer in possession of their civic rights, were qualified as *messieurs* in their burial certificates.

Very modest reforms so far, but soon to be reinforced by a change in manners. Certain newspapers were already accusing government clerks of 'monsieurizing' too easily, and people

[1] Saint Roch devoted himself to nursing victims of the plague, contracted the disease himself, and was saved by a dog, whose master sheltered and cured him. [Translator.]

in society adopted the habit among themselves, now that the thousands of *émigrés* who had been allowed to return were there to set the tone. There were still placards outside the restaurants bearing the legend 'Here we honour one another with the title of Citizen', but inside, the customers used the word only to give orders to the staff: 'Citizen Baptiste, clean my boots!' 'Citizeness Angot, open a dozen oysters for me!' Which was hardly enough to prove their love of democracy.

Other anecdotes were current, to the amusement of Parisians. Two friends broach the eternal subject. 'How can you expect me', says the first, 'to be proud of the title of Citizen when it was borne by Marat and Joseph le Bon?'

'But after all,' says the other, 'Cartouche and Desrues were known as *messieurs.*'[1]

When people start joking on a subject, it soon loses its importance. Revolutionary forms of language were going the same way as the out-of-date festivals, together with the Décadi, the new calendar, in short all the articles of the Jacobin creed. With the approach of the Empire their last partisans would become more and more rare. Some of them would even allow themselves to be converted by grace, like the composer Rey, a young musician attached to the chapel of the Tuileries.

In spite of his post at the Château, he still retained the most ardent republican convictions; a bust of Liberty was enthroned on the mantelpiece in his bedroom, and it was to this that he paid his devotions every evening. But it happened that after a concert at which one of his works had delighted the audience, Bonaparte gave orders that the artist should be presented with a gratification of 6,000 francs. Wild with joy, the young man went home, mounted the stairs four steps at a time and spread his treasure before the eyes of the bust.

'See what the tyrant has given me! And you were teaching me to hate him! What have you done for me, false goddess? What have you given me, heart of plaster?' And as the statue made no reply, he hurled it to the ground with a blow of his fist and broke it in a thousand pieces.

We may safely bet that many Frenchmen passed from one regime to the other with equal ease.

[1] Cartouche was the famous chief of a band of robbers (1693–1721), Desrues a notorious poisoner, broken on the wheel in 1719. [Translator].

CHAPTER III

HISTORY SEEN FROM THE STREET

Events and public opinion – Paris celebrates Marengo – July 14, 1800 – The festival of the Peace – Transparencies – Bonaparte's little boats – From the moat of Vincennes to Notre-Dame – The Coronation – Stendhal rinses his mouth

THE home life of a country is always bound up with its history and its politics. A generation that has waged war differs from one that has sat about in slippers, and a man who spouts *Vive l'Empereur!* does not breathe in the same way, does not eat with the same appetite, does not sleep the same sleep as he would if he shouted 'Down with the tyrant!'

To understand the French between 1800 and 1815 one must always bear in mind the events of which they were witnesses. During those perpetual wars they went through alternations of enthusiasm and lassitude, and their daily life was affected by the rebound. To follow this reaction of events on opinion, and of opinion on life, to trace the curve of this collective fever, would lead us too far from a simple chronicle of manners; but we may take a look at those occasions during the Consulate and the Empire when popular feeling expressed itself most forcibly.

Great events in which whole towns were involved, departure and return of armies, celebrations, public ceremonies, following on one another in quick succession for fifteen years, came to seem a part of daily life. They were history seen from the street, a series, as it were, of popular prints in simple, garish colours, in the first of which we behold the huge joy of the capital at the news of Marengo.

No success could have been more brilliant or more unexpected. Unpleasant rumours had been rife all the week. It was known that Masséna had capitulated in Genoa, and only the day before Carnot had received a message that made a retreat by Bonaparte seem likely, and the funds had dropped ten points. But suddenly, on the 2nd Messidor, a second courier, arriving in the morning, announced that the Austrians had been crushed: the Armistice had been signed, it was a dazzling victory.

At two o'clock the cannon thundered, and soon posters appeared confirming the event. *Italy is taken!* The words echoed everywhere in a continuous murmur. People came pouring out like a waterspout from the houses, the shops, the workrooms, spreading over the squares, dancing in circles, lighting bonfires. They were all embracing, congratulating one another 'as if on some happy family event'.

In the evening rejoicings started afresh. When Mme Permon and her daughter, whom we met at the Théâtre Feydeau, returned after dinner from their country estate of Saint-Mandé, they guessed the great news from the general intoxication of the crowd. All the inhabitants of the Saint-Jacques quarter, of the Place Maubert and of the Cité, had gathered on the site of the old Bastille, the place where Paris had grown accustomed to dance, and the workmen of the Faubourg Saint-Marceau had crossed the Seine by boat to join them there.

On entering the boulevard the Permons' carriage could hardly move, and Mme Junot jotted down the words of the passers-by. 'Did you see what he wrote to the Consuls?' said one, ' "I hope the people will be pleased with their army".' And everybody that overheard began shouting, 'Oh, yes! We're pleased with it, all right!'

Another eye-witness, Cambacérès, declares that this was 'the first spontaneous public rejoicing' for nine years. He was recalling the great day of the Federation, when all classes shared the same delirium – as they were doing now. They thought then that the Revolution was over, and now they believed peace was assured for ever. The error, alas, was equally great in both cases: in 1790 the Revolution was just beginning; in 1800 wars had started that were to last a whole reign.

How was the country to suspect this, with reports coming in from Italy of so many conquests and so much glory? In future its life would revolve round the young Chief who had taken its destiny into his hands and for whom many people were beginning to entertain a kind of idolatry.

(*above*) Île du Palais and Notre-Dame

1   Early nineteenth-century views of Paris

(*below*) View from the Pont-Neuf

2 Napoleon receiving the representatives of the army after his coronation (Painting by Serangeli at Versailles)

Two years earlier, when he was in Egypt, an old peasant woman had vowed to give six francs to the poor if he came back safe and sound. Now the blind patients of the Quinze-Vingts[1] were lamenting the fact that they would be unable to see his face. 'Deign at least to let us hear the sound of your voice!' they pleaded. And an honest inventor about to receive an award in an exhibition found a no less vivid way of expressing his admiration: 'If the First Consul, instead of giving me a medal, would beget a child on my wife, I should be much better pleased!'

Each successive review on the Carrousel aroused an outburst of enthusiasm on the part of the Parisians, but this was never so lively as on July 14, 1800, the day of the Fête de la Concorde. When the Government marched from the Tuileries to the Invalides, and from the Invalides to the Champ de Mars to present the colours taken in Italy and Germany, an immense crowd surrounded the procession. Frenzied people – old men, women, children – dashed among the horses' legs to get near the General, to touch the gilding on his saddle and kiss the skirts of his uniform. 'I've come forty leagues to see him!' cried one man. And those that had seen him ran along behind him, trying to overtake him and see him a second time.

On the Champ de Mars people went mad again. Every now and then they broke through the barriers and invaded the track prepared for horse racing and chariot races. The spectacle itself, grandiose though it was, interested them less than the man providing it. They could not take their eyes off the tribune where the figure of the First Consul stood out, slender and wiry in his scarlet coat. They stared unceasingly at the litle red patch, the 'magnetic point' that was electrifying a whole population.

*   *   *   *

The hopes cherished by this population soon appeared to be realized. Having got the better of Austria, France at last obtained the famous 'natural frontiers' which, from having been so ardently desired, had come to seem almost supernatural. A few months later the preliminaries of an equally

[1] The famous hospital founded by Saint Louis in 1260 as a home for the blind. [Translator.]

C

desirable settlement were signed with England. Between the
Treaty of Lunéville and that of Amiens, Paris, killing two
birds with one stone, set about preparing a great Festival of
Peace for the anniversary of the 18th Brumaire.

During those three weeks the stage coaches arrived
crowded with passengers. There was a general fight for seats
to view the show. 'My house is to let at twelve hundred francs
for twenty hours', so ran the bills posted by one landlord
along the embankments. And a single window, near the
Préfecture of Police, was booked for twenty-five louis. People
had begun admiring the triumphal arch erected on the Pont-
Neuf, the festoons of greenery on the Louvre, the open-air
theatre in the Place de la Concorde and the huge colonnade
on the roundabout of the Champs-Élysées.

On the great evening itself, while the public monuments
were being lighted up, together with hundreds of yew-trees
in the Tuileries Gardens, a pantomime of War and Peace,
with chariots and horsemen, was being performed on the
Place de la Concorde. After which fireworks were let off on
the banks of the Seine, dotting the sky with a thousand stars.

Quite as important a part in the nocturnal *décor* was
played by the innumerable fairy lamps lighting the windows
of the houses, and the legends on the transparencies hung
outside them. All these, of course, extolled the fame of
Napoleon and the joys of peace; but competition was intense
between the inhabitants of the various quarters. Some chose a
lapidary style, like the chemist of the Rue Saint-Honoré, who
wrote simply:

Pax vobis!

A riverside dweller on the Quai Malaquais put more feeling
into it:

He deprives himself of the repose he gives us.

At the corner of the Rue Saint-Florentin a calligrapher,
who must have been the father of Joseph Prudhomme,[1] had
hung a transparency bearing these lines in a fine copperplate
hand:

[1] A ridiculous character invented by Henri Monnier (1805–77), much given
to the utterance of solemn banalities. [Translator.]

*Hail and Glory to the Hero of two Worlds! He is at once
citizen and conqueror, soldier and general, avenger and pro-
tector; a Lycurgus in the Senate, in the field an Achilles. Let
us carve on a trophy the surname of Invincible, and let us
never forget that he was our saviour!*
Long live the Republic and all its allies!
Signed: D. F., 18th Brumaire, year X.

But the palm must be given to the transparency in the Rue
Choiseul, showing an English and a French flag tied together
round an olive branch, with the legend:

Forever united!

What would the author of this fine prophecy have thought
if he had been told that eighteen months later everything
would be upset again? For suddenly the atmosphere was to
change. After the short-lived Peace of Amiens both countries
realized that their understanding had been based 'on a mis-
understanding'. Without any declaration of war the English
seized part of our merchant fleet, and Bonaparte, by way of
reprisal, flung himself into the great adventure.

His one idea now was to enlarge the squadron of Boulogne
and build a flotilla of flat-bottom boats. The Esplanade of
the Invalides was soon covered with sheds in which a legion
of workers were employed. From La Rapée to the Gros-
Caillou the entire left bank of the Seine was nothing but an
enormous naval shipyard. A fascinating spectacle for the
crowd it attracted daily.

During the whole summer of 1803 the flotilla grew, and
one afternoon in Vendémaire the First Consul came to in-
spect it. Great was the emotion when he was seen to go
aboard a barge, upstream from the Pont de la Concorde,
direct manœuvres, examine the new paddle system invented
by the engineer Marguerie, wield the oars himself, make a
mock landing, and then have himself taken back to Saint-
Cloud, along with Mesdames Bonaparte, Leclerc and Caroline Murat, by a company of the Guard who had seated themselves in two longboats.

After this demonstration the public was convinced that
the Boulogne game was as good as won. It strained its ears

for the cannonade announcing the victory. And sure enough, a few weeks later, salvoes of artillery did resound.

Everybody supposed that we had at last reached the shores of Ireland. Café strategists announced that we had landed 50,000 men. Others, the 'exaggerators', went as far as 150,000. . . . After all, with a fair wind, you know. . . . People remained under this delusion for two hours; then they heard there had been no landing: the guns had merely announced the return of the Chief Magistrate of the Republic to the Tuileries.

'It is a happy event,' said a Parisian lady who never lacked wit, 'but you know how one feels when one has made up one's mind to a thing. The truth might be a hundred times better than what one had expected, but one is angry and ashamed at having made a mistake. We were very chapfallen. But it's all over now, we've forgotten all about it.'

* * * *

Some dramas of the past seem to have made far less impression on the people of their day than they do upon ourselves.

On March 21, 1804, Norvins, having gone out early, heard someone in the Faubourg Saint-Honoré saying that the Duke of Enghien had been court-martialled during the night and shot. 'Who's that?' inquired a voice. To which a bourgeois replied, with a vague gesture, 'Probably another of those foreigners.'

That evening, in the boxes of the theatres, women showed by their remarks that they knew very little more themselves about the family of the Condés.

Although royalist circles were shattered by this event, and diplomatists disturbed, it is therefore probable that there was far less dismay among the other classes of the population. Burning questions of the moment, such as the trial of General Moreau, the suicide of Pichegru, the arrest of Cadoudal, were far more in people's minds than the execution of an unfortunate prince hardly known to the public.

In a few months' time they would think of him still less, for the Empire would by then have been proclaimed. The whole country, no excepting royalist Vendée, would have voted for the 'Pacifier', and the sole subject of conversation in France would be the ceremony of the Sacring, or, more fashionably, the Coronation of Napoleon.

In preparation for the great day thousands of jobs were being feverishly completed in Paris: gravel spread in a great many streets, the kennels of the boulevards filled in, part of the Carrousel cleaned up, the approach to Notre-Dame laid open and a painted canvas gateway erected in front of the Cathedral, which some people took for a copy of Saint Peter's in Rome, but which Messrs. Percier and Fontaine had merely intended as a *décor* 'in the Gothic style.'

Long before the fixed date, thousands of provincials invaded the capital, some delegated by their home town, others simply as onlookers. When they found the hotels full they camped haphazard with private people who had turned their apartments into dormitories.

December 2 came at last. The cold had been intense the day before, and the morning opened with ice on the ground and flakes of snow in the air. It was only by Napoleon's usual luck that the sun broke through the fog at nine o'clock and the weather became bearable again. And it was at nine o'clock that the Pope's carriages left the Pavillon de Flore and drove towards the Cathedral by way of the Rue Saint-Nicaise, Rue Saint-Honoré, the Pont-Neuf and the little streets of the Cité, filled since early dawn with an immense multitude. Let us mingle with the crowd behind the triple rank of soldiers lining the way, and try to note what it will remember of the spectacle.

First of all, no doubt, the jovial face of Monsignor Speroni, cross-bearer to the Holy Father, astride a mule. The Imperial stables, not possessing the orthodox female, had only succeeded in hiring a male of the species for the sum of sixty-seven francs. But the public was not particular on the subject, and gave it a long ovation. 'The Pope's Mule! The Mule [slipper] one kisses!' they shouted, and a gale of laughter saluted, accompanied, pursued the good prelate, who had the sense to laugh himself. 'He knew the Parisians!'[1]

Perhaps he would have known them still better if he had

---

[1] For his trouble, the vendors of caricatures made him popular, and the makers of thermometers forced him to predict bad and fine weather, like Saint Anthony, by going up and down the Papal crozier.

seen them, a few minutes later, suddenly change their attitude and bow as one man at the approach of the Pontiff. Visible to all through the eight windows of his coach, Pius VII, very simply robed, leaned towards the spectators and made the gesture of benediction. Before him, many who were not religious bowed the knee. And the great coach went on its way, at the slow pace of the horses, bearing on its roof the pontifical tiara supported by gilt doves.

Patience would be needed by those waiting to see the other great coach go past, on the roof of which stood the crown of Charlemagne held by eagles. The Emperor was not due to leave the Tuileries until an hour after the Pope, and the infinite complexity of the procession was bound to delay it on its route. In streets, some of which were barely seven yards wide, how would it be possible to keep things moving without collisions – squadrons of riflemen, cuirassiers, mamelukes and above all, the immense coaches with six horses, carrying pompous dignitaries and bridling princesses, with the finest horsemen of France caracoling alongside?

When at last the procession began, when, after the trumpeters, the kettledrummers, the carabineers, after Murat and his staff, after the main body of cavalry, after the long line of carriages, the huge gilded crate came into sight, in which Napoleon and Josephine were seated, the crowd was less amazed by this monumental coach-building effort than by the strange gala uniform in which its owner was rigged out. Oh, the artists had done their work well! While the architects had been making up the face of Notre-Dame, Isabey and his team had been disguising the Emperor. His Spanish jacket and velvet cap made him look like a character out of the *Henriade*, And this vaguely troubadour get-up, with feather hat-bands, ruffs and lace shirt-frills, was worn by all those taking part in the ceremony, from Joseph and Louis to Talleyrand and Fouché and the least of the chamberlains.

Perhaps under the vaulted roof of the church, aided by the majesty of the ceremony, all this fine company would assume the meditative gravity lent it later by the brush of David the painter. But for the moment, in the harsh daylight of the Paris street, the masquerade seemed almost indecent. Many people wondered what had become of the heroes of the Wars of Italy. They looked for the Bonaparte of Marengo and could not recognize him.

Their feelings changed when, towards the end of the afternoon, the procession left the cathedral again. The crowd had only been able to catch the echoes of the long ceremony, but this consecration by Rome of the Emperor of the French made a deep impression on them, none the less. Many families had already dined, for it was now five o'clock, and the December night was falling on the square when the procession was re-formed.

It returned to the Tuileries in the same order as in the morning, but preceded by a multitude of torches and making a wide detour through the quarters of the Right Bank, the better to satisfy the curiosity of the city. Napoleon appeared to be saying to his people: 'Behold my glory; it is your work.'

And in the narrow Rue Saint-Martin with its lighted windows, near the gate of Saint-Denis, decorated with a gigantic N, all along the boulevards, the people responded with a tremendous ovation. As the chain of horsemen, carriages and torch-bearers unrolled its links like those of a giant *Tarasque*,[1] the cheers broke out in an endless roar, and the day, so unpromising to start with, ended in an apotheosis.

Amid the general enthusiasm, however, certain heads remained cool. Only royalists could have been guilty of publishing lampoons such as *Pie se tache* [Pius soils his hands], or talk of 'A performance given by the Imperial Players: *The Emperor in spite of Everybody*, followed by *The forced Consent*.' Only a La Fayette could express astonishment at the whim that had seized Napoleon 'to have a little phial broken over his head . . .' Only a man of Stendhal's temperament could write on coming home that evening: 'I've been thinking all day about this so obvious alliance of all the charlatans. Religion coming to consecrate tyranny, and all that in the name of human happiness! I washed the bad taste out of my mouth by reading a little of Alfieri's prose.'

[1] A mythical amphibious monster said to have haunted the Rhône near Tarascon, often represented in popular processions. [Translator.]

CHAPTER IV

THE RELIGIOUS QUESTION

*Three classes of priests – Religion of the rural districts and of
the world of fashion – Political reasons for the Concordat –
Anger of the Philosophers – Intolerance of the former clergy –
Pius VII in Paris – Surprises for the Holy Father – Religion of
the State*

ON THE threshold of the nineteenth century the Catholic world was still far from having recovered its tranquillity. The new Government, it is true, had made a show of almost liberal intentions towards it; the day was past when refractory priests were regarded as fodder for the guillotine, and so was the morrow of Fructidor, when seventeen hundred of them were deported to Cayenne to die of fever. Theoretically, the freedom of religious observances was recognized, but under what strange conditions!

In the service of a Church of which unity had always been the main principle, there were now three different clergies hurling anathema at one another. First the refractory priests who, having never accepted any authority but that of Rome, were living as outlaws, hidden somewhere in the country, or as refugees abroad. This was the case with most of the bishops, who, having emigrated to London or Germany, had lost contact with their dioceses. Among the priests that had taken the oath, some had adhered from the first to the Civil Constitution of 1790, the others, five years later, to the Republic of the year III, which brought about differences of opinion on many points.

At last, after Brumaire, the Consulate replaced the oath by a more elastic formula: 'I promise fidelity to the Constitution.' Some of the original refractory priests accepted this, and were called *promissaires*; but the orthodox church disavowed them, as it had disavowed the 'jurors'.

On the other hand the Government, faithful to the Republic, continued in principle to deny the refractory priests the right to exercise their ministry. For the sake of appeasement it had gone so far as to reopen a certain number of religious edifices and hold them at the disposal of the faithful. As most of these wanted to recall their former pastors, a policy of wide tolerance was adopted towards the latter. Without authorizing their return, the Government looked the other way. And soon, in many districts, the non-juring curé settled in again opposite his Constitutional rival, contending with him for his parishioners, administering the sacraments to them, rebaptizing and remarrying them if necessary – because some articles are worthless if they do not bear the proper trade-mark.

When an inquiry was instituted into the feeling prevailing in the provinces, it showed that the refractory clergy were more successful than the others. In Eure-et-Loir, in Seine-et-Oise, a report by Lacuée tells us that 'the Roman Catholic religion is practised in nearly all the communes'. In the Vaucluse and Provence, Françoise de Nantes found that 'one-tenth of the inhabitants follow the Constitutional priest, and the remainder those returned from emigration'. Finally, what Barbé-Marbois tells us of Brittany is conclusive. 'In Vannes,' he says, 'on the day of the Epiphany, I went into a cathedral where the constitutional mass was being celebrated. There was only one priest and three or four poor people. A little further on I came upon such a crowd that I could not make my way through. These were people who had been unable to get into a chapel, already full, where the mass known as that of the Catholics was being said.'

This competition between the two clergies inevitably started little battles in many parts of the country, worthy of the *Lutrin*.[1] Relying on the law, the submissive curé claimed the church for his alone. If the Prefect sided with him, he was execrated by those under his administration. If he tipped the balance the other way, as at Troyes, he was reproved by Fouché. This duality of religions was a veritable nightmare. 'It is amply demonstrated now', said Beugnot, 'that it made for trouble. Where there was only one priest, of no matter which persuasion, he was very badly paid, but he managed to satisfy everybody. If you introduced a second priest, of a

---

[1] A comic poem on a quarrel between the treasurer and the precentor of a church as to the position of the lectern. [Translator.]

different persuasion, you introduced discord at the same time.'

In Paris itself and in many other towns the quarrel was complicated by the celebration, still persisting, of the cult of *Théophilanthropes*, a philosophical doctrine of which Lareveillère-Lépeaux had attempted to make a sort of official religion under the Directory. Its devotees were no longer very numerous, but they still had the right to assemble, every Décadi, in fifteen churches of the capital, renamed for their sake Temples of Concord, of Genius, of Hymen, of Commerce, and so forth, and to listen to fine discourses on morality and the civic virtues, pronounced by orators in surplices in front of the busts of great men.

If these practices were not to the taste of certain Roman Catholics, they could avenge themselves by smashing the noses of Jean-Jacques Rousseau or William Tell in the choir of Saint-Eustache or come to blows with the Theophilanthropists in Saint-Nicholas-des-Champs. But as a rule these little disturbances were avoided; religion had grown used to such strange *rapprochements*! In the year IX, had not the Temple of Victory, alias Saint-Sulphice, been the scene of a festival in honour of Confucius, dedicated to the Chinese in Paris?

Among so many different cults, God himself must have lost his way.

*   *   *   *

Was Bonaparte driven to the Concordat by an irresistible wave of public opinion? The desire for an open resumption of the old religious observances was certainly unanimous in the provinces of the Ouest, but in many other regions the reviving piety of the countryside seems to have been far less ardent.

On a visit to Lorraine and the Midi, a German remarks that the peasants treated the Mass as a mere amusement. Lacuée says the same of the Île de France. 'The needs of the people', he says, 'seem confined for the present to an empty spectacle, to ceremonies. Going to mass to hear a sermon, or to vespers, all very well – but confession, communion, fasting, meatless days are not to their taste. They would rather have bells without a priest, than priests without bells.' And Beugnot, referring to Bar-sur-Aube, a region he knows well since it is his own, paints it in even less mystic colours. 'My native region is gaily religious. The men get drunk. Their wives give them horns. The girls have babies fairly frequently. All these people go to mass, many of them even to confession. . . . Don't imagine there is any fanaticism in Bar-sur-Aube. There is a taste for theatrical display, for the old music of the *In exitu Israel* and in addition to a devotion to the Republic on which you can rely.'

With the Parisians too the interest shown in the churches was mainly compounded of curiosity. People wanted to see the chapels newly restored to religion, like those of Saint-Pierre de Chaillot, the Filles-Saint-Thomas or the Carmelites; to attend the ceremonies presided over by the Bishop of Saint-Papoul, one of the first prelates to return; to listen to the sermons of the Abbé Bossu, the fiery curé of Saint-Paul, soon to be curé of Saint-Eustache; to admire Mme Récamier taking up the collection at Saint-Roch, or to hear the last of the Couperins playing the organ in Saint-Gervais.

For many people the pageantry of the liturgy was a novelty, and they flocked to the Easter celebrations and to the midnight masses, the tradition of which had been revived. That at Saint-Merri, in the year X, was marked by a dramatic interruption, the noise of a detonation spreading panic throughout the congregation. Some took it for a pistol shot, others suspected some new infernal machine, and they were all making for the door when the beadle discovered that the disturbance had been caused by the bursting of a horse-chestnut in an old lady worshipper's foot-warmer. 'The crowd rushing out of the church turned back again, and sang thanks in chorus to the Child Jesus for letting them off with a fright.'

Services with full orchestras, paid admission on certain days, reserved seats, all suggested fashionable curiosity rather than true piety. On serious occasions, such as the forty-hour adoration, the churches were always empty. Children were beginning, here and there, to make their first communion, but the great majority of adults stayed away from the sacraments. They paid no attention, either, to fasting or abstinence, and there had to be ecclesiastics among their guests for them to order meatless dishes.

In this society of the days of the Consulate a sort of 'aesthetic and sentimental' religiosity came into flower at the time of the publication of *Atala*, followed by *The Spirit of Christianity*, a sort of lyrical mysticism of which Chateaubriand was to be the prophet. But most people were not yet looking so far ahead. The spectacles offered by the Church were among the attractions of Paris in which it was considered good taste to take part. This is how a young blood lists his day's pleasures to come. 'Oh, there's no denying it, no day will ever have been better spent! Listening to a *Passion* that will make me cry, while everyone is bound to notice me; after that, dining well at Rose's; then taking my charmer Sophie to Longchamp in an elegant phaeton, and eating an ice with her at Garci's on the way back; going to hear Garat sing Pergolesi's *Stabat*; then spending a few hours at the masked ball, thoroughly roasting Mme X . . . , who is to be disguised as a lay sister, then . . . Upon my sacred word! It's delightful!'

If Bonaparte was feeling his way to the Concordat, it was doubtless not for the sake of assisting the development of such a peculiar form of devotion, any more than to please his colleagues of the Institute, nearly all of them enemies of the Church, nor the generals of his army, all ferocious anti-clericals. The reasons for this great step, one of the most daring of his whole career, were exclusively political. He knew that in governing a people the spiritual power was the most valuable auxiliary of the temporal. One would think he had read this saying of Rivarol's: 'Philosophy divides men, religion unites them in the same principles. . . . Every State, if we may say so, is a mysterious vessel whose anchors are in Heaven.'

Up to then the Catholic world had mostly worked against the Consulate, born of the Revolution, and part of the country was still in a state of armed insurrection of moral opposition. The object of the manœuvre, therefore, was to set men's consciences at rest the better to enslave them. Bonaparte's idea could not be more accurately defined than by the – more or less apocryphal – confession that Julie Talma ascribes to him: 'Is it not true that the non-juring priests have the greatest influence in such and such departments? Is it not true that these priests belong to Louis XVIII? That he is therefore more powerful than myself in those regions? By treating with the Pope, therefore, I am robbing Louis XVIII of this army of priests; they are mine instead of his.'

The original idea of the Concordat can be entirely reduced to this consideration. There were still the innumerable difficulties to be solved which the negotiations with Rome would present at every moment – persuading the Pope to consent to the division of Church property among the purchasers of national property; obtaining the substitution of the bishops of the old regime by prelates chosen and paid by the Government; introducing among the regular clergy a part of the Constitutional clergy and marrying two elements that had always fought against each other – so many thorny problems destined at last to be solved, thanks to the goodwill of the Holy Father and the persistence of the First Consul.

But all this is wide of our subject. We are only concerned to know how the country was going to accept this spiritual *coup d'état*, and what effect it was to have on everyday life.

❋ ❋ ❋ ❋

On Easter Day 1802 a grand ceremony took place in Notre-Dame. With the tenor bell of the cathedral ringing again after ten years' silence, a *Te Deum* celebrated the alliance concluded between France and the Holy See.

A considerable number of soldiers and mounted police were drawn up round the church, and the wits insinuated that this was to prevent God the Father from being burgled. At eleven o'clock, preceded by four regiments of cavalry, a succession of coaches drove up, with grooms in full livery for the first time, bringing the three Consuls, the Ambassadors and the Ministers. Received on entering by the recently appointed Archbishop – the old Monsignor de Belloy – with holy water and incense, Bonaparte, Cambacérès and Lebrun took their seats in the choir, under a dais, while Mme Bonaparte throned it in one of the two ambos.

The Cardinal-Legate said mass. At the moment of the elevation the onlookers were surprised by a spectacular innovation: the troops presented arms and the drums beat a general salute. During the sermon several of the generals laughed derisively, especially Lannes and Augereau, who had just lunched too well, and had been almost forcibly dragged there by Berthier. Another, General Delmas, asked that evening by the First Consul what he thought of the ceremony, replied without hesitation, 'A fine piece of Church flummery! The only thing missing was the million men who gave their lives in order to destroy what you have just re-established!'

That phrase summed up the feeling of a large number of military men, for the army of the Revolution found it hard to understand the sudden right-about turn it had been ordered to execute. Feeling was no less acute in certain intellectual circles, especially in the Institute, where the spirit of the Encyclopaedia still held sway. We need only recall the motion proposed by Cabanis during a session 'I demand that the name of God shall never be pronounced within these precincts!' And the still more singular declaration made by another member 'I swear that God does not exist!'

But these belated disciples of the philosophers, who included Guinguenet and Parny, Garat and Marie-Joseph Chénier, were after all only a small group; their protestations were hardly taken seriously, any more than the fantasies of Lalande the astronomer, who had such fine things to say of the heavens, and such bad ones of their principal occupant. There was certainly little religious belief among the people of that day, but the mere fact that religion had now been given legal existence soon helped it to gain ground, because the general concern was for correct behaviour in such matters.

This explains the rebirth of fashionable piety on the morrow of the Concordat. It soon became the custom for certain very important persons to go to Mass, like Cambacérès, or to be appointed honorary churchwardens, like Murat; for certain leaders of fashion to take round the plate at Saint-Roch in full evening dress, like the wife of the banker Delarue – with a Russian Count leading her by the hand and two lacqueys carrying her train, followed by a negro – or to tender the bread for consecration at Saint-Ambroise, like Mlle Duchesnois, or even to set up a temporary altar on the day of Corpus Christi, like Mlle Contat at her country house at Ivry. The Paris populace was not a little astounded by

these unaccustomed sights, but more surprises were in store
for it. The priests were about to reappear in the streets in
ecclesiastical garments, first in short cassocks, like the abbés
of the old regime, then in the long soutanes formally recommended by Bonaparte.[1] On feast days the service would be
performed outside the church; the Holy Sacrament would be
carried along the Boulevard Saint-Antoine, or the procession
would go to worship the Calvary at the Hermitage of Mont-
Valérien.

Since the clergy were now officially recognized, they must
obviously be free henceforth to pursue their calling in a
variety of ways, such as blessing the cadets of the Military
School of Saint-Cyr (who greeted the Bishop of Versailles
with somewhat comical verses[2]), confirming the young ladies
of Saint-Lazare, and assisting condemned prisoners on the
Place de Grève, an innovation witnessed by the populace,
according to the *Journal des Débats*, 'with as much pleasure
as respect'.

And all would have been well if it had not been for the
persistent intolerance of some old-fashioned priests, which
gave rise to a number of unnecessary disturbances.

Why deny the Constitutional abbés the right to say mass,
now that they had been recognized by the Pope? Why should
the Abbé Bossu turn an honest man out of Saint-Eustache,
with insults, for having committed the crime of dressing his
two little boys as mamelukes, rather as we might dress ours
as sailors or Scotsmen? Why, above all, should the Curé
Mardruel forbid the funeral procession of poor Chameroy to
enter Saint-Eustache, thus incurring the anger of the theatrical world and the indignation of the public at large? So many
blunders that might easily have been avoided in the interest
of the Sacred Union!

Unfortunately these clashes were even more numerous in

[1]At Brienne in 1805 Napoleon met an old priest who had been his school-
master at the Military School. Seeing him in a brown overcoat, he pretended
not to recognize him. 'The soutane was given to the priests so that everybody
should know who they were. Go and dress!' he said. Then, when the other
had changed, 'Ah! Now I recognize you, and I'm very glad to see you!'

[2]O, respectable leader of a sacred enterprise,
Guide, oh guide our steps towards the Promised Land!
Our thirst is a burning one, oh, deign to assuage it!
Be to us our Moses and strike upon the rock!

the provinces. Some towns, like Avignon, publicly burnt the Concordat. In others, as in Saint-Flour, the new curé, who was accused of having been a juror, was hooted at, and the military had to intervene. The parishioners of Vitré pillaged the church, under the pretext that it had been profaned during the Revolution. Those of La Panissière, in the Loire, took the belfry by assault to the number of four or five hundred, and pelted the curé, the mayor and the police with stones from above. At Orleans, they went one better. As the new bishop, Bernier, had not only taken part in the negotiations of the Concordat, but was said, no doubt wrongly, to have had a hand in the massacres of the Vendée, his flock had a pail of blood deposited in front of his door during the night. A delicate manner of bidding him welcome.

As a rule things did not go so far, but the Roman clergy meddled too much with politics. A priest in Lot-et-Garonne refused to baptize an infant because the godfather 'did not belong to his party'. Another, in Sambre-Inférieure, used the holy-water sprinkler to cudgel those of his parishioners who displeased him. And if we may believe the Archbishop of Besançon, certain confessors of his diocese ordered their penitants to restore Church property in exchange for absolution, and forced dying soldiers to beg God's pardon for having served in the armies of the Republic.

❊   ❊   ❊   ❊

One thing alone could succeed in calming opinion and inculcating mildness and tolerance – the white-robed figure from Rome that was greeted by Paris on November 28, 1804. Even in the days of the Most Christian Kings, the city had never set eyes on a Pope, and although little religious as a whole, it could not remain indifferent to such an unaccustomed sight. In the general reaction to the pontifical presence, the mildness, the evangelical simplicity of Pius VII played a great part. When visiting our churches or officiating in them himself, receiving the grand Corps d'État and the flower of society in the gallery of the Louvre, shown round the sights of Paris – the Invalides, the Monnaie, the Hôtel-Dieu, the Quinze-Vingts, the Jardin des Plantes – he appeared interested in everything and spoke kindly to everybody. Prejudice fell away in the presence of this frail old man, whose hand seemed made for blessing.

Without a moment's hesitation the fiercest Jacobins of yesterday bowed their heads before him, from François de Neufchâteau, saluting him in the name of the Senators, and François de l'Aude, bringing him the homage of the Tribunate to the melodramatic Lalande, who laid his hand on his heart when presenting the members of the Bureau des Longitudes. David himself, the former friend of Robespierre, having obtained a few sittings from the Sovereign Pontiff, was loud in his praise. 'He really *is* a Pope, that man,' he said, 'he's a *true* priest: the gold trimmings on his robes are just a sham!'

For four whole months Pius VII garnered tokens of respect, of enthusiasm even, such as he could hardly have looked for. And when a last ovation greeted him on the balcony of the Pavillon de Flore, on the day of his departure, he was finally convinced that this eldest daughter of the Church no longer had anything about her of the *enfant terrible* he had been led to expect.

The Pope's visit had enabled the Emperor to be anointed after the fashion of Charlemagne, and the Paris vendors of rosaries to do a roaring trade. One of them is said to have sold more than a hundred dozen a day; another to have made a net profit of 40,000 francs in the month of January alone. Was this not a proof that piety was beginning to make serious progress?

This progress was soon to be rapidly accelerated, as may be gathered from accounts of the religious movement up to the end of the Empire, which tell of the organization of parishes, the development of preaching and missions, encouragement given to welfare work like that of the *Filles de Charité*, and the creation at Saint-Sulpice of the *Congrégation* by the Abbé de Freyssinous, all of which represented appreciable victories for the Church, signs of a rebirth of which the Concordat had provided the germ.

But a paradoxical situation developed three or four years later when Napoleon, disrupting the harmony he had taken such pains to create, despoiled the Pope of his States, interned him at Savone, got himself excommunicated and

D

remained, in spite of all this, the official master of the clergy.

An extraordinary situation if ever there was one! The most powerful Catholic sovereign of Europe excluded from the Divine Law (*He shall be in your sight as a heathen and a publican*), and continuing nevertheless to celebrate the mass every Sunday in the chapel of the Tuileries, to appoint bishops, and to be greeted, every time he entered a church, by the traditional *Domine, salvum fac imperatorem!*

How did the faithful react to such a spectacle? 'If the truth must be told,' wrote a future minister of Louis-Philippe's, of most orthodox opinions, 'nobody gave it a second thought.' Such was Napoleon's authority that his quarrels with the Holy See were looked upon by his contemporaries as mere incidents in foreign politics. 'We paid little attention to it,' confesses the Duchesse d'Abrantès, 'firstly because we always do take everything lightly, and then because the Emperor himself did not want people to concern themselves with what he did or ordered to be done.'

And after all, there was no reason for astonishment. Bonaparte had not really contradicted himself since the day when, as First Consul, receiving some of the Vendéean leaders at the Luxembourg, he said to them, 'I intend to re-establish religion, not for your sake but for mine'.

The programme had been fully carried out. The spiritual was under the control of the temporal, which dictated its will to it. Let nobody attempt to work against it! Napoleon had certainly restored religion, but rather after the fashion in which a road full of pot-holes is repaired by driving a roller over it.

CHAPTER V

SOCIETY AND THE SALONS

Society upside-down – The salon of Mme Montesson – Talley-
rand's evening parties – The new Society: Legion of Honour
and Empire titles – Receptions at the Tuileries – Literary and
artistic salons – A night at Melpomene's

A SOCIETY cannot be improvised. That of the old regime
had almost ceased to exist in 1800, and its successor
was still a topsy-turvy affair. The financiers now in
possession of all the money, and occupying the finest houses,
would always lack certain talents that are not to be bought.
When they attempted to give parties, their dinners, at which
people gorged themselves, were more like public banquets,
their balls were *kermisses* of the *nouveaux-riches*. They mistook luxury for good taste, good living for *savoir-vivre*.

A woman's charm is not enough to make her a good hostess.
People went to Mme Récamier's as if to the theatre, to
applaud the beautiful Juliette, whose glances and attitudes,
whose whole person, in fact, suggested she was on the stage.

Her entourage was not so much a circle as a crowd; the
crush was so great that Julien, the mulatto *chef d'orchestre*
could hardly handle his bow, and his band, when they accompanied a bolero, were obliged 'to hook their scores onto the
shoulders of some of the onlookers sitting near them, using
their backs as music stands'.

There was the same scrimmage at Thérèse Cabarrus's. She
too took a pride in packing her house with people, 'without
considering whether there would be room to talk, or whether
her guests would not be suffocated'. When the last of them
had left, she would drop on a sofa, moaning, 'I'm exhausted,
I'm dead!' – and a minute later, exclaim with satisfaction,
'We were quite a crowd, weren't we?'

Where was any reminder of the old regime to be found?
Not so much in the drawing-room of the de Luynes, where
far too much card-playing went on, as in the little select
gatherings of the Faubourg Saint-Germain described by

Countess Potocka, in the friendly parties of a dozen persons
playing charades, or amusing themselves by organizing fights
between pug-dogs round a pie baked in the shape of a fortress. Probably also in the apartment of the Princesse de
Vaudemont, with the conversation of Narbonne and Talleyrand to enliven proceedings. Or again at the Princesse de
Beauvau's in the Rue Saint-Honoré, whose modest apartment
is thus described by the Vicomtesse de Noailles:

'On leaving the dirty staircase, common to all the inhabitants, you felt as if transported into a world apart; everything in those little rooms was aristocratic and well kept.
The few servants you saw were old and rather helpless; you
always felt they had seen such good company that their
opinion was to be respected.'

Another drawing-room, much less select, could also claim
relationship with the *ancien régime* – that of Jeanne de La
Haye de Riou, widow of the Marquis de Montesson, but
better known as the morganatic widow of the last-but-one
Duke of Orleans. It was public property that this pseudo-
Maintenon of the great-grand-nephew of Louis XIV was not,
nor ever had been, a model of virtue; but the tone of her
household was nevertheless very Old France. It was at her
house that the men first reappeared in shoes and silk stockings, while the servants donned the liveries proscribed by the
Revolution.

As the Government had given orders that some of her possessions should be restored to this affable dowager, she still
enjoyed a certain amount of luxury, and was at home every
Wednesday. First Josephine, and soon afterwards her husband, found their way to her receptions, where they could
rub shoulders with people like the Montaigus, the Saint-
Aulaires, the La Feuillades and the Noailles. A bridge was
thus thrown across from one world to the other, and the Consular personnel came to learn good manners at the house of
the marquise, rather as some young men learnt to tie their
cravats under the tuition of professional beauties matured by
long experience.

A useful lesson for the new Society, especially for certain
military men about to play their part in imperial celebrations.

Many of his brothers-in-arms whom Bonaparte was soon to turn into field-marshals or highnesses were hardly, as they say, out of the top drawer. Ney was the son of a cooper, Lefebvre of a miller, Murat of an inkeeper, Augereau of a mason, Lannes of an ostler. Before appearing at Court and living in grand style, they needed a serious course of training. The same could be said of many of the ministers, whose first attempt to hold receptions were anything but brilliant. An English diplomat, George Jackson, attending an evening party given by Fouché, was struck by the bad style of the company. He mentions muddy boots, doubtful linen, and conversations suggesting that the Minister of Police had recruited his lady dancers from under the arcades of the Palais-Royal.

Fortunately some members of the Government made up for their colleagues' lack of experience. The fête given by Berthier at the Ministry of War for the anniversary of Marengo was long remembered. And the evening parties organized by Talleyrand, two years in succession, at his country house at Neuilly, may be said to have really marked the renascence of Paris life. The second, which took place in the year XI, was later described by Norvins as 'the most splendid festivity yet seen in our day'.

Not only was the party admirably organized, with its illuminations, its concert and its pastoral ballets, but for once people were enjoying themselves. For the first time, we may suppose, the fair ladies of the foreign colony were meeting the brilliant officers of Napoleon's entourage. While some of the couples went on dancing in the drawing-rooms, others wandered off to the end of the park, where the Bengal lights were less frequent and there was some hope of a little darkness. And when at last it was time to go, 'there remained a belated cluster of pretty women in a circle of attentive gallants, huddled together like gazelles rounded up by the hunters. Breathless men came running up from all sides, one after another: these were the husbands. And both parties exclaimed at once, so perfect was their understanding, 'I've been looking for you for the last two hours!'

* * * *

What was needed in this brand-new Society, if it was ever to rival the old one, was an officially recognized *élite*, an aristocracy not of birth but of merit, bringing together in a group all men of worth, and furnished with a distinctive sign. The creation of the Legion of Honour was to supply this.

Why did this institution, which was later to have the approval of the most democratic of regimes – often to the extent of abuse – arouse such violent opposition at its inception? Because for many people, even those that had rallied to the Consulate, the principle of equality was still the most sacred article of the Revolutionary creed. This became obvious at the Council of State, where the urgency of the project was passed by a majority of only four votes; at the Tribunate, where its adversaries amounted to more than a third of the Assembly, and in the Legislative Body, where 110 deputies declared themselves resolutely hostile to it, as against 136. The fate of the millions of ribbons that were to redden French buttonholes in the course of the century was really hanging by a thread.

At first it was regarded much less as a decoration than as a sort of League of Honour. The law of the 29th Florial, year X, does not mention any insignia. There was no talk of crosses, ribbons or stars until two years later, after the proclamation of the Empire. And even then many of the first thirty thousand legionaries wore their ribbons and rosettes with obvious embarrassment. Some of them, Lafayette, Lemercier, Ducis, Delille among them, went so far as to refuse them. 'They say that people with the most *Honour* are refusing to enter the *Legion*. On a principle of equality, no doubt? One should give to the poor. They, so enormously rich, are not in want of anything. So the others will look like *nouveaux-riches*.'

Meanwhile the young bloods of the Boulevard des Italiens had been trying to bring the cross into ridicule by wearing a crimson carnation in their buttonholes. But the mockery withered away when sentinels were seen presenting arms to decorated soldiers and war-scarred pensioners; when women took to stopping Captain Coignet in the street, wanting to touch his medals, begging to be allowed to embrace him; and when the café proprietors of the Palais-Royal said to him,

'We will serve you with anything you like. Members of the
Legion of Honour are treated gratis.'

In the town it became the custom to address the legionaries
as 'Monsieur le Chevalier', or 'Monsieur l' officier', which was
a bit over-ceremonious when offering a pinch of snuff or
asking the time; but the interested parties were none the less
flattered. 'They call these things baubles', said Bonaparte one
day to the Council of State, 'but after all, it's with baubles
that one leads men by the nose.'

It was in virtue of the same axiom that, a few years later,
he created the Empire nobility with its 1,000 barons, its 400
counts, its thirty-two dukes and its three princes, to say
nothing of its 48,000 knights. The major dignitaries received
endowments, estates in tail, fine châteaux of the Île de
France; and 30,000,000 francs were set aside yearly for
their benefit, from the revenues of the domain. The aristocracy was thus re-created all of a piece by the 'fourth
dynasty'. With a stroke of the pen the victor of Brumaire
cancelled the night of August 4.

But what a magnificent Court would gravitate around him
henceforth! This was the dawn of the grand festivities in the
Hall of the Marshals, described by the Duchesse d'Abrantès:
'On both sides of the room, three rows of women covered
with flowers, diamonds and waving feathers. And behind
them the line formed by the officers of the Emperor's household and those of the princesses'; then the generals in
uniforms glittering with gold, the senators, the councillors of State, the ministers, all richly dressed, their breasts
covered with the stars and ribbons that Europe offered us on
its knees.'

There was the same display of luxury at all the imperial
receptions, but they all retained the somewhat military organization that suggested 'reviews with ladies taking part',
as the Comte de Saint-Aulaire remarked.

The Comtesse de Boigne's description of the ball given in
1806 on the occasion of Stéphanie de Beauharnais's marriage
certainly does not suggest a very enjoyable evening. The
guests were parked in the two ballrooms, the Galerie de
Diane and the Galerie des Maréchaux, according to the
colour of their tickets, and were not allowed to go from one

to the other. Nor were they allowed to dance, at any rate before a certain hour, their role meanwhile being restricted to watching the quadrilles performed by sixteen ladies and sixteen chamberlains, led by Hortense and Caroline.

The Emperor, the Empress and the princesses took their seats on a platform. When the ballets were over, the Emperor stepped down alone and went the round of the room, addressing himself exclusively to the ladies. He was wearing his 'Francis the First' costume, more or less the same as for the Coronation: white satin breeches, feather-trimmed cap trimmed with a diamond clasp. 'This costume may have looked well in the design', says Madame de Boigne, 'but on him, short, fat, and awkward in his movements as he was, it was decidedly unbecoming. I may have been prejudiced, but I thought the Emperor looked hideous, he reminded me of the King of Diamonds.'

Having completed his round, Napoleon returned to Josephine, and the procession departed 'without mixing at all with the plebs'. By nine o'clock it was all over; the guests were now free to dance, but the Court had gone. 'I followed its example', adds the young woman, much taken aback by the imperial behaviour. 'I had known other monarchs, but none of them treated the public so cavalierly.'

The same criticism might be applied to many of the festive occasions at the Tuileries, especially the singular ball of 1812, given in the Salle des Spectacles, at which such a rigorous demarcation was established between the personnel of the Court and the bourgeois guests, that not only did the latter take no part in the dancing, but they were forbidden to approach the buffet, and were obliged to wait in their boxes for the lacqueys to bring round refreshments.

Goddess of Equality, so dear to the preceding generation, how sadly you must have veiled your face!

Nearly all the official receptions had another defect in common – their stilted nature. At Josephine's concerts, at Marie-Louise's evening parties, when Murat or Pauline threw open their doors, or Junot, Berthier, Bessières and Cambacérès gave balls, there was always the same ceremonial luxury, the same 'regular explosion of magnificence'.

There was nothing to suggest the easy manners, the natural

elegance that characterized the salons of the eighteenth century, nor anything to enliven or vary social entertainment. It had been disciplined like everything else, and its formula would remain unchanged. Up to the end of the Empire, the only diversity allowed in the recurrent fêtes was the introduction of novel subjects for the quadrilles, such as the *Vestals*, given by Caroline in 1808, and *Chess* at the Italian Embassy the following year, with living chessmen performing evolutions on a gigantic chessboard; and most famous of all, that of the *Hours*, which created a furore at Court on the eve of the Russian campaign.

All this was brilliant, magnificent – but how many couples would have preferred a less pedantic choreography, such as the *Boléro*, the *Allemande*, the *Mont-ferrine*, the *Monaco* – a former favourite of Bonaparte's – the *Grand-Père*, which he still asked for at times, or simply the *Valse*, introduced into France by Trémis, and described by Kotzebue as 'a dance of familiarity demanding the amalgamation of two dancers, which runs as smoothly as oil on polished marble'.

*   *   *   *

In the rest of Paris, however, from the days of the Consulate onwards, a score of social circles had rubbed shoulders with one another, each with its own habits and pleasures – much to the advantage of social life, which thus lost its uniformity.

There existed at first a few political salons, but now that Fouché had his eye on them they kept out of the limelight as much as possible. Mme de Staël had tried to have one of her own, the one of which Bonaparte said: 'It's not a salon, it's a club', but she was soon given to understand that the air of Paris was not good for her.

The authorities took less umbrage at the little literary societies. Towards 1800, Pauline de Beaumont hired an apartment in the Rue Neuve-du-Luxembourg and started her *salon bleu*, or as she might have called it, her menagerie and aviary, since the nicknames of her guests were derived from natural history. Pauline herself was known as the 'Swallow', Chênedollé the 'Raven of Vire', Chateaubriand the 'Illustrious Raven', and Fontanes the 'Wild Boar'.

There were many celebrities to be met with, too, at Sophie Gay's. She had not yet moved to Aix-la-Chapelle, and was on familiar terms with Népomucène Lemercier and Jouy, with Coupigny, the king of ballad-singers, Musson the mystifyer, Frédéric the horn-player, Dalvinar the harpist, and the inimitable singer Garat, whom Piccini called 'Garat la mousique', to distinguish him from his namesake.

Composers and virtuosi were also among the habitual guests of the Comtesse Merlin, a beautiful, witty *grande dame*, with a singing voice they delighted to hear. The painters, for their part, met chiefly at David's house in the Rue de Seine, at Carle Vernet's studio, where the awards of the Salon were celebrated by balls, and at the hotel of Baron Gérard, where visitors were welcomed by a whole gallery of celebrities – Canova, Talma, Ducis – even the Emperor himself.

Parties were also given in dramatic circles. Mlle Duchesnois entertained a brilliant gathering one evening in 1805, on the occasion of her birthday. But how imprudent of her to invite that scandalmonger of a Stendhal! *A Soirée in Buskertown* might have served as a title for the reportage that Ariane's party suggested to the future author of the *Chartreuse de Parme*.

Beyle arrived too early. In the tragic actress's drawing-room he found four or five 'cads' sitting in a circle, with an old dwarf lady who prided herself on playing the piano, and a family from Valenciennes whose daughter 'had nothing remarkable about her but two big tits, very hard and very round'. The centre of interest was the hostess, 'weighed down by her long robes and her *Cyrus*, which was giving her a stiff neck'.

Soon a tall young man made his appearance, whose manner of bowing 'was as utterly foolish and ridiculous as Fleury's is gracious'. This was Millevoye, an elegiac poet. Wearing enormous spectacles, he peered about everywhere for the actress, and ended by seating himself on the knees of another guest.

Many people who were expected had cried off, including Legouvé, Mlle Bourgoin, Mme de Saint-Aubin. Instead, there was Baptiste junior kissing the hand of the Duchenois, and 'looking as usual like a great, solemn fool, very pleased with himself, as he does on the stage'. Close at his heels came Mlle Contat, accompanied by her lover, Parny's nephew, and by her daughter, the young Almaric, a love-child burdened with a name less natural than her birth. Their arrival was a noisy one, heralding the entrance of a *femme d'esprit* 'at the sort of party a fool would give for her'.

The *pièce de résistance* of the evening was a little improvisation acted by Baptiste junior, Armand and a few others. Seated in front of footlights composed of eight candles, Duchesnois and her female friend heard themselves proclaimed in doggerel verse that praised them to the skies. Duport, the great dancer, was then applauded for a few pirouettes, and this kept them going till it was time for supper, which was served on the second floor, in a miserable little room where the men, for want of space, were obliged to 'remain upright'.

Although the feast was somewhat meagre, the health of the hostess was duly proposed. Chazet improvised a couplet in which he informed the century that Melpomene and Thalia were sisters. Mlle Contat stopped her ears, and turning to her hostess, cried, 'My dear, they could have come for your sake without coming for mine!' 'How charming!' exclaimed everybody. And after more poems, arousing fresh applause, the effusions, embraces and enthusiasms knew no bounds.

Supper over, they went back to dance in the drawing-room, but by four in the morning it was time to think of going home. Beyle, always practical, was one of the first to slip away, with one of his friends.

As these gentlemen had no cab, and were not inclined to walk two miles in dancing-shoes, in Siberian cold, they treacherously took possession of a carriage that was waiting for Millevoye. The cabby remonstrated in vain. 'We made him start off in a furious hurry, in spite of his reluctance, promising him anything he liked to ask.'

So much the worse for the author of the *Falling Leaves*! If he got inflammation of the lungs it would merely be an opportunity for him to compose an elegy on the ill fortune of poets, the cruelty of prose writers and the impudence of the drivers of cabs.

CHAPTER VI

A RUINOUS CAPITAL

*Life in the ruins – An epidemic of demolitions – Saint Michael
and the Devil – Mud – Kennels and pavements*

A TOWN that is no longer kept up, whose streets are
left unswept, its houses unplastered, its walls and roofs
unrepaired, soon becomes unrecognizable; it takes on
the ruinous, catastrophic aspect presented by Paris at the
beginning of the nineteenth century.

Many of its wounds, of course, were mementoes of the
Revolution: eight years after August 10, the holes made by
cannon-balls and the marks of bullets were still to be seen
on the façade of the Tuilleries. The stones of the Bastille
choked the moats of the ancient fortress; pedestals bereft
of their statues were still standing in the middle of many
squares, while convents like that of Saint-Lazare, and houses
of the high-living nobility like the former Hôtel de Castries,
still showed the marks of pillage.

But what had done more harm than any act of vandalism
was the complete neglect from which the town had suffered.
Absorbed by the triple worry of internal politics, war and
'rations', the authorities had never had the leisure or the
means to bestow the requisite care on it. They had allowed
time to do its work, to heave up the paving-stones, hollow out
ruts, choke the drains and make circulation almost impossible. The result was heart-rending. 'It is easy to imagine',
wrote Sainte-Beuve in his *Biographie de Frochot*, 'what Paris
was like in 1800, after ten years of anarchy, sedition and
laxity, during which no useful work had been undertaken,
not a street had been cleaned, not a residence repaired,
nothing improved or cleansed.' And in another place he
quotes the evidence of a contemporary: 'Not a courtyard gate
was left on its hinges.'

This was hardly surprising, since most of the houses of the
aristocracy, deserted by their former owners at the time of
the emigration, had been either put to business uses or de-

clared national property and sold to the *bande noire*, an
association of house-breakers that robbed them of their
panellings, mirrors and pier-glasses, and made a fortune by
reselling them, before allowing the unfortunate property to
collapse. Paris had in fact been turned into one immense
house-breakers' yard, combined with an equally huge junk
shop.

For more justifiable reasons the new Government began
by following the example of the *bande noire*, pulling everything down as fast as they could. Because many monuments
were threatening to fall, or standing in the way of traffic, they
decided to hack them down without asking themselves
whether some of them might not deserve a better fate.

The tower of Saint-André des Arts was the first to be sacrificed. Then came the church of Saint-Nicholas and the hotels
of the Coignys and the Baudoins in the little streets of the
Carrousel; in the Tuileries, the poky little houses lining the
terrace of the Feuillants; elsewhere, the Seminary of Saint-
Sulpice, the old buildings of the Chapter of Notre-Dame
and the Grand Châtelet, with the tower of the Temple to
come.

So many memorials lost, so many regrets for the artists and
historians of the twentieth century! But at the beginning of
the nineteenth, people set little store by the relics of Old
Paris. They were being suffocated in a cramped, inconvenient
city, and every time they were given more air, promised new
streets and wider vistas, they were delighted to see the walls
falling.

The newspapers of the day always found excellent reasons
for justifying the demolitions. When work was started on the
Manège of the Tuileries, they said that this scene of so many
cruel conflicts 'was already tottering under its own weight'.
When Notre-Dame was to have a space cleared round it, they
accused the neighbouring buildings of masking half the
cathedral. When the Grand Châtelet was pulled down they
declared it was 'a shapeless mass, offensive to taste, obstruct-
ing the public thoroughfare and injurious to the health of the
citizens'. And when there was talk of getting rid of the houses
still bordering the Pont Saint-Michel, a poet seized his lyre
and published in the *Journal de Paris* this *Desire of an in-*

habitant of the Quai des Grands Augustins fond of fine views:

> As we all know, Saint Michael,
> Armed with his terrible spear,
> Aimed such a blow at the Devil
> As made him fall into a swoon.
> But the Devil, being immortal,
> Was soon convalescent, and well;
> May he soon raze to the ground, out of
>   vengeance,
> The houses on Pont Saint-Michel!

He was to raze many more yet, but we cannot stop to enumerate the thousand and one works undertaken during the Napoleonic era, the architectural history of Paris being only somewhat distantly related to our subject. Confining ourselves to social history, therefore, let us see how little modern the capital was in 1800, and what scanty means it disposed of for guaranteeing the material existence, security and hygiene of its 600,000 inhabitants.

＊　　＊　　＊　　＊

With the addition of a lot of dirt, the streets at that time were just as they had been under the old regime, that is to say, of an almost medieval narrowness. The point of view changing with each epoch, people then talked of the Rue du Bac, the Rue de Lille and the Rue de l'Université as we should speak today of the Avenue Foch or the motorway of Saint-Cloud. Except for the main boulevards, the Rue Royale and the Rue Saint-Antoine, Paris had as yet no really wide thoroughfares. Nearly everywhere there spread a network of by-streets, blind alleys and passages – a labyrinth in which only old Parisians contrived to find their way. But people found fault with the capital less for its lack of air and space than for its extremely dirty condition.

Mercier had complained of it even under Louis XVI, but the dirtiness merely increased with the Revolution. Was it because the carts were employed on other duties during the Terror that sanitary tasks had been neglected ever since? At any rate, countless heaps of garbage piled up before the

doors, waiting for the next thunderstorm to spread themselves over the middle of the road and turn it into a slough.
When bad weather took a hand, the appearance of most of
the streets, with their big, disjointed flagstones, their single
central kennels and their lack of pavements, was indescribable. Lost in this swamp, drenched by water off the roofs,
which long gutter-pipes, pretending to be gargoyles, spouted
to a distance of three feet from the houses, pedestrians ex-
perienced some tragical moments.

'However good a walker one may be,' moaned one of them,
'one hesitates to wade through streets full of refuse and
covered with thick, glutinous mud. . . . Yesterday, going on
foot to the national Jardin des Plantes, I went through some
lanes where the poverty, filth and indecency of the passers-
by were such that it makes me feel sick merely to think of
them. . . . This is the first time, in my peregrinations through
Europe, that I have discovered I have a stomach, and understood the sensation described as *mal de cœur*.'

A few improvements were tried out, however. In certain
streets the middle of the roadway was cambered, and the
central kennel replaced by gutters on the right and left. This
method was said to have given good results in England; but
whereas London had pavements, Paris still had none, which
meant that every shower produced floods, and the water
poured down into the cellars and found its way into the
shops.

'Let's make pavements at once!' thought the engineers; but
the first they laid were paved with great flagstones that made
walking difficult, dotted with unsightly mark-posts and suddenly interrupted at every entrance gateway, forcing pedestrians to step up and down continually.

Taking everything into consideration, the innovation did
not seem particularly useful. The famous Dillon pavements,
as they were called, were therefore only very slowly adopted
under the Empire. A few made their appearance here and
there, in streets 'as great and wide as the Rue du Mont-
Blanc' – the Chaussée d'Antin of today. Elsewhere there was
no change: walkers continued to hug the walls to avoid
being run over, and the little Savoyards went on throwing
planks across the gutter with their traditional cry of *Passez*,

payez! A piquant subject for the painters, but a most unpleasant necessity for the fashionables of both sexes, for ever
threatened with a glissade and an evil-smelling footbath.

Stendhal went through this ordeal one evening, trying to
cross the gutter in the Rue de Poitiers. He came out of it so
covered with mud that he had to spend the night with his
friend Crozet to get his breeches dry. And the adventure was
still fresh in his mind, no doubt, when seven or eight years
later he wrote in his diary: 'We ought to shout at these
Parisians, who think themselves so advanced in the matter of
their police and their cleanliness, 'You are barbarians; your
streets stink aloud; you can't take a step in them without
being covered with black mud, which gives a disgusting
appearance to the populace, forced to travel on foot. This
comes of the absurd idea of turning your streets into a main
sewer. It's *under* the streets that sewers should be laid.'

An idea that appears somewhat commonplace today, but
was much less so under the First Empire, since throughout a
reign in which architects and engineers played such an important part, only five kilometres of new sewers were laid
down. Five kilometres – hardly a three-hundredth part of our
underground system of today!

4   Armed robbers on the roads of France

A roulette table

CHAPTER VII

PUBLIC SERVICES

*Antediluvian public services – Lack of water and lack of light
– The markets – The police – The post office – The fire service
– Scarcity of carriages – His Excellency's coach*

THE dirtiness of the city was also due to the lack of water. In face of this, the Prefect of Police was merely wasting his breath when he enjoined the owners to have the streets cleaned in front of their houses, and the campaigns started in the newspapers were equally useless. It was with a certain irony that their readers took note of articles like this in the *Observateur Français* of the 1st Thermidor, year IX – a pleasing sample of the literature of the dog-days:

'Citizens of Paris! clean your city! It is hot, very hot, the street surface is burning, the gutters are stagnant and stink of putridness. Water them, therefore! Your own interest calls for it, and the police has ordered it. We have no water, say some of you. We have no arms, say others. But you all have two sous with which to save yourselves from the heat of reflected sunlight, from falls, illnesses, doctors' visits and so on.'

Two sous – this was, in fact, the price of a water supply consisting of two pails containing about three gallons. But for the family kitchen, for housework, for personal cleanliness – no question of baths – this provision was slender. Besides which, many people reckoned that two sous a day made one écu a month, that is thirty-six francs a year.

In the courtyards of many houses there still existed a few wells, while the various quarters possessed between them about sixty public drinking-fountains; but most of these were charged for, functioned only in the daytime and often ran dry. So that if they were not to die of thirst, the Parisians were obliged to have recourse to the good offices of the Auvergnats perambulating the town, dragging their little

E

water-butts mounted on wheels, or carrying a pair of buckets hooked on to a wooden ring.

In theory these buckets had to be filled at so-called 'purifying' fountains, but many of the carriers found it simpler and more economical to go and draw water fom the river, and it is easy to imagine the swarm of microbes to which they treated their customers every morning.

By some miracle of grace our grandparents did not seem to be the worse for it. Although it was already terribly polluted,[1] they still looked on the Seine as a 'beautiful, limpid river', and they were grateful to the pumping stations of Notre-Dame, the Gros-Caillou and the Périer Brothers for feeding their fountains.

But among foreigners visiting the capital, the water of Paris had a bad name. Sir John Dean Paul blamed it for the violent attacks of colic from which he suffered in the course of his travels in 1802; and a year earlier, the King and Queen of Etruria suffered the same sort of disaster. As for their young heir the Contino, he invented a picturesque way of expressing his woes: whenever people inquired how he was he turned a pirouette, lifted the skirts of his little coat and pointed politely to his behind. They had no need to know Spanish to see where the shoe pinched, in a manner of speaking.

Various kinds of filters were suggested from time to time in the hope of purifying the drinking-water after a fashion, foremost among them that of a certain M. Cuchet, of which the papers told wonders. But for really drinkable water the people of Paris had to wait for the completion of the important public works ordered by Napoleon, such as the building of the reservoir at La Villette, of the canal of the Ourcq and the water supply of the Beuvrone, which finally ensured the abundant, regular output of our drinking-fountains.

A city does not only need water, it also needs light. Unfortunately no serious progress was made in this direction during the Empire. With its 4,000 lanterns swinging at the end of a rope – miserable argand lamps only too often ex-

[1] There were, of course, no such things as sewage farms, and the most horrible refuse – spoilt goods from the market halls, garbage from the Hôtel-Dieu, and so forth, fell straight into the river.

tinguished by rain and wind, or even left unlighted because the licence-holder wanted to burn as little oil as he could – Paris was to remain, up to 1815, what it was in 1800: not the City of Light but the city of candle-ends.

There were times when Napoleon lost his temper. 'The non-lighting of Paris', he wrote one day to Fouché, 'amounts to an embezzlement. We must make an end of an abuse of which the public is beginning to complain.' But these fits of anger had no effect. A few new devices were tried out for form's sake, such as the mirrored lamps of Saver and Fraiture, and the 'parabolic reflectors' of Bordier the engineer. The thermo-lamps of Philippe Lebon, the earliest form of gas lighting, were looked upon as mere curiosities, and people remained faithful to the old lanterns, which continued to afford the Parisians intermittent illumination.

Some of these were known as 'variable burners', which meant in plain language that they did not function on moon-lit nights. But even when they deigned to be lighted, their rays were so feeble that the streets were as dark as before. This was why, under Napoleon as under Louis XIV, lantern-bearers still waited for the audience coming out of the theatres. And also why Caulaincourt, Master of the Horse, fell carriage and all, one night into a pot-hole in the Place Vendôme.

A fine advertisement for the Highways Department and what was then grandiloquently labelled the Service of Illumination!

* * * *

Every step taken in the Paris of that time shows how primitive its life still was. Going to the Seine, it is found cumbered with floating mills and boat wash-houses. There were embankments in only a few places, and bridges were no less rare. Upstream from the Pont de la Tournelle and downstream from the Pont de la Concorde there was nothing to connect the two banks. The quarter of the Arsenal was completely severed from that of the Jardin des Plantes, and when a citizen of Chaillot wanted to go and court a young lady of Grenelle, he had to hail the ferryman or re-enact in person the adventure of Hero and Leander. This lack of bridges and

embankments was one of the first deficiencies to strike
Napoleon, and he was determined to remedy it, however
long it might take to accomplish.

He was shocked, too, by the medley of sheds, booths and
red umbrellas lying between the parvis of Saint-Eustache
and the fountain of the Innocents. 'The Paris market is unworthy of Paris!' he declared; but unfortunately he did
nothing about it, and up to the end of his reign the strange
jumble persisted, like a Flemish kermis, in which were sold,
almost side by side, meat, fish, vegetables, coal and old
hats.

The surrounding quarter was rich in picturesque, if often
rather repulsive, sights. You might come upon many of the
horrible butchers' shops to which animals were brought alive,
to be slaughtered on the spot. Every morning, according to
Prudhomme, herds of twenty or thirty oxen came in from the
outskirts, driven by one man and two dogs, setting all the
neighbourhood in an uproar and completing the congestion
in streets already full of carts. This was followed by the bel-
lowing of 'the victims being immolated almost in sight of the
passers-by'. So much the worse for sensitive souls! The Paris
that lacked clean, hygienic markets had no abattoirs either.

The other essential services of urban life that were non-
existent or still at a rudimentary stage would make a long
list. Public transport was conspicuous by its absence, colleges
were like prisons, the Stock Exchange was housed in a
church, hospitals had prehistoric appointments; the whole of
this poor capital seemed really to be installed among ruins.

Most of the public services had also retained the kindly
dilatoriness of the past. Foreigners smiled at the leisurely
ways of the post. 'I declare', says Yorke in his travel notes,
'that according to the official documents I have on my table,
I could sail to Jamaica with a fair wind before a letter reached
a post office in the provinces.

There were complaints, too, of high postal rates: a letter to
Lyons or Bordeaux cost fourteen sous. Some people, it is true,
got out of paying. As stamps had not yet been invented, and
it was not the sender but the addressee that was made to pay,
cunning people agreed among themselves on a clearly visible
mark to be made on the cover – a star, a cross, a blot – which

was to signify 'I'm coming tomorrow', or 'Marie has just had a baby'. The letter was delivered, the addressee examined it, learnt what he wanted to know and coolly returned it to the postman, keeping his fourteen sous.

* * * *

A slow-motion postal service may be a bearable nuisance, but that a body of citizens entrusted with the maintenance of order should set an example of indiscipline was a far more serious affair. And this was precisely the case of the militia, another legacy of the Revolution which the Consulate would gladly have done without.

Day after day, Dubois's reports were full of criticisms of these so-called auxiliaries of the police, who neglected their guard duty, constantly roping in boys under sixteen to take their place, or deserted their sentry-box to spend the night carousing. 'Yesterday,' notes the Prefect, 'towards eleven at night, a patrol from the post at Gravilliers made bold to enter a tavern known as the *Petit-Trou*, underneath the Paphos dance hall, and drink there with prostitutes.' When another patrol came up and attempted to put an end to the scandal, a regular battle ensued. And similar scenes became so frequent that many peaceable people were afraid to go out of an evening.

Another no less fantastic body was that of the Fire Brigade. To the 293 men belonging to it, divided into three companies, the decree of the 17th Messidor, year IX, had nominally given a military organization, but as there were no barracks available the firemen were in practice allowed to live at home. They took advantage of this to ply their usual trade, which for some unknown reason was generally that of shoemaker. Seldom attending drill, badly commanded by a certain Ledoux, whose slackness was proverbial, these fine fellows made a show of stirring their stumps when the fire alarm sounded; but what assistance could they render with hardly any material means available?

Their corps possessed only two fire-escapes, one stored at the library in the Rue de la Loi, the other at the house of the market superintendent. Moreover, as we have seen, water was hard to come by in Paris, especially at night. So that in

1808, when a fierce fire broke out in the Faubourg Mont-martre, the hydrants on the main boulevards, which were supplied by the pumping station at Chaillot, could not be used because an employee of Périer Brothers had turned off the mains and taken the key away in his pocket.

That same year the Cornmarket was allowed to burn down with little attempt to save it, and its famous dome collapsed with a resounding crash. But the most serious catastrophe of all took place in 1810, when the ballroom at the Austrian Embassy blazed like a match, and the body of the lovely Princess Schwarzenberg was discovered among the ruins, while some ten other victims died of their injuries.

This time the lack of safety appliances really roused the indignation of Napoleon, who had witnessed the tragedy, and he wrote at once to the Minister of Interior: 'On Sunday, at the party given at the Austrian Embassy, there were only six firemen, several of whom were drunk. I have discharged the colonel[1] for not being present and not having organized the service himself.'

Pour Ledoux! Unaware of all that was happening, he had spent a peaceful night outside Paris. But since he was so fond of the country, why was he not given the firemen of Nanterre to command instead?

*   *   *   *

Nearly all the views of Paris at that period have one char-acteristic in common. Whether you are looking at a canvas by Etienne Bouhot, an illustration by Garbizza or a *gouache* by Nicolle, you cannot help being struck by the small number of carriages circulating in the streets. Except for the shop-ping centres, like the Raubourg Saint-Denis, and the main thoroughfares, like the boulevards or the Champs-Élysées, Paris was mainly a world of pedestrians, which accounts for the quiet, provincial appearance of many quarters.

Vehicles were so scarce that sometimes in the course of their walks, people amused themselves by counting the num-ber they saw passing. On his way from the Odéon to the Louvre the day before, so one good man tells us, he only

---

[1] Ledoux was only a major, actually, but a band more or less was all the same to the Emperor.

came across eight cabs. And this scarcity of transport, deplored by the youth of the Directory, was equally inconvenient when the fine ladies of the Consulate wished to go out at night. 'How many charming women', wrote Norvins at a later date, 'have we had the happiness of accompanying to balls, holding an umbrella over their heads and carrying their shoes in our pockets!'

Little by little the Parisians were to have fresh facilities provided for them, but up to the end of the Empire the number of carriages remained very restricted. To begin with, as we have said, there was no sort of public transport service in common. The only vehicle available for getting about was the old *fiacre*, which people had complained about as far back as the reign of Louis XV, and which had gained nothing from the Revolution except rather rustier springs, a rather more worm-eaten body, a rather dirtier seat. The chroniclers of the time describe it in detail:

> An old coffer all to pieces,
> Badly hung on its four wheels,
> Drawn by two raw-boned horses
> Through the dust and the mud;
> The cabby, mostly tipsy,
> Flogging, cursing, swearing,
> Here you have the very picture
> Of the carriage called the *fiacre*.

After a time, however, it had a rival, the *cabriolet*. More up-to-date, lighter, faster, it was the vehicle for people in a hurry. They had to be nimble enough to climb into it without too much difficulty, and undeterred by the cold in winter, or the proximity of the driver in all weathers; but one can put up with many discomforts for the pleasure of travelling at speed, a pleasure of which the cabbies never deprived themselves. The accidents they caused even made the prefecture show its teeth at times. It ended by subjecting hired carriages to regulations in which the smallest details were laid down, from the colour of the number painted on the rear of the body to the size of the little bell dangling from the horse's collar.

Regular fares were fixed as well — twenty sous a journey for cabriolets and one franc fifty for fiacres. Hired by the hour,

the former charged one franc twenty-five and the latter two
francs. Theirs was an institution destined to a hard life, for
these fares remained stationary until the advent of the motor-
car.

There was little to be said, however, for the cab-ranks, of
which there were only three under the Empire – one each in
the Rue Le Peletier, the Rue Taitbout and the Champs-
Élysées. How did the inhabitants of the other quarters man-
age, especially those of the Rive Gauche, when they needed
a cab?

In a city so large, but so poor in means of transport, happy
were those Parisians possessing a carriage of their own, or
able to hire one by the month. The latter luxury cost Yorke
ten louis a week in 1804. At about the same time, Stendhal
hired his livery carriage from Quesnay, in the Rue de Babylone, at the rate of fifteen francs for the half day. He found it
more economical to buy the latest thing in cabriolets for
2,200 francs, as soon as his salary as a Councillor of State
allowed him to play the dandy.

Certain privileged persons travelled more cheaply – the
high dignitaries of the Empire whose office provided them
with a coach for nothing. But some of these, like Decrès, the
Minister of Marine, displayed decidedly too much arrogance
in their official equipage. One day when a hailstorm was
drenching pedestrians to the skin, his friend the Chevalier de
Panat, who was sitting beside the Admiral, saw him suddenly
burst out laughing, and asked him the reason.

'I'm laughing because here we are in a comfortable carriage, properly closed, while all these men and women go
wading through the mud.'

'Upon my soul,' exclaimed de Panat, 'if there are other
people who think like you, you can boast of being the only
one that dares to say such a thing!'

'I'm only saying it to you, you idiot!'

'Yes, but I shall tell everybody!'

And the fact that we know the story proves that he kept
his word. Nothing gets about so fast as a piece of gossip in a
provincial town, and the capital of the Empire was really
nothing more.

CHAPTER VIII

ON THE HIGHWAYS OF FRANCE

An epidemic of broken wheels – The misadventures of a Prefect – The ladies of Malmaison go travelling – The tyrannies of the road – The hell of the diligence and the purgatory of the inn – Highway robbers – The Grassini and the brigands

'TRAVELLING is a fine thing,' wrote Diderot, 'but one must have lost father, mother, children and friends, or never have had any, to make a profession of wandering over the surface of the globe.'

Thirty or forty years later, the French do not appear to have thought otherwise. But they had a good excuse for travelling so little – the execrable state of the roads.

Left unrepaired throughout the Revolution, as we have seen, they presented a pitiable appearance at the beginning of the new century. A few old royal highways still held together here and there, such as the road from Paris to Calais, along which English tourists were soon to drive their hooded coaches. But for one more or less carriageable road there were many others on which accidents occurred day after day.

The newspapers of the year IX tell us that on the road from Bordeaux to Bayonne nothing was to be seen but smashed carriages. A little later, police reports drew attention to certain stretches between Valenciennes and Cambrai, so bad that even the drivers of the mail-coaches were obliged to get down and walk to avoid breaking their necks.

Travellers coming from Strasbourg or Brussels were exposed to the same risks; none of them was ever sure, at the start of his journey, of finding himself whole on arrival.

The new Government would have liked to recondition all these lamentable roads, but the task proved such an enormous one that it was hardly even roughed out by the end of the Consulate.

When Prefect Beugnot took possession of his department of the Seine-Inférieure, he found only two high roads really worthy of the name, and he was not long in discovering what it cost to venture on any of the others. Having left Dieppe one morning with Lemasson, the chief engineer, to go to Neufchâtel, he had to drive along a so-called road that was no more than a beaten track. As a result, one of the shafts of his carriage was broken, and then, the body having become completely dislocated, the two men were obliged to continue their journey on foot. Policemen coming from the opposite direction asked them if they had seen the Prefect. 'We have been expecting him for the last two hours,' they said. 'That's me!' said Beugnot, pointing to the embroidered lapel of his coat. The mounted constabulary at once took the functionaries up behind and trotted off with them. A little too dashingly, no doubt, for the Prefect, who was no Franconi, soon lost his stirrups and found himself on the ground, swearing roundly, 'Oh, accursed dignity! Miserable glory!'

As no bones had been broken they started off again as best they could, but on reaching the neighbouring market-town, where the sub-Prefect, escorted by fifty troopers, was awaiting his chief, whom he had not met before, the state of the latter's uniform may well be imagined. 'Have you come across the Government carriages?' asked somebody. And one of the gendarmes replied, 'Here is the Government! Believe it or not!' Beugnot may have dreamed of a more sensational arrival, but at least he could flatter himself that he now knew what the roads of Normandy were like.

The Seine-Inférieure had no reason to envy the other departments. In the Nord, between Lille and Arras, we are told of a certain road with ruts three feet deep. On the Lyons road there were continual accidents. One day Bonaparte's carriage, coming down off the bridge at Montereau, upset in a ditch. Although two footmen were badly bruised, and Berthier's face was cut by glass from the broken windows, the First Consul was unhurt; but to get him out they had to heave him through one of the doors like a piece of luggage.

In the provinces of the East, through which so many troops had passed in succession during the last ten years, the roads had become even more impassable. Josephine would not soon forget her journey to Aix-la-Chapelle in 1804, nor the horrible road surface that shook her to pieces between Sedan and

Rethel. Next day, in order to climb a steep slope, her carriage had to be supported by ropes, and she howled with terror.

Three years earlier Josephine had found the journey to Plombières no pleasure excursion either, but at least it brought Bonaparte an amusing letter from Hortense, recounting the expedition. She and her mother had left home with Mme Laetitia, Émilie de Beauharnais, now Mme de Lavalette, and General Rapp, acting as escort to the ladies. As soon as they reached the Vosges, Hortense sent news:

'To the inmates of Malmaison.

'On leaving Malmaison the party was in tears, and this gave them all such a frightful headache that the day proved really an oppressive one for these amiable creatures. Mme Bonaparte *mère* went through this memorable day with the greatest courage; Mme Bonaparte the Consuless showed none at all; the two young ladies in the sleeping-carriage, Mlle Hortense and Mme La Valette, fought for the bottle of eau-de-Cologne, and the amiable M. Rapp had the carriage stopped every moment to relieve his little ailing stomach, which was burdened with bile.'

On the second day everybody's health seems to have improved, but the dinner they found at Toul consisted of spinach 'dressed with lamp-oil, and red asparagus fricasseed in sour milk'. They hoped for a better luncheon next day, at Nancy, but unfortunately the military authorities, coming to pay their respects to the travellers, interfered with their plans. 'We continued our journey, therefore, growing visibly thinner,' sighs Hortense. To crown all, the grand sleeping-carriage was nearly upset in the Moselle. Everything ended at last in a triumphal reception at Plombières.

❊   ❊   ❊   ❊

'This is the account of our journey, which we the undersigned certify to be true:

21st Messidor.

Josephine Bonaparte. Bonaparte-Lavalette. Hortense Beauharnais. Rapp. Bonaparte Mère.'

❊   ❊   ❊   ❊

If the journeys of the Bonapartes were as toilsome as this, it is easy to imagine the conditions under which ordinary individuals travelled. One of the nuisances they complained of was the number of toll-stages.

'The French', says Yorke, 'have recently discovered a means of raising the money needed for repairing the roads. They have set up barriers, at irregular intervals, that one can only open by paying from eighteen to twenty sous.'

Each section between two barriers counted as a stage, but the stage charges were higher on the national roads than on the others: between Calais and Paris, for instance, there were only twenty-six stages, but one had to pay tolls corresponding to thirty-four and a half.

What arithmetical problems the unfortunate traveller had to solve! He was for ever thumbing the official handbook of the stages with one hand and rummaging in his waistcoat pocket with the other.

Further taxes were imposed on him when he had to cross a bridge or be ferried over a river. The nearer he got to Paris, the greater the number of duties he had to pay. In the department of the Seine, ferry charges were as follows: six sous for a two-wheel carriage, fifty centimes for a four-wheeler, eight sous for a cart, fifteen for a wagon, ten centimes for a man on horseback, five for a foot-passenger, only three for a calf. Bipeds and quadrupeds thus had their special hierarchy.

Anyone crossing France from one end to the other would have time to compare these countless tyrannies of travel. He would be fortunate not to be held to ransom by some dishonest ferryman if he wanted to cross a ford, as was the case with the student from Périgord, the young Poumies, who has left us his recollections.

Having quitted his village in the early years of the Empire to go to Paris, where he intended to study medicine, the future Esculapius came to the bank of a stream which had just been turned into a torrent by a thunderstorm. A native declared that he knew a good ford. 'If you'll give me a hundred sous', he said, 'I'll take you across on my back.' The bargain concluded, Poumies was soon astride the shoulders of the peasant, who had discarded all but his shirt. They had reached the middle of the ford when the porter came to a dead stop, saying, 'It's a tougher job than I thought. Double the sum, or I drop you.' To avoid a ducking, the poor lad did as he was bid. But on reaching the farther bank with his bundle intact, tired of travelling pickaback, he hurried on to Angoulême and jumped into the diligence.

Not that there was anything attractive about these clumsy vehicles, which from one year's end to the other went grinding their axles along the roads, covering hardly more than seventy-five kilometres in twenty-four hours – taking six days, that is, from Lyons to the capital, and four and a half from Paris to the Channel coast.

Their Paris station was in the Rue du Bouloi, in the old stage-coach yard painted by Boilly. There, every morning and evening, laden with endless luggage, all sorts of travellers were to be seen arriving, from the bourgeois of the Marais, carrying his skull-cap for the daytime and his cotton nightcap for the night, to the touring actress, the commercial traveller and the pair of lovers. Some were departing, others being left behind, and touching scenes took place: like Fontainebleau, Paris had its Court of Farewells.

After much weeping and embracing, the hour of departure arrived; the coachman mounted his box, a bell rang, and the heavy conveyance moved off with a clatter, amid the cursing and whip-cracking of the postillions. It would rumble along for hours and hours, shaking up its occupants at every jolt, deafening them with the rattling of the windows, souring their tempers, provoking subacid dialogues between neighbours: 'Monsieur, your elbow is hurting me!' 'Madame, your box is in my way!' 'Do pull up the window!' 'Stop that child crying!' 'Wring that parrot's neck!'

When night came, these unfortunates would sleep, alas, with one eye open. They would wake next day with cramped legs and arms, stiff necks, puffy eyes. Such was the usual martyrdom of the patrons of a diligence. Little wonder if people thought twice before trusting themselves to it, or if the total number of travellers leaving Paris each day, under the Empire, hardly exceeded an average of 220.

Lighter, and therefore faster, carriages known as *velocifères* were placed on the road at the beginning of 1804. There were seven different models, from cabriolets and berlines to

the huge vehicles to seat thirty-five passengers, and drawn by
four horses, which in spite of their size beat all the records of
the ancient 'letter mail', reaching Rouen in seven hours,
Dijon in sixty, and Milan via the Simplon Pass in ten days.
They had moreover the no less appreciable advantage of
lower fares than those of the diligence – fifteen sous a league
at most. Besides which, the stages were reckoned so as to
allow their passengers to spend every night at an inn, sup on
something better than a snack, and sleep in a real bed.

Was it always a comfortable one? It would be unwise to say
so, for most of the French hostelries were still very indifferent. Apart from a few famous houses, such as the *Tête-de-
Bœuf* at Abbeville, the *Hôtel de la Cloche* at Dijon, the
Haute-Mère-Dieu at Châlons-sur-Marne, the *Poste* at Beaune
and the *Tivollier* at Toulouse, the innumerable *Cheval-
Blancs*, *Grand-Cerfs*, *Chapeau-Rouges* and *Cadran-Bleus*
thronging the provinces at that time had only very meagre
resources at their disposal.

One could sometimes have a reasonably good meal there,
especially if one had taken the precaution of announcing one's
arrival in advance. Sir John Dean Paul was very pleased with
the dinners provided by the *Dessein* in Calais, and the 'Occitanienne' had an enthusiastic memory of the cooking of M.
Villeminet, the excellent master cook of Lavaur. But in most
of the inns either the customer was fleeced or he found the
larder empty, and ran the risk of being told, as Théophile
Gautier was, somewhat later, when he said he wished to *take
something*: 'Well, then, monsieur, take a chair!'

But the question of accommodation was even thornier than
that of food. People usually had to be satisfied with a miserable room, badly furnished, and a bed with coarse sheets. As
for the sheets themselves, it was better not to look too closely.
When young Barante, son of the Prefect of Carcassonne, went
one morning to call on Élisa Bacciochi, who was travelling
through the district, he found her at the hotel, lying on a
mattress that she had been obliged to throw on the floor, to
avoid the bugs infesting the bedstead.

Few people complained, however, for they were inured to
the dirtiness of the inns and the bad state of the roads, and
these rooms, however indifferent, often found more patrons

than they could accommodate. On a very busy night it was fairly usual for two complete strangers to agree to share a bed. If they were of the same sex the arrangement might appear admissible, but we may imagine the feelings of a certain Mme de Nouaillé mentioned in a chronicle by Lenôtre. On arival at Niort she found, in the room she had engaged at the inn, a young man of the name of Patrot who had just had his luggage brought up there.

'*I*'m going to sleep in that bed,' he declared.

'I'm not saying *you* won't sleep in it,' retorted Mme de Nouaillé, 'but *I*'m going to sleep there too.'

And to avoid a quarrel, they both spent the night in it.

A far more serious drawback to travel than these little discomforts was the lack of safety on the roads. Armed attacks had become less frequent than at the beginning of the Consulate, but they were far from having ceased. Several were reported in the very year of the Coronation: in September 1804 Marshal Lefebvre, on his way to his country house after a session of the Senate, was twice shot at, almost point-blank, coming out of the woods of Saint-Martin; his horses bolted, and he was only saved by the presence of mind and strength of wrist of his coachman.

In the following year Talleyrand had a similar adventure in the neighbourhood of Strasbourg. Three months later the Rouen diligence was attacked near Saint-Clair by five robbers wearing smocks 'under which uniforms could be detected'. They searched the carriage, and robbed one of its occupants of four thousand francs.

'I'm sorry to see that some diligences are being held up,' wrote Napoleon from Berlin. 'You must stir up the police and send out some of the force. This will reassure the good citizens.'

They certainly needed reassurance, for even in the heyday of the Empire the highway pirates were still in the news. One of their most celebrated victims was the fair Grassini, robbed in her berline on the road to Avallon on October 19, 1807.

The artist was on her way from Milan to Paris, to sing before the Emperor. She was accompanied by Charles, her *carissimo fratello*, and by her servant, Filippo. All had gone well up to then, and towards eleven at night the travellers were asleep when, after the relay at Rouvray, the carriage suddenly stopped, the doors were opened and two men climbed in, pointing enormous pistols at the occupants, while two others, armed to the teeth, kept the postillions covered. 'Quick, out you come! Quick, your money! Otherwise . . .'

Grassini held out fifteen louis she had about her person; Charles let them take his watch and Filippo gave them his. All the baggage in the carriage was thrown higgledy-piggledy on the road. In the singer's 'ridicule' the robbers discovered another thirty-five louis, and in her jewel-case they found two miniatures, one of which, set in gold, represented Napoleon.

A personal present from the Emperor! This was too much. Grassini burst into tears. 'I beg you, my good bandits,' she pleaded, 'take everything I *poossess*, but leave me *oon* thing that I love more than you can: the *poortrait* of our dear *Goovernment*. I don't want the diamonds, but leave me the *poortrait*!'

Of course the rascals did not let themselves be affected by these politico-sentimental considerations. 'Hurry up, hurry up, Bianchi, let's be off!' cried one of them, and the gang gathered up their booty and disappeared in the darkness, while the travellers, more dead than alive, re-entered the carriage and drove on to Avallon, where they roused the police.

The story had its epilogue, to be read at length in the admirable study devoted to Grassini by M. André Gavoty. Here we learn that the bandits were four Italian deserters who had got their hands in earlier by pillaging the Bourges diligence. But their second exploit did not bring them luck.

On the following day, on the Dijon road, a certain M. Durandeau, in command of the national guard at Vitteaux, was struck by the suspicious appearance of four exhausted pedestrians. He lured them into an inn, warned the mounted police and fetched his own gun. A terrible struggle ensued, in which a policeman was killed, but it was put an end to by the Commandant, who laid two of the bandits low. A third had already been bound hand and foot. The fourth, who had taken to his heels, was caught the following week.

The law thus retained the upper hand. Though Grassini had lost the portrait of her 'dear Government', she had at least the pleasure of reading in the *Moniteur* of October 29, 1807 that the Veterans' Cross had been awarded by Imperial Decree to Jacques Durandeau, her avenger.

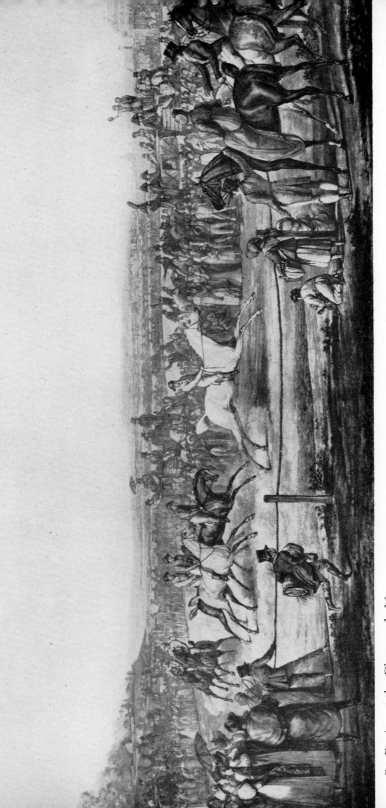

5　Racing at the Champs de Mars

a A luxury bed   *b* A 'gondola' bed

6 Empire Furniture styles

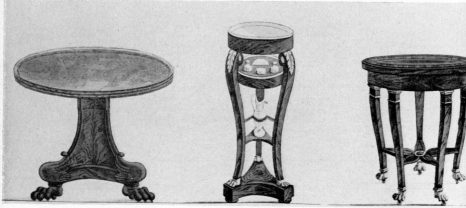

c Tea table   *d* Toilet table   *e* Double-topped table

f and *g* Drawing-room furniture

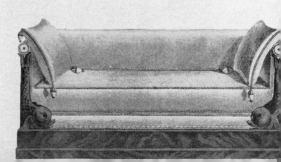

CHAPTER IX

HOUSES AND FURNITURE

*Numbering of houses – The hierarchy of floors – More luxury
than comfort – Empire furniture – Mme Récamier's sanctuary
and Julie Talma's mousehole – Lighting and heating – Great
men in nightcaps*

HAVING an address would seem a simple matter, but
the most elementary problems have not always been
solved at the first attempt. Who would think that the
Consulate authorities had so much difficulty in numbering
the houses systematically?

A few years earlier the Revolution had gone the wrong
way about it. Instead of proceeding by streets, it had proceeded by sections, including all the properties in the same
quarter in a common enumeration. If a street ran through
several sections, this enumeration came to an end every time
it went from one to another, to begin again a few yards farther on with that of the neighbouring quarter. The same
numbers might therefore be repeated several times over in
the same street, or on the other hand, if the street was a very
long one, the numbers might mount up astronomically. A
certain Isaïe Carus, mentioned in a police report, lived at
No. 1,087 Rue du Bac. Pity the messenger sent to deliver a
parcel to him!

To make an end of these complications, various systems
were considered by the new Government, but several years
of discussion were needed before they could come to an
agreement, and not until 1805 was the modern principle of
enumeration adopted: a single series for each street, with odd
and even numbers on alternate sides.[1] This sensational invention had taken five years to work out.

Even then it was not much to the taste of some house
owners, who regretted the old customs. Before 1789 anybody
of any importance, nobleman or financier, considered that his

[1] Frochot had advised a different system: all the numbers, odd and even,
were to follow along one side of the street and then down the opposite side
in the reverse direction, as is still the practice in Rome today.

F

gateway was sufficiently well known to need no distinctive
sign. But habits had changed since then: most houses had
been let out in floors, and some egalitarian method was called
for, since, owing to this division, very different social classes
were housed in the same building.

From this point of view the Paris of the future – the one
we know today – in which the rich and poor quarters have
definite frontiers, differs essentially from the Paris of the
Empire. In the latter there were fewer watertight compart-
ments; tenants of every degree lived close to one another,
though the hierarchy of the floors was strictly observed. 'The
tradesmen occupy the shops; rich people the first floor; well-
to-do people the second; salaried people the third; workpeople the fourth, and the poor the upper stories.'

Later on, much later on, this local geography had to be
revised. A day would come when the top stories would be
the very ones most in demand. But the Napoleonic era knew
nothing of the use of lifts or the fashion for roof-gardens.

Without climbing so high, therefore, we may content ourselves with taking a look at some handsome apartment in one
of the new houses going up on the fringe of the Tuileries or
near the boulevards. It may be more or less luxurious, but we
can be sure, alas, of finding the same defect everywhere: an
inconvenient lay-out, with rooms opening into one another
and an almost complete lack of comfort. Even if the emulators
of Percier and Fontaine have provided drawing-rooms of
pleasant proportions, with a multiplicity of mirrors, large
marble fireplaces, neo-Greek cornices round the ceilings, they
have obviously sacrificed everything to show. Abodes of this
kind might be suitable for giving grand receptions, but as
regards the amenities of ordinary life, little progress appears
to have been made since the century of Louis XIV.

Almost everywhere we find the same plan. You enter from
the staircase straight into a large room, the floor of which is
often flagged in black and white, and which does duty as
antechamber and dining-room combined, for the dining-room
as we understand the term does not yet exist.[1] This room

[1] Even at the Tuileries there was no regular dining-room for the daily use
of the Emperor, who gave orders every morning as to the room in which he
wished the table to be laid, whether in his own apartment or in Josephine's.

opens into the drawing-room. As for the bedrooms, they were nearly always interdependent.

Let us not ask to see the dressing-rooms, still less the bathrooms; nine times out of ten they will prove to be horrible cubby-holes in which the lighting is as poor as the water supply. As often as not there will be just a little basin and a tiny water-jug hidden behind the door of a wall-press. As for another place, of a still more intimate character, it is better not mentioned, for it has been relegated no matter where – on the landing or the half-landing. Sometimes it is non-existent, replaced by a chair which has nothing in common with a *chaise de poste.*

To complete the inventory we may note that the kitchen – unfortunate transition! – is often situated outside the apartment, and that most houses have no back stairs. Servants, tradesmen, modest tenants of the garrets, everybody must go up and down the main staircase, which is pretty badly kept in consequence. 'You know,' writes an Englishwoman, 'the houses in Paris are inhabited by a lot of different people, and their stairs are streets – dirty streets at that.'[1] She was not altogether wrong, but her criticism should have been directed to the architects rather than to the doorkeepers.

* * * *

For the furnishing and decorating of these houses, so often incommodious, but handsome in appearance none the less, a new style had been evolved, resembling that of the eighteenth century no more than a period of Fontanes' resembled a phrase of Voltaire's. Although this so-called new style was an obvious imitation of the antique, arising so to speak out of the ashes of Herculaneum, the treatises of Winckelmann and the pictures painted by David even before the Revolution, it was nevertheless to be known as Empire style, and it deserves to retain the title, so well did it express the aspirations of an epoch enamoured of force and majesty.

By simplifying their lines, by returning, or thinking they were returning, to the purest classical forms, the artists had blazed the trail. Certain cabinet-makers, the Jacob brothers at their head, contrived to follow it; and soon there came

[1] Maria Edgeworth, *Personal Letters.*

from their workshops those fine masterpieces in mahogany, citrus-wood, maple and ebony, which master-carvers such as Thomas and Raviro decorated with matchless bronzes.

Their stocky forms, their gilt motifs represent a symbol, that of Victory. This is the significance of all these crowns, trophies, lions' heads, griffins with clenched talons supporting tables and brackets, proud caryatids with breasts swelling like sails.

Furniture of this type was not only found in the houses of every member of the family, at the Hôtel Thélusson where Caroline and Murat lived, at the Folie Saint-James, Élisa's residence, and at the old Hôtel Dervieux, Parisian home of Louis and Hortense, it invaded the homes of ordinary people who prided themselves on following the fashion.

Many a *cocotte*, as a reminder of her *liaison* with some celebrated military man, adopted a model from the catalogues of the *Mésangère* described as the 'Bed of a General's Wife'. Two lances crossed behind a shield supported the curtains of the bed-recess, and an upturned Roman helmet served as a toilet-tidy at night.

Another very odd bedroom was that of the actor La Rive. At his house at Montlignon he had a camp bed set up under a tent hung with portraits of Spartacus, Genghis-Khan, Bayard and Tancred, his most famous roles. It seems a miracle that he could sleep peacefully in such company.

But in the heyday of the Consulate the most celebrated bedroom was Mme Récamier's. The incomparable Juliette made a point of showing it off to visitors as a museum of elegance. When she gave a party she greeted each guest with the same question: 'Would you like to see my room?' And a handful of the faithful would accompany her to the sanctuary.

Always easily astonished, Reichardt describes it with somewhat naïve admiration. 'This very lofty room was entirely surrounded by tall mirrors all in one piece, with an immense mirror forming the end partition. Here, with its head to the wall, stood the ethereal couch of the goddess of the place – a cloud of muslin, a white vapour!'

Perhaps this profusion of mirrors in the bedroom of an honest woman might seem a little questionable to modern taste. But the learned traveller was not so particular. He was wonder-struck by the antique bed, draped with curtains of violet silk and crowned by a pelmet of bronze satin. He noticed a statue of *Silence*, bathed in the rays of a lamp into which a genie poured oil, drop by drop. Alongside the bedroom was the bathroom, with the bath hidden under a sofa upholstered in red morocco, in the inevitable looking-glass recess; and close by, too, was the boudoir with a frescoed ceiling, chairs covered in corded silk of Tours, and in each corner an Argand lamp on a metal stand. Double curtains in all the windows, drooping veils everywhere. A great deal of mystery for a bedroom and a boudoir in which, if repute is to be believed, nothing ever happened.

The same could certainly not be said of the bedroom of Mme Tallien, who had reverted to the name of Thérèse Cabarrus on becoming Ouvrard's mistress. In her house in the Rue de Babylone, which she owed to his liberality, she too liked showing off her bed, a bed of ebony ornamented in bronze, sheltering under a sort of tent held up by a pelican's bill. This modern Cleopatra believed the decorations of her bedroom and drawing-room to be in the purest Egyptian style; but her upholsterer – possibly the famous Boulard, later employed by Josephine – had chiefly supplied her with miles of gold fringe and trimmings in decidedly Parisian taste.

The junction of Consulate and Empire was a happy time for luxury trades, with fashion evolving and furniture changing from day to day. At one moment the craze was all for polished wood. A few months later no self-respecting drawing-room could have mahogany or citrus-wood furniture; it must be made of 'ordinary wood covered with several coats of matt white paint, relieved by ornaments in burnished gold'. Or again, in the summer, 'for the sake of coolness', some young lady might demand a set of furniture in painted iron, 'Her clock is of iron, her antique vases of iron, the ornaments on her mantelpiece and her window-sills, even her bed is of iron.' And the junk shops of the future would be the richer by some amusing curiosities.

A thousand infectious caprices prove that Parisians could refuse nothing to their wives, still less to their mistresses. Though Madame was not musical she would discover all at once that she could not live without a large-size piano or a gilt-edged harp. Off went the gentleman to Érard's;[1] the handsome harp cost a hundred louis, the grand piano about double, but it meant that a woman was satisfied, while all her friends turned pale with jealousy.

Another lady might have a mania for flowers. She had so many in her apartment that besides the valet and the floor-polisher she would soon need an indoor gardener. Meanwhile she had a conservatory built on, where she spent her days. No matter if she mistook geraniums for hydrangeas, or mixed up pistils and stamens, she would plume herself on botanical knowledge, and declare with intense seriousness: 'I used to love literature, music, dancing, my husband; now I have only one passion in the world. . . . Flowers! Ah! They are the joy of my life! I can only exist in my hothouse.'

But at this same period, fortunately, there were many women who did not need so much luxury to feel happy in their homes. They had chosen them and furnished them without much regard to fashion, and they liked them because they suited their tastes. Julie Talma, for instance, on going to live in the Rue Neuve-du-Luxembourg, has this to say to her faithful friend Benjamin Constant:

'A great problem has been solved. They have managed to make an apartment small enough for me. You thought I had no furniture, but you were much mistaken – and anyhow it all depends on the apartment you take. Mine is so well suited to my size and my fortune that I have been obliged to distribute my furniture to all my friends. The joke of it is that I had gone begging all round for things to ornament my rooms. Nobody refused, but instead of giving me anything, each of them went off with what took their fancy. To tell the whole truth, however, I'm having some mahogany furniture made for a little room I call my drawing-room. Did I tell you that my windows look straight on to the boulevard? Did you know that the looking-glass over my fireplace will reflect either the green or the dust of the trees? For such

[1] Érard's reputation was increasing at that time. He sold small pianos of the harpsichord type for 59 louis, and large ones, lavishly decorated, for up to 200. These were delivered to all countries 'accessible by water transport'.

advantages as these I would have been content to live in a mouse-hole.'

This little note, almost in the style of de Sévigné, is surely worth any number of the lyrical dissertations of that intolerable phrasemonger in her greenhouse.

❋   ❋   ❋   ❋

When we said that the First Empire was little more advanced than the age of Louis XIV, we were thinking partly of two problems equally badly solved: the lighting and heating of the houses.

All foreigners passing through Paris agreed that the houses were icy, and curiously enough it was the people from the north that complained the most. Thinking with regret of their comforting stoves, they referred ironically to our fireplaces with a few miserable logs burning in them.

The larger the rooms, the loftier their windows and doors, the more difficult it was to protect oneself from draughts, and this was true of course of all official apartments. In the drawing-rooms of the Luxembourg and the Tuileries Bonaparte was always to be seen handling the tongs.

It was by the fire that he once received Fortuné d'Andigné and the heads of the Royalists; he gave many of his audiences leaning against the mantelpiece, for in his case chimney-corner conversation was by no means a metaphor. When the Court went into residence at Saint-Cloud, all this fine company found their teeth chattering at the first frosts of autumn. 'In spite of the greatcoats piled up on the beds it is impossible to get warm.'

A few inventors had new ways to suggest for fighting the cold. In the Great Hall of the Institute, for instance, which was undergoing alterations by Antoine Vaudoyer, steam pipes were being installed, as like our modern radiators as two drops of hot water. But all this was done mainly by way of experiment, and for many years to come private individuals would continue to heat their rooms by log fires.

The peasant trader at the corner shop charged thirty-eight francs for a load of wood, the contents of a medium-sized cart.[1] One could also burn blocks of peat, costing only

[1] A load was the equivalent of two cubic metres.

seventy-five francs for 4,000. It was poorish fuel, but our ancestors had not yet been spoilt by progress. They thought it quite natural to use flint and steel to light their fires, and to end their evenings by candle-light, in front of a fireplace in which smoked a few charred embers.

In most middle-class houses the lighting was no better than the heating. The pump lamp and the Carcel lamp – the latter in need of considerable improvement – were reserved for grand occasions. The rest of the time people used candles, taking care not to burn them at both ends, since they cost four francs a pound. There were two kinds, known as the ordinary and the bastard, and the wags remarked that it was just the same with children.

With such rudimentary comfort, the most critical hour was that of bedtime. Because there were no matches (they were not invented till 1809, and did not come into common use until the reign of Louis-Philippe), night-lights had to be kept burning. Because the bedrooms were cold, head-coverings were needed – Madras handkerchiefs for the gentlemen, caps with strings for the ladies.

To the French of the twentieth century, enjoying central heating and sleeping every night with an electric switch within reach of their hand, these habits must appear rather strange. They will find it difficult to imagine the heroes of the First Empire transformed at the hour of the curfew into comedy characters, and appearing next morning, after getting out of bed, in the costume of the *Malade Imaginaire*. Yet the most august personages set this example. It was with his handkerchief tied round his head, its two corners falling on his shoulders, that the Emperor spent hours every morning, working beside his secretary and even receiving a few ministers in his back room.

Audiences held in this sort of costume would not surprise anybody, for people of all ranks behaved in much the same way. Until a good fire had sent the thermometer up, dressing-gown and nightcap were perfectly admissible as morning wear. It was one of the features of the time, one of the little freedoms of family life, far more numerous under the Empire than is generally supposed.

Because in the paintings and prints of the time we are

shown rooms of exemplary tidiness, furnished in a rather
stiff fashion, we are apt to forget that a room in which people
sleep and dress is not an exhibition stand, and that this edifying scene must often be upset. Many a kerchief, many a
gorget, many a vulgar flannel waistcoat must have littered a
Jacob sofa, many a pair of boots have been left about on those
handsome carpets with their flowered rosettes. The material
conditions of life, lack of water, poor lighting, dust from wood
fires, insufficiency of toilet utensils, resulted in a certain disorder, even in apartments that were well kept; and many
were probably very badly kept.

For proof of this, we have only to accompany Maria Edgeworth and Mme Récamier on a visit to that old mountebank
La Harpe, who received them in a horrible little room dig-
nified by the name of office, clad in a dressing-gown 'that
had once been red' and a 'superlatively dirty nightcap'.

Or let Norvins show us Fouché – now Duke of Otranto –
at his toilet, his cotton nightcap lying beside a shaving-brush
on a corner of the mantelpiece, himself in shirtsleeves, his feet
in down-at-heel slippers, stropping an old monk's razor before
shaving off a beard as yellow as his face, in front of a looking-
glass costing thirteen sous. Or to complete our edification, we
might push on to the Arsenal, to take Mme de Genlis by sur-
prise and glance at her worktable. There, among volumes of
verse and watercolour sketches, we should see a medley of
toothbrushes, an inkstand, two pots of jam partly consumed,
eggshells, a roll, the remains of a cup of coffee, some paper
flowers, a candle-end, a tress of false hair and a piece of Brie
cheese.

Poor Mme de Genlis! Napoleon used to say of her, 'When
she talks of virtue, she seems to be making a discovery.' If
she had been talking of cleanliness the subject would have
seemed no less novel to her.

CHAPTER X

PARIS AT TABLE

A generation of big eaters – Time and nature of meals – Cam-bacérès's dinner-parties – Grimod and his Almanac – Other famous epicures – Talleyrand's two salmons – Middle-class tables – The hardships of the Continental System

WHENEVER we suffer from stomach trouble, we have the right to make a grievance of it against our grand-parents of the First Empire, for their appalling voracity is at the root of many of the gastric affections of today. Dinners like Cambacérès's, lasting five hours, must inevitably be paid for sooner or later. It is only rather tire-some that we should be the ones to clear the debt.

Let us try to be good losers and recall that generation at its meals without too much bitterness. We shall soon dis-cover that their ideas and habits in gastronomical matters were not in the least like our own. Everything will seem odd to us, the hours of meals to begin with.

The morning of a bourgeois who liked doing himself well included two separate breakfasts: the cup of coffee or choco-late taken on rising and, towards ten or eleven o'clock, a more copious meal of eggs and cold meat – sometimes grilled meat – called for some unknown reason *déjeuner à la fourchette*. This was a little, unpretentious meal, dispatched in one's dressing-gown, which intimate friends often dropped in to share, whether they had been invited or not. No mark of friendship was more appreciated than this brief explanation of a ring at the door: 'I've come to ask you for some break-fast.' It might not delight a Parisian of today so much.

The hour of dinner, which in the past had been fixed at the beginning of the afternoon, while we have since moved it to the end, seems to have varied a great deal under the Empire. The table was laid more or less early according to the per-son's rank, the quarter in which he lived and the profession he followed. 'I bet they get up at seven and dine at two,' says somebody in a play by Alexandre Duval, of some good people

living in the Marais. The same rule obtained for workpeople
and small shopkeepers, but people of higher condition waited
till five or six for the important meal of the day.

A few people, attached to their old ways, may have complained of the new, but they were forced to admit that the
restaurants were never empty till the end of the afternoon.
As for fashionable occasions, the hour mentioned on the
invitation cards was usually five or half-past. But one had
to read between the lines: *five o'clock*, by itself, really meant
six; *five o'clock precisely* meant half-past five. Only the term
five o'clock very precisely was to be taken literally.

Anyone ignorant of these subtleties of etiquette ran the
risk of arriving ridiculously early at his host's house and
finding the domestics laying the table.

With dinners so late as this, the fashion for suppers, so dear
to the old regime, naturally lost many of its followers. There
were so few of them among the general public that henceforth most restaurants closed at the same time as the theatres.

It was only in households that liked going to bed late that
suppers of a sort were still improvised, under the more up-to-
date name of English teas. But their menus were so ample,
and their accompaniments so luxurious, that they were less
like our little snacks of the twentieth century than very
copious evening dinners. The first course usually consisted of
a huge roast, such as a twenty-pound leg of mutton, two
other no less considerable dishes, eight smaller ones and six
hors-d'œuvres. Roast meats appeared in the second course as
well, besides side-dishes, dessert and ices. Very strong coffee
and numerous liqueurs completed the programme of a well-
filled day.

The acrobatic feats performed by the stomachs of the Consulate and the Empire were astonishing. Their owners had
not even the excuse that the French of the time of Louis XIV
could proffer, that of imitating a sovereign possessing a formidable appetite. Bonaparte was, on the contrary, a model
of frugality.

Minor history gives us precise details of his way of life at
the Tuileries. His daily menus were hardly more complicated
than those of an ordinary man of means. As a rule he dispatched his meals at military speed: fifteen minutes at most

for evening dinner, in Josephine's company; a little less haste
on Sundays for the feast that brought together the entire
Bonaparte family and a few dignitaries of the Court.

Napoleon himself seems never to have been very appre-
ciative of the pleasures of the table. He cared so little for
them that sometimes, if he had work to finish, he would take
no notice of dinner-time, to the great distress of the palace
scullions, who were obliged, one evening, to spit twenty-
three chickens, one after another, so that the last one might
be eatable. When a man can throw away twenty-three chickens, it is fair to conclude that he knows nothing about food.

Such was actually the monarch's own opinion. 'If you
are a small eater,' he said to a certain diplomat, 'come to me.
But if you want to eat a lot, go to Cambacérès.' And even
after a century and a half this advice seems judicious, for the
sight of the Second Consul playing the part of host was not
a little comical.

A foreigner who dined with him towards the end of 1802,
when he was still living in the Hôtel d'Elbœuf in the Carrousel, describes the scene with full details. Thirty-six guests
were gathered round a huge table, covered with flowers and
silver-plated chafing-dishes. The footmen were in full consular livery, the butlers wore maroon coats with gold-
chequered buttons. They seemed to be acting as supers only,
for the host took it upon himself to carve all the main dishes,
offering each guest the morsel most likely to please him. A
heavy task for the head of such an assembly, with a succession
of more than sixty dishes to cope with. The session ended,
reckon the number of times the amphytrion plunged his knife
into the legs of mutton and the fowls, and how many times
he asked the same questions of each guest in turn.

'May I give you this little wing, Monsieur le Conseiller
d'État?'

'Which do you prefer, Excellency? The parson's nose or
the merrythought?'

But Cambacérès did not mind the trouble. People had come
to his house to eat well, and he was determined that everybody should do his duty. The trial was a bit severe, however,
for those with a middling appetite. The young Norvins,
Napoleon's future biographer, discovered this one evening to

his discomfort, when dining at the Hôtel d'Elbœuf after his return from Santo Domingo. Under the pretext that his digestion had been impaired by his travels and the doctor had prescribed a diet, he was placed beside his host, who had little fancy dishes prepared for him. 'I accepted all his favours', wrote Norvins later in his *Memorial*, 'with the discretion of a eunuch in the harem, seizing the opportunity to get rid of my plate every time he turned his head.'

Another drawback to these parties was their lack of gaiety, such special food having to be savoured with profound concentration. Woe to the imprudent guest daring to raise his voice while the famous partridges, roasted on one side and grilled on the other – a speciality of the house – were being sampled! He was called to order, as the obese Aigrefeuille was one day. 'Don't talk so loud, my friend! Really, one can't tell what one's eating!'

To Cambacérès gastronomy was really a sort of religion. He not only ransacked the forced-vegetable shops of Paris, he not only had the most delicate specialities of the provinces sent him – game from his estate at Livet, ducks from Strasbourg, potted meats from Nérac – but for certain consignments he even mobilized the State Messengers. This practice nearly got him into trouble during the Congress of Lunéville. Bonaparte, having discovered that several individuals were misusing the official dispatch box, gave orders that it should be strictly reserved for the transport of dispatches. That evening the Second Consul entered Bourienne's office looking very pale. 'I've come to ask you for an exemption. How do you think one can make friends if one can't give them choice food? You know yourself that it's mainly by means of the table that one governs.' For him, good politics was synonymous with good cooking. The idea had the good fortune to amuse Bonaparte, who settled the business himself. 'Cheer up, my good man', he said, 'and don't get in a state. The Messengers shall continue to convey your truffled turkeys, your Mayence pasties and your red-legged partridges.'

* * * *

If the title of Prince of Gastronomes had existed at that time, it would not have been awarded to Cambacérès, in spite of his pretensions and his big belly, but to Grimod de la Reynière, for this original heir of a celebrated Farmer-General surpassed his rivals by a hundred cubits. Uniting theory with practice, he made of the culinary art a branch of literature. With his *Almanach des Gourmands*, which had a good sale for eight years in succession, he put poetry into his sauces, wit into his condiments – and made his readers' mouths water. 'Let us lay down our principles,' he says. 'You will agree, Messieurs, to begin with, that the pleasures afforded us by good food are those that we experience the soonest, that we relinquish the latest and enjoy the most often. Could you say the same of the others?'

As a practical application of these ideas Grimod founded a sort of little Academy, of which he was to be the perpetual president: *le Jury dégustateur*. It consisted of a dozen members, elected unanimously, who assembled once a week – round a table, of course. They were given newly invented dishes to taste, on which they were to bestow *certificates of official recognition*, which were collected with the utmost seriousness by a secretary. Actresses sometimes attended the sessions of this Areopagus – Émilie Contat, Mlle Volnays, Mlle Mézeray, Mme Belmont and the celebrated Fanchon la Vielleuse, who played godmother to a new cake: la Fanchonnette.

These dinners which, as we said, lasted no less than five hours, took place in winter at the Hôtel de Grimod, No. 1 Champs-Élysées – where the nineteenth century would see the *Cercle de l'Epatant*, and the twentieth the United States Embassy – and were improvised, in summer, at his château of Villiers-sur-Orge. The table was laid out of doors, under a magnificent catalpa tree, and practical statements went the round, such as 'There's more wine than is wanted for the mass, and not enough to work a water-mill, so it must be drunk.'

Our Epicurean's guests were glad to obey him, for he owned an admirable cellar. His wines were not, like those of the Emperor, standard types at six francs a bottle, supplied by the local grocer,[1] but old bottles bearing impressive dates,

[1] Whether Chambertin, Napoleon's favourite wine, or Clos-Vougeot or Château-Lafite, all the wines for the Tuileries were bought at this fixed price at Souppé and Pierrugues, 333 Rue Saint-Honoré.

to which one must take off one's hat. As for the liqueurs,
Crême d'Arabie, Crême des Îles, and so on, that Grimod had
served at table together with very hot coffee, he got them
from Mme Amphion, an old lady of Martinique for whom he
wore mourning in 1802, when she ended by dying at the age
of a hundred and eleven. Which shows that if alcohol can kill
a man it sometimes takes a long while to do it in the case of a
woman. But to return to the Almanac. . . .

He could not have chosen a better time to glorify the art
of cooking, for every class of society had its famous gourmands.
The theatre boasted the huge, enormous des Essarts, who
played Molière's Orgon very well, but incarnated Rabelais's
Pantagruel even more naturally in real life.

'An honest man', he said, 'must make the fame of his table
his first care. Good food is the fertilizer of a clear conscience.'
Then he goes into details. 'The leg of mutton must be looked
forward to like a lovers' first rendez-vous, beaten as tender as
a liar caught in the act, blond as a German girl and bleeding
like a Carib. Mutton is to lamb what the millionaire uncle is
to a poverty-stricken nephew . . . spinach is not worth much in
itself, but it is susceptible to every impression, it is the virgin
wax of cookery. . . . Use the egg as an amiable conciliator
insinuating itself between all parties in order to bring about
difficult *rapprochements*.'

In dramatic circles, furthermore, the critic Geoffroy was
fond of his stomach, and this weakness led him to accept
presents from his tradesmen. Next day he would slip a free
advertisement for their benefit into the *Journal des Débats*,
by way of postscript to his article. But the practice was
severely criticized by Étienne, the Censor, who launched this
protest: 'Only a few days ago a *mustard-seller* came to the
office of the *Journal*, under the impression that he could
insist on having his merchandise advertised because M.
Geoffroy had accepted samples from him. This is of the
utmost indecency!' His indignation is easily understood:
Accepting *pots-de-vin*, well and good, but pots of mustard,
fie!

The great houses of the Faubourg Saint-Germain, which
were doubtless victualled by more admissible procedures, included some first-class gormandizers among their inhabitants.

The duc de Luynes eclipsed them all by reason of his name, his wealth and his girth. Those who dined with him noticed a sort of little internal gulf hollowed out of the table; this indentation was required to house the august abdomen. Although no longer young, its owner still ate voraciously, but his head sometimes felt a bit heavy. Wishing to help his guests, he might dip the ladle into the soup tureen and fall suddenly asleep before he had filled it. A servant would tap him on the shoulder; he would awake with a start, complete his polite effort and sink into lethargy again. An illustration of the proverb *Qui dort dîne*.

With every year of the Empire the luxury of the table assumed fresh forms. Not only were the provision shops in the Palais-Royal raided – Chevet's, whose cramped premises were always crowded, Hyrment, famous for his fish and his stuffed tongues, Corcellet, whose sign was painted by Debucourt and who sold such exquisite larks from Pithiviers and such succulent pasties from Toulouse – but it was now sought to please the eye: people demanded fine glass and fine linen, and the wife of Marshal Ney bought four thousand francs' worth of tablecloths and napkins in a single season from a certain Mlle Théoville. The decoration of a dinner-party demanded a sumptuous display of candelabra and centre-pieces supplied by the firm of Odiot, and often hired out by them. The middle of the table was often ornamented by some masterpiece in nougat, sponge cake or spun sugar, representing the passage of the St Bernard or the episode of the bridge at Lodi. An edifying collaboration of confectionery and history!

As for the details of the service, the procedure was almost invariable. Dishes were always handed round three times; this was the rule. Glasses must never remain empty, as soon as one threatened to dry up a butler hastened to refill it. Every guest found his place marked by a card bearing his name, but the use of hand-written menus had not yet come into fashion. It was thought sufficient to have the dishes announced by the major-domo, who usually played his part with the seriousness of a heavy father on the stage. And after all, in many houses, people were rather like the audience at a theatre. Talleyrand's guests must have felt like this, the day that a certain salmon was offered them with great pomp.

It was a gigantic fish, a real product of a *pêche miraculeuse*. When it appeared, carried at arm's length by a major-domo, everybody exclaimed, 'Marvellous!' 'Unique!' And Talley-rand, rubbing his hands, said, 'I've certainly been lucky; there's not another salmon like it.' But he had hardly said this when the sound of smashed crockery was heard. Having caught his foot in a chair, the major-domo had fallen full length on the carpet, amid the ruins of the salmon. Faced with this disaster, prearranged no doubt by himself, the prince alone remained unperturbed. With a slight shrug of his shoulders, he looked at the unique object, of which, as if by chance, he possessed two specimens, and said simply, 'Bring the other one!'

* * * *

Not everybody bought their fish at Hyrment's nor their fruit at the widow Fontaine's. Besides the tables of high society, Paris contained countless others, more modest but no less good, those of unpretentious middle-class people, who appreciated good cooking for its own sake, and treasured their old recipes. Their menus often afford us amusing dis-coveries: had you ever heard of toasted dough, beef between two dishes, grilled fricassees, cream cheese *à la rose,* straw-berry coffee? These were some of the specialities of the ex-cellent Mme Moitte, with whom we shall soon make closer acquaintance. Whether going to market or watching over her kitchen stove, her only ambition was to do her family well, in her little apartment on the Quai Malaquais.

Another very attractive household was the one near the Observatory, where Reichardt was entertained to dinner one evening and was delighted to find the patriarchal customs of pre-Revolution days still observed.

Here children and parents addressed one another by 'thee' and 'thou'. A pretty girl of fifteen, not above taking a *'canard'* from her father's cup when coffee was served, told the visitor that he had once taken her to the theatre, but disguised as a boy in her brother's clothes, to save the expense of a frock. As for her mother, although a Parisian, she had never been to

G

the Opéra, but she loved music all the same, and proved it by singing a little song over the dessert. Here was the kindly gaiety of the old days.

It was all the more suited to the occasion, in that the Carnival had just begun. An excellent opportunity to introduce their guest to the game of *beignets*. In the lovely golden fritters being passed round, some pieces of playing cards had been slipped under the slices of apple. Every time one of the guests pretended to choke there was a shout of 'Caught!' and everybody laughed. Reichardt, who evidently liked simple jests, laughed like the rest, grateful for the excellent dinner he had just been given; he had counted no less than sixteen dishes, washed down with generous wine.

Anybody who might be surprised to see people in such modest circumstances offering such a copious bill of fare, would only have to look at the account-books of the housewives of the First Empire, to see that food was ridiculously cheap at that time. Eight pounds of boiling beef cost about five francs; two pounds of ham, two fifty. For twenty sous one could pluck a partridge; for twice that sum, roast a chicken or a duck. A pound of butter cost twenty-eight sous, a quarter of ordinary eggs twenty-two. If you liked oysters you could get ten dozen at the market for four francs. And heavy drinkers were fortunate in France, for claret cost them twelve sous and ordinary brandy three francs.

The only produce costing a little more seems to have been that imported from a distance, such as oil and oranges from the Midi. The continental blockade was to prove a far more important factor in the increase in market prices. All colonial products, such as rum, coffee, chocolate, would suddenly go up, and sugar, that unfortunate sugar that people found it so difficult to do without, was to become one of the heaviest expenses for small purses.

So as not to waste it, some families had recourse to a most ingenious plan. From the ceiling of the room where they drank their coffee they hung a piece of sugar at the end of a string, and each person had the right to dip it in their cup for a moment before passing it on to a neighbour.

A very old lady we knew in our childhood told us she had seen this sort of egalitarian sugaring being practised when she herself was very young. The duration of each dip was carefully checked, with no mercy shown to the egoist who exceeded the legitimate time and had to be called to order by his neighbours.

And our venerable friend could still hear the reprimand addressed to her by a cross-grained uncle. 'Zenaïde, I kept the piece for twenty seconds less than you. That sort of delicacy is the sign of good breeding and true family spirit.'

CHAPTER XI

THEATRE AUDIENCES

*Fondness for the theatre – Time of performances – The golden
age of gate-crashers – Actors and managers – Pit audiences –
The* claque *– Mlles George and Duchesnois – The origin of
the* crochet *– Tragedy and its applications – A drama at Grosbois – Whims of the censorship*

W E ARE fond of the theatre today, but to nothing like
the same degree as under the First Empire. With
many of our contemporaries this ancient passion has
dwindled to a mild, intermittent temptation – with women
when they have a dress to show off, with men when they have
been given complimentary tickets.

It was otherwise in the days of Talma and Mlle George.
The theatre was then considered by all classes of society as
the essential element of their daily pleasures. Not a bourgeois,
not a shop assistant, not a student but could be reduced to
tears by a drama of Pixérécourt's, or to helpless laughter by
some farrago of nonsense by Brunet.

The reason for this concentration of evening amusement
behind the footlights is not far to seek. We have only to
picture Paris to ourselves as it was around 1800: a Paris without a cinema, without a music-hall, and with cafés which,
in spite of their reputation, would remind us today of provincial pubs. Picture this city of feeble lanterns, lugubrious
after nightfall, and ask yourself where our great-grandfathers
could have found a little liveliness, noise and light except at
the theatre.

There was usually one at their door, offering every attraction – convenient hour of opening, cheap seats within the
reach of every purse, frequent change of programme.

It was towards the end of the afternoon, when the family
dinner had been dispatched, that the curtain went up everywhere. Six o'clock was still the usual hour towards 1800. Later
on there was a tendency to delay the three hammer-strokes
at some of the theatres, notably at the Comédie-Française,
where the signal was not given till seven.

But a more radical reform attempted by Devismes, the manager of the Opéra, met with no success. The rash man had conceived the extraordinary idea of waiting till nine o'clock to open his doors, which he announced in a style inspired by Jean-Jacques Rousseau.

'Audiences and artists', he wrote, 'will thus have time to dine at their ease with their friends, to visit walks and gardens and admire the bewitching sex whose grace and elegant dress contribute to the ornament of these places. After breathing this pure air they will take their seats at the Opéra, which will not open its spectacle until Nature has closed her own.'

This romantic effusion aroused universal mirth, and Geoffroy, in his article in the *Débats*, dealt it a shrewd blow. 'When it granted you protection, Monsieur, the Government had no intention of sheltering you from censure, or even ridicule.' The subject was dropped, and the Opéra remained faithful to its old habits.

It was also ordained by the Central Bureau of Police that all performances should end more or less at the same time. The curtain must be rung down everywhere towards half-past nine, to make the journey home through the dark streets less troublesome. A few theatres only, with very full bills, managed after a time to have the curfew delayed: the Ambigu, for example, with its interminable dramas in which murder was committed fifteen to twenty times every night. Steeled by so many emotions, the audience would be able to return to their homes without dread of nocturnal attack.

As far as the practical life of the theatre was concerned, many customs under the Empire were much the same as those of today. Multi-coloured bills announced the plays to be given, but instead of being pasted on Morris pillars they were stuck up at street corners, on sixty-seven specially reserved sites familiar to all theatre-goers.

Then as now, ticket-sellers plied a shameless trade outside the box-office. In 1802 the unfortunate Reichardt complained of having been robbed, near the Français, by 'a sort of commissionaire, fairly well dressed', who sold him tickets at three times their original price.

As in our day, too, the theatres took a day off at intervals, but the official ones had not yet formed the habit of long

holidays; they merely allowed themselves a short respite
when the weather was too hot. The posters then referred
prettily to the 'fineness of the season'.

Other more important problems were already troubling the
managers, foremost among them the 'right of the poor', which
from 1800 to 1807 was to deprive them of an average of
400,000 francs a year, and above all, in the big theatres, the
number of free tickets they were obliged to grant. It was
useless for Bonaparte to insist that all seats must be paid for,
that 'nobody had the right to gratuitous enjoyment of an
entertainment that the contractor sold to all and sundry';
useless for him to practise what he preached and pay 20,000
francs yearly for his box at the Opéra, 12,000 francs for that
at the Opéra-Comique, and the same for one at the Italiens;
the majority of civil servants set so much store by their
precious *entrée* that they pretended not to understand. And
when one evening a scrutiny was made at the Opéra, it was
found that out of 150 orchestra stalls only twenty were paid
for, twenty-six out of 150 in the amphitheatres, and of the 200
occupants of the fourth row at the sides not one had a paid
a red cent. How could they make ends meet under such
conditions?

Taking a look behind the scenes, we shall find the poor
managers having difficulties, too, with the members, male
and female, of their companies. Elleviou's annual salary, towards the end of his career, amounted to 84,000 francs, and
he was demanding 120,000. The Emperor had at last to put
his foot down, deciding that the king of singers had begun to
practise blackmail.

Even more frequent were the dramatic interludes, such as
the refusal to play a certain part, diplomatic attacks of influenza and departures at a moment's notice that upset the
whole show. When Mlle George started out in haste for
Amiens, under the pretext that her father was at death's door,
it was really because a series of lucrative engagements were
awaiting her there. Talma and Mlle Duchesnois too were for
ever asking for leave, and the papers deplored 'the scandalous
disappearance of most of our leading actors and actresses
who, never satisfied with their share, run off to the country
to seek a supplement of fame and money'. As for Mlle

Contat's tours, someone was heard to say that 'the Théâtre-Français will soon be no more than a *pied à-terre* for our wandering Thalia, where she can take a rest now and again.'

Criticisms that might have been uttered yesterday, since they apply to behaviour which, unfortunately, belongs to all time.

However, as the Empire prided itself on being a forceful regime, it sometimes had recourse to strong measures for the suppression of too flagrant abuses. A comedian refusing to act, a singer masking his ill humour under a pretended attack of laryngitis, a *danseuse* leaving everybody in the lurch, all such unruly creatures ran the risk of penalties far more severe than being fined and held up to shame. They were made to spend a few days at the Fort l'Evêque, like political prisoners.

Such was the fate of Brunet for having perpetrated a bad pun on the Tribunate, of Roland the actor and his colleague Julien, for refusing to act, and of Martin, the famous baritone, as a cure for an imaginary cold.

Pretty women themselves were not safe from this military discipline. In a police report of June 23, 1810 we read that 'Yesterday, Friday, Mlle Chevigny did not appear at the Opéra, where she was to have played an important part in the ballet *Andromaque*. It was ascertained that Mlle Chevigny was at her country house with a young man aged twenty-four, a little-known individual.'

If it had been a Councillor of State, or even some brilliant member of the audience . . . But a young man of twenty-four, and *little known* at that! What were the *danseuses* thinking of?

❋   ❋   ❋   ❋

But the most capricious element, the most difficult to control, was actually the audience. In the days of the Empire, as we have said, the public was passionately fond of the theatre, and proved it by its regular attendance. A young writer who complained bitterly of his lack of money – 'the fault of an inhuman father –' and whose name was Henri Beyle, contrived to go to the theatre almost every evening. It was a great sacrifice for him, for a seat in the pit at the Français

cost forty-four sous. Having treated himself to the upper
circle for a performance of *Nicomède* on the 1st Germinal,
year XIII, he reflected bitterly that for another four francs
eight sous he could have had a seat in the orchestra, 'near the
woman he loved'. And he tells us at the same time that a seat
in the dress circle at the Comédie cost about seven francs. No
wonder the pit proved more attractive to young people.

The pit had always been the province of a sympathetic,
but often noisy, audience. They no longer came, as at the
time of the Revolution, pipe in mouth and wearing fox-skin
caps. On the contrary, they were great sticklers for the pro-
prieties, and when any of the audience transgressed them,
by neglecting, for instance, to leave the front seats in the
boxes to the women, or by appearing in shirt-sleeves, as two
Englishmen who had dined too well did one evening, they
treated them to a volley of whistling, to force the former to
change their places and the latter to change their rig.

But the din in the pit usually had some other cause; the
malcontents were nearly always demonstrating against the
play or against some member of the company.

One of their pet aversions was the *claque*. They detested
these 'market porters', as they called them, who applauded
at every turn, by order of the management or because some
actress had given them copious bribes. In many houses,
especially at the Comédie, their regular gang was reinforced
by some dozens of choirboys armed with sticks. To leave
themselves freedom of action, 'they lay their hats beside
them, put their cudgels between their knees, and go at it with
hands and feet till the exasperated audience forces them
to stop.'

Any number of other incidents might set the house in an
uproar: a maladroit announcement, a change in casting, a
well-known artist understudied by a duffer, all these aroused
indignant protest, only moderated in the case of *force
majeure*. When Dazaincourt got a friend to say that he 'had
a violent fit of colic', or when a young actress made her hopes
of maternity her excuse for non-appearance, the pill, so to
speak, was swallowed without too much difficulty, but in
most other cases less consideration was shown. Once past the
box-office, the audience demanded that the performance

should keep the promise of the bill. If in the absence of Mlle Mézerai the management tried to substitute *L'École des Maris* for *Le Séducteur amoureux*, or for some other reason, *Tancrède* for *Mithridate* – worse still, if the part of Aménaïde was played neither by Mlle George nor Mlle Duchesnois, but by their understudy, Mlle Gros – a storm would at once break out.

The rivalry between the two great tragic actresses who had disappointed them that evening gave the 'brawlers' many occasions to renew their exploits. The battle of the ladies was carried on in all seriousness, with the ovations and whistlings of their respective partisans, fainting fits during the performance, irruption of armed forces in the house and, following the imprecations of Clytemnestre, that of a half-crazy police superintendent, shouting from the balcony as though he were in the encampment at Boulogne, 'Arrest the brigands! Down with the English!'

A foolish theatrical quarrel, pitting against each other two women of talent who had each her enthusiastic admirers. Would these not have done better to adopt the opportunist advice given them by a manufacturer of doggerel verse:

> Between two new actressess
> The wits are divided;
> But those that have ranged themselves
> Under neither of their flags
> Will prefer, incontestably,
> With all respect to Melpomene,
> To hear one on the stage
> And keep the other in bed.

A game that was not without cruelty was much in favour, a few years ago, on the popular stages of the Third Republic. Modest amateurs of both sexes were invited to come and try their voices, the audience to play the part of jury. Tempted by a few prizes, the grand tenors of the house-painting trade and the nightingales among the dressmakers ventured to sing the *Chanson des blés d'or*, or the *Prière de la Tosca*. But at the first false note a growl went round the audience, a gong was sounded, and the next victim was called upon. This was called the *Crochet*.

There would seem to be little difference between this kind of torture and the treatment inflicted, under the Empire, on dramatic authors and their interpreters.

We have seen examples of cabals against the artists, and the demonstrations marking the first appearance of the young Plantou, of Auguste Thénard and Mlle Hordé might complete the series. These incidents were all the more exasperating in that the critics were so often at fault.

Audiences were not very knowledgeable. They might, for instance, mistake *Esther* for *Les Liaisons dangereuses*. One day when the former was being performed at the theatre of the Jeunes Artistes, the tragedian playing the part of Aman had hardly spouted the line: *Malheureaux, j'ai servi de héraut à sa gloire!* when a member of the audience interrupted him with

'We say *"de heros à sa gloire!"* '[1]

'*Tà sa gloire!*' repeated Aman.

'*Zà!*' persisted the other. And a violent altercation ensued between these two purists, each of them appealing to syntax and to the shades of Racine.

There was an even greater hubbub on the first night of *Pierre le Grand*, a tragedy by Carrion-Nisas given at the Théâtre-Français in 1804. But this time the pit had its knife in the author, and began shouting in advance, 'Down with *de Carillon!*' In spite of Talma's efforts the curtain had to be rung down before the end. As in *Esther*, a dangerous alexandrine had precipitated disaster. 'Whistles fetched a huge price on the day of Carrion's play,' wrote Julie Talma. 'One of the lines contained the words:

'*Le vizir à tout craint*. [The vizier feared the worst.]

'The audience took this for *à tous crins*, [with flowing mane and tail] and someone suggested cutting off his tail! A poor playwright is much to be pitied when he is thus misunderstood. I saw people laughing three days after the performance as though they were still there. Carrion may say with pride that he has contributed more than anybody to the amusement of his fellow-citizens.'

On another occasion the new piece presented was *Octavie*,

[1] Mistaking *herald* for *hero*. [Translator.]

a horrifying tragedy, in the last act of which Nero's wife is seen taking poison. As she raised the fatal cup to her lips, some wag shouted, 'The Queen drinks!' The unfortunate princess was shattered by the blow, and so was the play.

Dramatic works without number suffered the same misfortune. Nearly all the authors of new tragedies – Arnault with *Don Pedro*, Népomucène Lemercier with *Isule et Orovize*, Aignan with *Polyxène*, Marie-Joseph Chénier with *Cyrus*, learnt to their cost that the bear-pit in the Jardin des Plantes had a branch establishment in the House of Molière. In the year 1812, out of six new works produced in the Rue de la Loi, two never reached the last act, and in the case of the other four, the pit refused to let the authors be announced. The *Crochet* might have begun.

Why did the Empire generations show so much severity towards some productions and so much indulgence to others? Why was *Les Templiers* by Raynouard considered a masterpiece? Why did the arch-critics of the Opéra go crazy over Lesueur's *Les Bardes* and fail to appreciate Gluck's *Alceste* and Mozart's *Noces de Figaro*?[1] Why should such inane productions as *Fanchon la Vielleuse* and *Le Pied de Mouton* make all Paris rush to the theatre? Such things cannot be explained. Good taste and fashion seldom agree; they were never more at variance than between 1800 and 1815.

The most that can be said of the theatre at that time was that it still found a good deal of room for the old repertory, for tragedy especially, restored to honour by Talma. Tragedy was liked firstly for its own sake, and secondly because many lines of our great classic authors could easily be applied to events of the time. Lovers of allusions drew attention to them by cheers or laughter. If the passage applauded celebrated the victories of Achilles or the moderation of Augustus, the demonstration was a tribute to the fame of Napoleon, and Dubois referred to it with satisfaction in his report next day. But under cover of Athens or Rome the little game was often imbued with a very different spirit.

[1] Geoffroy's verdicts in his *Débats* articles are beyond belief. Writing of *Alceste*, he deplores 'the prostitution of Mme Armand's beautiful voice to this disagreeable, noisy music'. As for the *Noces*, he says that Mozart 'has preserved none of the gaiety, comedy and wit of Beaumarchais' play'.

When Mlle Bourgoin, whose liaison with Chaptal was common knowledge, poured forth Junie's lament:

'My Lord! I will go join the company of the Vestals!'

the whole theatre rocked with laughter, and the Minister of Interior, seated at the back of his box, looked somewhat embarrassed. From the lips of Mlle George, too, Emilie's retort:

'If I could seduce Cinna, I can seduce many others'

was all too clearly a reminder of Napoleon's extra-conjugal fancies. Not many months before the Coronation, when the pit acclaimed the distich spoken by Cinna:

'And the name of Emperor,
Concealing that of King, does not lessen the horror . . .'

people at the Tuileries had the right to consider the joke in doubtful taste.

But one 'application' was to outdo all others. The incident occurred, not in a public theatre but at Grosbois, Berthier's house, in the course of a performance given by the Prince of Wagram to the Imperial Court.

In December 1809 the news of the impending divorce, already in the air, lent an atmosphere of discomfort to the party. In the hope of cheering things up, Berthier had asked Brunet to come and give a performance of his latest farce, *Cadet Roussel*, with the company of the Variétés.

In the presence of Napoleon and Josephine the plot unfolded more or less smoothly until the moment when Cadet's father says to his son, to put him on his guard against the machinations of a countrified gallant, in love with his wife, 'Do you know what it is that attracts this libertine? It's your divorce he's aiming at!'

The audience was startled, but worse was to come. Cadet explains why he got married. 'Do you suppose it was for pleasure? It was for something far more solid – not to allow the perpetuity of my family to die out; to see myself reborn, and to have *predecessors*!'

It was as though lightning had struck the gallery at Grosbois. Josephine turned pale behind her fan. Napoleon had ceased to laugh. Berthier tore his hair behind the scenes, and exchanged acid remarks with the chamberlain, M. de Saint-Cyr. 'Who chose the play?' 'Yourself!' 'I didn't know anything about it!' 'You ought to have read it!' 'How absurd!' 'What a disaster!'

But they were joined by the Emperor, who had already recovered his equanimity. 'I see, messieurs,' he said, 'that my secret has been well kept. If these good people had known it, they would certainly not have uttered the things I have just heard.'

Not for the first time, Napoleon was determined to prove that of all the actors of his day he was still the best.

*   *   *   *

It is always very risky for the theatre to meddle with politics, for politics will hit back, and it will soon feel the smart. During the Revolution a number of theatres had made use of material that smacked of public meetings. Under the Consular regime they were early subjected to fairly strict supervision, and had to make shift with this up to the day when the Emperor, by his decree of 1807, decided to authorize the existence of only eight Paris theatres, suppressing all the others at a single blow, much as one might tear up the undergrowth of a wood to facilitate the work of the game-keepers.

On the morrow of Brumaire, apparently for the sake of allaying public excitement, certain topical plays were banned, such as *La Pêche aux Jacobins* and *Mariniers de Saint-Cloud*, which were considered impolitic. A few days later the Minister of Police demanded that 'new dramatic works be submitted for examination by the Central Bureau before their performance'. This was the birth certificate of an institution that was to be only too often in the news; the Censorship.

No doubt the mischievous spirit of the audience and its fondness for 'applications' had something to do with the excessive zeal of the officials who thereafter wielded the scissors – dim hack writers richly rewarded for lending the Government their assistance. In justice to them it must be said that they did not spare themselves trouble, and that their scruples were sometimes touching.

In a play entitled *Henry IV et d'Aubigné*, one of them asked the author to replace Henry by Francis the First, 'who at least did not belong to a fallen royal family'. Another insisted on the substitution, in *Le Mari prudent*, of the titles of *chevalier* and *baron* for those of *vicomte* and *marquis*, unknown to imperial nobility. But the finest specimen of all was furnished by Nogaret, who flatly forbade the performance of a comedy in which a servant had the audacity to bear the name of Dubois – that of the Prefect of Police himself!

So long as the censors concerned themselves only with the insipid productions of their contemporaries, they might be forgiven, but their guilt became more serious when they proceeded to attack the classics, banning *Mérope* without even giving a reason for it, pruning *Athalie, Cinna, Britannicus* and *Le Marriage de Figaro*, turning *Sganarelle, ou le Cocu imaginaire* into *Sganarelle, ou le Mari qui se croit trompé*, returning *Heraclitus* shorn of a number of passages but enriched by a long tirade in which the poet-censor Esménard vindicated Napoleon's right to the throne:

'The worthy Emperors whose footsteps we follow,
    Children of Fortune, children of the Legions,
    Counted, instead of forebears, their own great deeds.'

This posthumous collaboration with the author of *Le Cid* must have astonished some people. But after all, as Fouché said, 'were not Esménard's lines as good as Corneille's?'

A chronicler in the pay of the Government asserted one day that there was no censorship in France. 'Freedom of thought is the main conquest of the century, and the Emperor wishes it to be respected.' An assertion not easily reconciled with the exploits of the champions of expurgation. It may be said, however, that they pursued their activities in the sphere of politics far more than in that of morals, in which the audience itself played the part of censor.

Very broad-minded in real life, it evinced the most sensitive prudery as soon as it entered a theatre; and this was not the least paradoxical side of this singular epoch. 'People are determined to have virtue on the stage', said Geoffroy, 'because there must be some somewhere.'

In conformity with this principle, the dramatist must not introduce a woman deceiving her husband, nor a girl being seduced, still less a divorced wife. Behind the footlights, henceforth, there must be no more illegitimate couples, amorous adventures or even ill-matched unions – one of which, between a gallant colonel and a widow too young for him, was hissed at the Théâtre-Français. Only edifying comedies were called for, as a restful change from an existence that was usually not edifying at all.

The playwrights of the Empire were to be pitied, for their profession cannot have been an easy one. If those of the following generation had been obliged to observe the same rules, we should have had neither the romantic dramas, nor the plays of Dumas, nor even those of honest Émile Augier.

As for our authors of today, without the providential resource of adultery and a few other minor sins on which their fancy feeds, they could not write two scenes. Or else they would be as boring as the works of Étienne, or of Alexandre Duval.

CHAPTER XII

THE SPIRIT OF THE AGE

The way people talked – Napoleon's malapropisms – The style noble – The sensational novel – The lachrymose mania – Jean-Jacques's walking-stick – The fashion for practical jokes

WIT and taste are riches that revolutions are not apt to set much store by. When a country has spent ten years trying to shed its skin, when its life has moved from the drawing-room to the street, it is hardly surprising to find a generation like that of the Empire springing up as a result of the experiment – with a somewhat summary culture, an almost childish sensibility, and a fondness for high-sounding words and hollow phrases, in short, rather lacking at times in a sense of humour.

It was what circumstances had made it, admirable in some ways, a trifle ridiculous in others, very different in any case from the France of the eighteenth century, whose nimble, versatile spirit had reigned so long supreme.

Some people accused the newcomers of talking a strange language. Poor Mme de Genlis had little hair left, but it stood on end when she heard expressions such as *Cela est farce, Cela coûte gros,* or *une bonne trotte* instead of *une bonne course; un castor* instead of *un chapeau; votre demoiselle* instead of *votre fille.*

Imagine her feelings if she were to be told that Bonaparte often made much more serious mistakes; that he might even say – so Chaptal declares – *armistice* for *amnistie, rentes voyagères* for *rentes viagères, îles Philippiques* for *îles Philippines, point fulminant* for *point culminant*! But these malapropisms – of which the last was perhaps merely the affectation of an artilleryman – were not really very surprising from the lips of a little Corsican gentleman who had begun rather late in life to speak the language of Paris, and might mispronounce certain terms he had not heard aright to begin with.

These trifling mistakes did not prevent him in any case

7　Opéra Comique in the Rue Feydeau

The Odéon

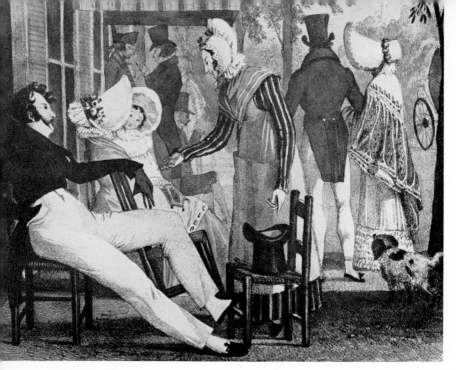

8 Chairs for hire

At the milliner's shop (Paintings by Chalon)

from proving, almost from the first, a great writer, capable when need was of hitting on a striking expression, a vivid, direct phrase. If among the 6,000 Frenchmen who boasted of wielding a pen during his reign, many had possessed the like gifts, the literary level of the Empire would certainly have been higher.

Save for two brilliant exceptions – Chateaubriand and Mme de Staël – it was decidedly low, but for this the mediocrity of public taste was no doubt responsible. An epoch has the writers it deserves, and this one suffered from serious defects that were sufficient to explain the situation.

If the high-flown oratory of La Harpe roused his hearers to enthusiasm, if a bookseller could offer Delille 30,000 francs for the manuscript of his *Pitié*, if a woman could think of saying to Chênedollé 'Your lines are as lofty as the cedars of Lebanon!', if the novels of Mme Cottin and Mme Krüdener shattered the nerves of thousands of readers, male and female, it was because these sorry productions gratified a triple passion shared by all their contemporaries: a passion for a high-falutin style, misnamed *noble*, a passion for dramatic situations and a passion for tears.

Never say anything simply: this was the first principle for both prose-writers and poets. As for the latter, one can hardly blame them, for they were only following the rules of the game when they called man a *mortal*, marriage *hymen* and war *Bellona*. Delille may even be forgiven the astonishing periphrases in which he specialized. This is his description of an umbrella:

> 'This precious, adaptable implement, displaying the art of both whalebone and silk . . .'

and he calls the pig

> 'The frigid celibate, inapt to pleasure,
> Of the table's luxury unfortunate martyr.'

But this florid language becomes insufferable in the theatre. When a lover in Raynouard's *Templiers* declaims:

> 'The flame has devoured the sacred characters,
> Of my written vows depositary witnesses',

H

we have some difficulty in realizing that the fool has let his love-letters fall into the fire.

Prose, therefore, the supreme quality of which is clarity, should have been all the more careful to spare us these riddles. But those that wrote it wanted to follow the fashion, and the journalists were the first to attempt it. For both leading articles and news in brief they made use of the same rhetoric. This is how a reporter expresses himself in an account of the Exhibition of Industrial Products:

'Slowly completed, these pompous monuments are a lasting evidence of difficulty overcome, and of the latest efforts of the spirit of man, rising by means of these marvels above all other creatures and drawing nearer to the Creator, of whom, it might be said, he becomes the most perfect emulator.'

Jealous of such fine effects as these, governmental literature itself leaned towards lyricism. When Dubois was appointed Prefect of Police, the manifesto he addressed to the people of Paris was really a masterpiece:

'Citizens! Everything that may at any time have been the subject of your complaint will henceforth be the object of my solicitude . . . Severity but humanity! My eye shall penetrate the innermost recesses of the criminal's soul, but my ear shall be open to the cries of innocence and even to the groans of repentance . . .'

We must not imagine that language of this kind provoked the risibility of the public. On the contrary, it was delighted with the prefectoral eloquence, and had no ambition but to talk in the same strain. It was its love of a flowery style that gave it such a taste for the lectures at the Institute and the courses at the Collège de France, and made it sneeze with admiration as soon as old La Harpe dipped his fingers into his snuff-box. It was for the pleasure of listening to fine periods, carefully cadenced, that so many people frequented the Lycée des Arts and the Portique républicain under the Consulate, and the Athénée de Paris, the Athénée des Étrangers and the Académie de Législation under the Empire.

The programmes of these establishments varied a great deal. One day Citizeness Constance Pipelet might be heard holding forth on 'the condition of women in a republic'; another day a certain M. Gallais would discuss the thrilling question, 'Is eloquence useful or harmful at the Bar?' On yet another occasion, Marie-Joseph Chénier would discourse on the history of the Troubadours – a subject foreshadowing Meilhac's *Petite Marquise*.

And when the Parisians of that day had absorbed all this spiritual nourishment, they were firmly convinced that never before had French literature shone with such brilliance.

*   *   *   *

It was not only at the theatre that dramas were to be seen. Real life had some very sombre ones to show, and an epidemic of suicides was especially noticeable at the beginning of the Consulate.

On the 3rd Ventôse, year VIII, a young pupil of David threw himself from the top of a tower of Notre-Dame. A piece of paper was found on him, on which was scribbled in pencil, 'When one considers the destiny of man on earth, one should water one's cradle with tears.'

Not long after, some despairing creature chose the Porte Saint-Denis for his spring-board, but he had the good taste to shout first to the crowd, 'Take care! Passers-by! It's not against you that I bear a grudge!'

Another, less spectacular, exit was that of Chappe the inventor, who, disgusted with life, and perhaps with his telegraph, drowned himself in the well in his house, leaving this declaration, 'I am seeking death to escape from the boredom of life, which is weighing me down.'

And the actor Beaulieu, who also committed suicide, wrote his last message in the style of the monologues of *l'Ambigu*: 'May my blood, that I am about to shed, be, like that of the pelican, of use to my children. In order that they may inherit the esteem the public felt for me, say something in favour of their unfortunate father! I am preparing to fall asleep in eternity!'

Farewells to life all strongly tinged with literature, but which were perhaps the first symptoms of the famous *mal du siècle*, of which the next generation was to complain so bitterly. 'Alas! They think I am happy, and I have an abyss in

my heart!' sighed a nine-year-old child even then, little
Albertine, daughter of Mme de Staël. Are we not, henceforth,
in the thick of romanticism?

Werther had had time to found a school, and his sorrows
had inspired the novelists with endless tragic love-stories. In
this pursuit of catastrophe the women authors were well
ahead. Apart from *Delphine*, the boring subject of which is
at least relieved by a brilliant style, people had to undergo
a perpetual avalanche of *Valéries*, *Clair d'Albes*, *Amélie de
Mansfields*, works by disillusioned Muses with morbid imagi-
nations. 'According to Mme Cottin,' says one of their readers,
'one cannot recover from love any more than from the plague.
In three novels she has written for us, six people are dead
already. If love was as it is painted today it would have
destroyed the world instead of preserving it.'

But the bluestockings had a good excuse: the public,
especially the feminine public, adored terrifying scenes.
'What a lovely sight!' said a lady one evening, coming out of
a place in the Rue des Petits-Champs where ghosts were
made to appear; 'I fainted three times!' She, at any rate, cannot have considered there were too many funereal incidents
in Mme Cottin's novels.

Another failing, which I have called a passion for tears,
affected both sexes equally. A word, a memory, a picture, the
slightest emotion, were enough to wet the eyelids of a soldier
with a heart in the right place, of a professor suddenly obliged
to interrupt his lecture, of a judge discomposed in the middle
of a hearing. While the advocate Bellart was defending Mlle
de Cicé, implicated in the Rue Saint-Nicaise plot, his eloquence affected the audience to such a degree that 'old
gendarmes, forgetting their orders, let go their rifles to mop
their eyes, which were full of tears'.

Another time, during the trial of the chemist Ternaux,
accused of having poisoned his daughter, it was the foreman
of the jury that fainted before pronouncing the verdict. And
people thought little of it, for by a strange contrast all these
men, who had witnessed the dramas of the Revolution, and
were now living through terrible wars, far from concealing
their sensibility, displayed it with a sort of affectation.

There were innumerable instances of this. Alissan de

Chazet tells us that on going to see the Grand Chancellor Lacèpède, to recommend the widow of a Legionary, he began to weep so violently that he was 'obliged to interrupt his recital for a time'. The same accident overtook the former Jacobin Lemaire when pronouncing the eulogy of Luce de Lancival at the École Normale, and the academician Alexandre Duval speaking of the young son of his predecessor Legouvé, during his address of welcome – even to the curé of Saint-Roch, who, on coming to tell Mme Récamier that she had been elected Lady Patroness, was moved to tears on the subject of her virtues!

People wept and wept, sometimes for an excess of sorrow, sometimes for an excess of joy. Guinguené sobbed as he listened to his little boy spouting congratulations to him on his birthday. Junot's mother squeezed out a tear when lunching with Mme Laetitia, at the thought that the two happiest mothers in France had come together. Hortense's eyes were reddened when writing to her brother Eugène, whose portrait she had just been looking at. Napoleon himself confided to Méneval that he had never been able to read Baculard d'Arnaud's *Épreuves du Sentiment* without crying – a work we should find difficult to read through today, even with tears.

In the prose of the newspapers the same sentimentalism appeared in every line. The subscriber had at all costs to have his emotions stirred by some touching tale – of a concert improvised in the street by the Ellevious for the benefit of some unfortunate blind man, or the funeral of Greuze, with a tearful young woman laying a bunch of everlasting flowers on the coffin. 'These flowers, given by the most grateful of his pupils, are the emblem of his fame.' Or again, in the same year 1806, a sensational sale – that of Jean-Jacques Rousseau's walking-stick, exhibited in a sale-room in the Rue Neuve-Saint-Augustin, which an Austrian bidder had come on purpose to buy, all the way from his own country.

A miserable cane, worth perhaps thirteen sous, but stirring up such great memories! After obtaining it for its weight in gold, the Viennese fell into a sort of ecstasy. 'So that is his stick! That's what he leaned on when he went gathering herbs in the forests, when he withdrew from the curiosity of men to devote himself to the company of owls! That was the support of his old age, the companion of his wild, wandering life; That was...' But as they listened to this stream of words, everybody began to reproach himself for having let Jean Jacques's stick pass into foreign hands, and as if to make amends 'they went up to touch it, caress it and water it with tears'. It was not for nothing that the French had learn to weep from the *Nouvelle Héloïse*!

* * * *

It must be confessed, however, that their emotions were somewhat artificial. The sobs they uttered, the eyes they dabbed, all that was merely a way of showing that they were well-educated and tender-hearted. The rest of the time they felt, on the contrary, very gay, and they proved this to their friends by playing more or less amusing tricks on them, known as *Mystifications*.

These fooleries had started at Lucien Bonaparte's house at Plessis-Chamant, where people amused themselves by squirting water or firing petards under people's noses, slipping a live fox between Fontanes's sheets, making beds rock or scattering them with teasel prickles – making, in fact, the old Château of Cardinal de Bernis into a forerunner of the shops selling hoaxes on the main boulevards, which were to be all the rage at a later date.

The butt of these jokes was old Ramolino, well-known for his superstitious fears. One night when he was in his bed, a spectre came and shook it.

'I'm your father's ghost,' it said. 'Swear to obey me in everything!'

'I swear! What must I do?'

'Never eat spinach!'

The poor man swore all that was demanded of him, and of course a magnificent dish of spinach was offered him next day at luncheon. He refused it; his host persisted, and Ramolino, his teeth chattering, ended by recounting the nocturnal tragedy, to the delight of the other guests. Lucien had to divest himself of his ministerial coat and disguise himself as a ghost again, to lift the interdict.

People were not much kinder at Mortefontaine, his brother

Joseph's house. There Pauline Leclerc and Caroline Murat
amused themselves by remorselessly pestering the octogen-
arian Casti, Joseph the Second's official poet. If they saw him
dozing under a tree, they approached on tiptoe to snatch off
his wig. If he was about to checkmate his opponent, they
would sweep the chessmen off the board with the back of
the hand and shoot them onto the carpet as if by accident.
Delightful young women!

More complicated hoaxes were perpetrated at Grimod de
la Reynière's country house at Villiers-sur-Marne, which was
as full of shams and booby-traps as Robert-Houdin's house
later on.[1] There were secret cupboards everywhere, trap-
doors opening unexpectedly, voice-pipes giving vent to mysterious summonses. Even when there was not a cloud in the
sky, a stage thunderstorm would break out in the middle of
the night: the curtains shook in the wind, the doors creaked,
a sound of chains being dragged along came up from the
cellars, skeletons appeared, and to the astonishment of the
guests, family portraits in their frames began putting out
their tongues.

But jokes of this kind called for lengthy preparation, and
not everybody had Grimod's skill or imagination. Instead of
working the thing themselves, many hosts preferred to call
in the assistance of some established practical joker like
Musson, Legros or Thiémet, who had made so to speak a
career of mystification.

When people wanted to give a dinner-party, they fixed a
date with one of these gentlemen, and for a fee of one louis –
plus the meal – he would undertake to entertain the gallery,
as he might have undertaken to supply the flowers or play the
piano. As a rule the host pointed out to him the intended butt
of the evening, who would be seated next to him. All the
guests were in the secret except the victim. Imagine his perturbation when Legros, disguised as an old general, told him
he had had his ear-drum broken at the battle of Marengo,
and kept asking him, all through dinner, to shout as loudly as
possible down an enormous ear-trumpet!

Thiémet simulated a different infirmity, imitating as he
talked the noise made by the hydraulic machine at Marly,

[1] J. E. Robert-Houdin, 1805–71, a famous conjurer. [Translator.]

under the pretext that his mother had been frightened during her pregnancy by the *tic-tac* of that famous apparatus.

As for Musson, he had a genius for travel. It was he that took a somewhat simple-minded personage, who wanted to visit Orleans, for a day-long drive in an enormous berline laden with luggage. Indefatigably, without ever leaving Paris, the carriage went in a circle. 'Where are we now?' asked the traveller. 'That is Chartres Cathedral,' (pointing to the church of Saint-Cloud). Farther on, the Seine became the Loire. Horses were changed at imaginary relays, and off they started again for miles and miles, until at last the man, dazed by twelve hours' jolting, with a splitting headache and bruised ribs, returned home without even realizing that he was not in Orleans.

Obviously none of this exceeded the average studio rag. The only piquant side of the affair lay in seeing grave personages, bursting with their own importance, easily given to flowery eloquence and complacently displaying treasures of sensibility, amusing themselves with such tomfoolery.

But such was the spirit of the age. Solemn, tearful and schoolboyish by turns, its physiognomy was made up of a singular combination of contrasts.

CHAPTER XIII

FASHION

Extravagance of the Incroyables – *The Englishman and his hairdresser – Dresses less transparent – The* courturier Leroy *– Court dresses – Napoleon and the ladies' rouge – A Marshal who refused to dress up – Furs, shawls and hats – Elegance at Longchamps*

THE *émigrés* who returned to France during the first months of the Consulate must have been greatly astonished by the strange disguises now affected by their compatriots.

The tail-coats of the *Incroyables*, with their leg-of-mutton sleeves and their wide lapels padded with wadding, breeches either tight-fitting or pleated like skirts, cravats strangling their necks, coiffures *à la Titus* sprouting from empty heads; the transparent dresses of the *Merveilleuses* with the waist-line almost under the armpits, fashions making women look like the nymphs of Jean Goujon, only a bit less shy, gauze tunics showing arms and bust and allowing the rest to be guessed at – all this constituted a complete break with the elegance of former days. And in the streets of Paris, themselves almost unchanged, all this baroque, fantastic society, speaking a barely intelligible language, must have appeared to unaccustomed eyes like a people come from the antipodes, or inhabitants of the moon fallen on our planet on a day of Carnival.

It was obvious that fashion, like politics, had had its Revolution, which was even lasting longer than the other. For men as well as women the rules of good taste remained incalculable for some years after Brumaire.

A journalist of 1803 summed up, rather wittily, the code of masculine elegance. According to him, every dandy must have a long foot 'or have it made so by his bootmaker'. It was the tailor's duty to shorten his arms and tighten his coat, the good cut of which was recognized by the number of creases it made in the back. A well-bred man would refuse to wear anything that was not crumpled; he would sleep, if need be, in the shirt he was to wear next day, and make his servant take the newness out of his clothes, 'as in a certain island slaves are entrusted with the marriage night'.

The beaux of the day were not only bent on looking badly groomed, they tried to make themselves look older. Taking little steps, with their shoulders bent and their chest drawn in, enormous spectacles astride their nose and hiding half their face, they ended by looking like their own grandfathers. The ideal of these pretended victims of short sight and decrepitude was the exact opposite of the eighteenth century. Thanks to powder, wigs and the elegance of their clothes, the contemporaries of the Maréchal de Richelieu could maintain the appearance of a juvenile lead well into the sixties. Henceforth, to be elegant one must look twice one's age.

Another important principle was to take no notice of the season or the weather. Was it raining? Were the streets muddy? The *Incroyable* would be seen walking in white stockings. Was it the middle of summer? He would keep to his boots, his heavy cloth coat and two or three waistcoats, which he wore one on top of another, like Molière's false marquis.

Fashion was ruled by incoherence. Headgear of every size, spencers copied from women's wear, box coats with triple collars that looked as if intended for cab-drivers, all this pretended to elegance, as the jazz band, in the twentieth century, pretends to musicality: then as now a studious disorder, a taste for discord and a great expense of effort to achieve a painful result.

The worst eccentricities could, however, be combined with the cult of Greco-Roman traditions. When the *Incroyable* visited his hairdresser, this artist would draw his attention to a number of little busts grouped together in his saloon, and then, after a moment's meditation, would ejaculate in inspired accents, 'I see what you need. A mixture of Titus, Caracalla and Alcibiades. Look at these busts: this lock of Titus's is *full of kindness*, but it's important to combine it with this one of Caracalla's, which is *very severe*, and enliven them both with a few *very coquettish* ones of Alcibiades's. You will look very well.'

The operation was sometimes successful, but certain customers were not so pleased – Redhead Yorke, for instance, the Englishman, when he went with his wife to have both their heads trimmed Paris fashion. Mrs. Yorke's hair was first tortured 'in such a way that she looked as if she had just come out of her bath'. The husband's turn came next; his powdered queue fell under the scissors, and his head was soon covered with a multitude of little curls that gave the poor man 'the look of the young orang-outangs to be seen at the Exchange in Exeter'. But this was not all. Taking a pair of whiskers from his pocket, the artist tried to gum them on the patient's cheeks. Yorke resisted, but was obliged for the sake of peace to pay eighteen francs to have done with the accursed hairdresser. 'After all, he had earned them', he sighed, 'by changing my wife into a savage, myself into a baboon, and making us reek of his pomades and perfumes.'

More than one Frenchman had been struck by the elegance of these Britishers who had come to France on the morrow of the Peace of Amiens, to be only very temporary friends, and their example soon wrought greater discipline in French fashions. Seized with anglomania, the *Incroyable* gradually forgot his extravagances and became the perfect juvenile lead of the Empire, as he is shown in the fashion books of the *Mésangère* and Carle Vernet's illustrations.

There we may admire him in his blue or black dress coat, pomaded like Élleviou, shod with riding-boots that would have been the envy of Franconi. He was already the type of the modern dandy. His elegance smacked somewhat of the other side of the Channel, but there was a military touch about it too; henceforth all formal dress would look like a uniform.

The most obvious result of this double tendency was that men now attached the utmost importance to the correctness of their attire. Stendhal confesses jokingly that he 'could only play the fop if his get-up was faultless'. His whole evening would be spoilt if a coat-button 'stood out too much'. But on the other hand, what a satisfaction there was in looking one's best! 'I think I was never so brilliant,' he notes in his diary on February 25, 1805; 'I was wearing a black waistcoat, black silk breeches and stockings, with a cinnamon-bronze coat, a very well tied cravat, a superb shirt-front. Never, I believe, was my ugliness more effaced by my general appearance.' And he adds without false modesty, 'I looked a very handsome man, after the style of Talma.'

* * * *

The change in women's dress was not unconnected with the evolution of masculine costume. Grecian nudities remained in favour for a time, but a campaign was soon started against them.

It was suggested to the Parisiennes that their too transparent tunics offered too easy discoveries to prying eyes. One chronicler, J.-B. Salgues, even pointed out what might in plainer terms be called the dangers of standing with their back to the light. But the passage is worth quoting:

'When the beautiful orb that illumes us stands almost perpendicularly above our heads no harm is occasioned; the shadow is projected on the ground in a vertical direction and the modesty of our ladies is in safety. But when, changing its position, its chariot leans to the horizon, its sparkling rays, passing through the thin veils opposing them, light up their too pervious texture, and unknown to the fair one, lay open to profane glances those charms, the sight of which was not intended for them.'

If the emulators of Phryne did not understand (and they might be excused for not doing so), the lesson took a much plainer form on the day when one of them, literally naked, was greeted by whistles in the Jardin de l'Élysée and forced to make her escape amid the hooting of the onlookers. She had mistaken the Consulate for the Directory, Bonaparte's regime for that of Barras.

From the moment of his accession to power, the new Master had expressed his intention of suppressing this masquerade of gallantry. He wished the women of his entourage to display a luxury in better taste. Mme. Tallien was seriously scolded for having been seen in the balcony of the Opéra semi-clad as Diana. And one evening, in the drawing-room at the Luxembourg, Josephine's friends having exaggerated their *décolletage*, the First Consul made a show of cramming

the fireplace with logs. 'The ladies are naked, as you see!'
They did not need to be told twice, and dresses soon began
to change their appearance.

The metamorphosis was already discernible at the party
given by Berthier in 1801. The fair creatures present were
already worthy to take their places under the vaulted roof of
Notre-Dame on the day of the Coronation, and the main lines
of Empire fashion were more or less settled: the waist still
very high up, the sleeves short and puffed, the tunic falling
straight, moulding the forms without stressing them, the feet
shod in thin buskins, the coiffure very small, enhanced by
ribbons and gems – such was the canon of official dress,
fixed at the first attempt.

It needed only a few years of the reign to extract from these
elements the most they had to offer. By that time there would
be a Court surrounding the new Caesar, made to his order
and to his measure, brilliant, magnificent, setting an example
to the oldest monarchies of Europe; and at the service of the
women of this Court, of Josephine in particular, a man of inventive genius to create models without number, and to repeat
at the Tuileries the miracles performed by Rose Bertin at Versailles – a role that fell to Leroy, couturier to the Empress.

This Napoleon of fashion lived at No. 89 Rue de la Loi, at
the corner of the Rue Ménars, familiar to our century for a
little dark shop selling old books. He had a partner to begin
with, a certain Mme Rimbault, a linen-draper, but once his
fame was established the style of the firm was reduced to a
single name. Leroy's triumph as the maker of the most beautiful dresses for the Coronation was so overwhelming that
nobody afterwards dreamed of disputing his supremacy.

He employed a numerous staff, well-paid for those days;
his fitters earned from six to eight hundred francs a year, and
his sempstresses from two to three hundred, and they were all
given board and lodging, as was the custom. He did not only
dress Josephine, but nearly all the women of the Court, with
the exception of the Maréchale Lannes, who had been
offended by his insolence, and the Maréchale Lefebvre, who
had no liking for the heights of elegance.

Despite his insufferable self-conceit, the man was the
oracle of Paris, the obligatory supplier of all the Napoleonic

Courts. Couriers and diligences carried his delivery boxes to Cassel, Naples, Madrid and Lucca. In the course of a few years, although he was an inveterate gambler, and spent some time every night in the gaming dens of the Palais-Royal, he had saved more than 760,000 francs.

His prices, laughable today, were considered extravagant at the time. He hardly ever charged more than 18 francs for making a dress, but as he provided the materials and trimmings, he made a large profit on these as a set-off. An ordinary dress of Josephine's ended by costing 3,000 francs, and the Imperial bill for a single year amounted to the pretty total of 143,314 francs, 10 centimes. Note the ten centimes.

For the ladies of the Court the reckoning was of course more modest. When Mme de Rémusat paid 1,200 francs, and Mme Maret 1,500 for a Court dress it was considered an event. As a rule the extravagances of these ladies hardly exceeded fifteen louis, and the same can be said of Mme Duchâtel, Mme de Brignolle, Mme de Montmorency and the Duchess of Rovigo.

In course of time dresses became a little heavier. There would still be a vogue for sequinned tulle, but silk and velvet materials, recommended by Napoleon for the sake of helping the industry of Lyons, would also be much in demand. It remained to be seen whether they would adapt themselves to straight lines as well as thin veilings, and whether in some cases they would not accentuate embonpoint.

As soon as Josephine began to put on weight, especially after the divorce, the dresses that had looked marvellous on her pretty Creole figure had a much less felicitous effect. 'A certain part of her person, in particular, has increased in size to an extraordinary degree,' says Mme d'Abrantès, 'and the way she dresses helps to make her look stouter still.'

It is clear that fashion under the First Empire would have nothing to do with the concealments offered by panniers, which the crinoline and the bustle would again permit, half a century later. For the moment no trickery was possible; women had to show themselves as they were, with the very short corset hardly supporting the breast. With heelless buskins there was no hope of adding to one's height, either. It was 'a sincerity fashion', as someone said very justly.

'Dressed in this way, an ugly woman becomes more so, a pretty woman looks prettier, a really beautiful woman scores a triumph.'

*   *   *   *

There was, however, one artifice not disdained at the Tuileries, but even employed to excess, and that was make-up. Though a few notorious beauties had attempted to renounce it in the early days of 1800, Josephine soon restored it to honour. She made herself up like any actress in the attempt to retain a youthfulness already on the wane. The thick layer with which she plastered her face and neck peeled off sometimes as it dried, covering her bodice with starch. She attributed this drawback to an irritation of the skin, and when people inquired after her health she would say, 'I'm not well, as you can see. *I'm all over flour!*'

Napoleon was probably alone in considering this riot of rouge and white grease-paint natural. His eyes were so accustomed to it that he could no longer imagine a woman's face without the borrowed brilliance, of which Jezebel knew the secret before the days of Martin the perfumer. 'Why are you so pale?' he asked a lady one day. 'Are you just recovering from a confinement?' And to another he said even more bluntly, 'Go and paint your face, you look like a corpse!'

No wonder Josephine bought more than 3,000 francs' worth of rouge every year from the afore-mentioned Martin, from Mme Chaumeton and others. Since Napoleon liked make-up, he must have his money's worth. Even so he must have found other items of the budget, such as jewels, lace, furs and shawls, infinitely heavier to meet. Without going into details of the sumptuous frivolities that Frédéric Masson has studied with so much care, it can be said that the Empress possessed a prodigious wardrobe. When it was inventoried in 1809 it was found to contain 666 winter dresses, 230 summer ones, and sixty cashmere shawls, some of which had cost 10,000 francs, while her trousseau included 500 chemises trimmed with Valenciennes and Malines lace, but only two pairs of drawers.

On the latter point, though not on the others, Empress number one was beaten by many lengths by Empress number two, for four years later Marie-Louise is known to have bought two dozen pairs of drawers and twenty-two pairs of pantaloons, proving that young ladies were not brought up at the Court of Vienna as they were under the banana-trees of Martinique.

But whatever the personal tastes of the two sovereigns may have been – and Heaven knows how different they were! – the feminine luxury of the Court was maintained till the end of the reign. Leroy and his official designer Auguste Garneray went on thinking out, for Mmes the Duchesses and Mmes the Maréchales, the 'grand overdresses' with long trains, the gowns of silk or *lamé* tulle, with the *chérusque* fastened between the shoulders, which were the dazzlement of the Imperial receptions.

So that men's dress should harmonize with that of the women, etiquette soon prescribed, for civilians and military alike, a gala costume reminiscent of pre-Revolutionary elegance: the coat, embroidered in bright colours, differed from that of Louis XIV's day only by the width of the collar and facings.

Cambacérès was laughed at when he appeared in this guise at one of the first balls given by Mme de Montesson, his full suit of cloth of gold 'lighting up the whole drawing-room'. But since the Emperor had ordained that work must be given to the silk-mercers and embroiderers, everybody was bound to obey orders, and at Court festivities even Marshals no longer appeared in uniform. One of the strangest sights was that of Augereau in white satin breeches and Junot in a dress coat of dove-coloured shot silk.

Ney was the last to give in. Before an entertainment at the Trianon in 1811 he even had a domestic scene on the subject, the Maréchale begging her husband to don a handsome embroidered coat she had had made for him on the sly, while he, in a fury, hung this Shrove-Tuesday rig-out on the shoulders of the maidservant and swore that he would keep to his uniform. Like everybody else, he probably gave in in course of time, since such was the will of the Master. But what an odd appearance some hardened warriors must have presented in such gallant accoutrements!

❋   ❋   ❋   ❋

9 A Ball at Sceaux

Hair styles
and fashions,
c. 1800

10 A water-carrier

Fashions of
1809

The fashions of the town remained more sober. During the last half of the Empire they even tended to become a trifle middle-class. Warm quilted wraps were seen on the women's shoulders, and ample Grecian cloaks suggesting the fear of colds rather than a wish to imitate the antique models of David.

It was also the heyday of furs: lynx capes, tippets of Siberian lamb, every sort of pelt was worn, in every sort of shape. The fur shop A la Reine d'Espagne drove a roaring trade, and fashionable women greeted one another with descriptions of their latest acquisitions. 'Ah, you should see my ermine!' 'What sort of fur is yours, dear, blue fox or silver fox?'

But they were all united in their longing for the skin of a certain wild cat from South America, called chinchilla. There were only twenty of them in the whole of Europe, apparently, and only four or five Parisennes had the good fortune to possess one.

With the advent of spring, shawls reappeared from the cupboards; they were now worn three-corner fashion. As for hats, small to begin with, or replaced by turbans, they soon assumed the most varied shapes, and sometimes the most preposterous ones. Hats *à l'Anglaise*, toques like Doctor Gall's, headgear *à la Sphynx*, helmets *à la Minerve*, hats *à la Clorinde*, *à la Babet*, *à la Glaneuse*, top hats *à la Pamela* garnished with a peak and, if desired, a 'curtain' – masterly confections of straw, felt or satin, ranging from the minute *bibi* to the huge poke bonnet, there was something for every taste, even, alas, for the worst!

Paris offered innumerable opportunities to the coquettes wishing to show off these masterpieces, but the finest was undoubtedly the Promenade de Longchamp during the three days before Easter. The traditional parade was less brilliant than under the old regime, being hardly more than a procession of carriages, cabriolets and horsemen, among the latter a wag or two riding a donkey. But for the women Longchamp still had its prestige; they longed to shine there. 'Ah, my dear,' sighed one, 'I've been told I must not spend more than 20,000 francs on that day, including my carriage. Isn't it mean?'

I

But in spite of their husband's niggardliness, the ladies' dresses were as magnificent as ever, and their carriages most luxurious. Some coach-builders agreed among themselves to obtain a harmony of colours. In 1805, for instance, the interior of many carriages was upholstered in pale blue, and this was one of the most successful parades ever seen. Starting at eleven in the morning, it went on till nightfall. With the return of the procession in view, Garchi had opened new rooms at Franscati, and they were packed all day long.

Press reports, however, were somewhat critical. Too many soldiers keeping order, it was said, a fashion review must not be just a 'review'. And then instructions had been carried out with disagreeable severity. Under pretence of preventing pedestrians from crossing the roadway, they had been roughly handled, as the Prefect of Police was obliged to admit. In after years he drew attention himself to the exaggerated zeal of the men on duty. One infantryman drew his sword on an individual who was not moving fast enough; a citizen had his coat torn; two guardsmen ran after a man on horseback and pricked him with their bayonets.

Even if one is living under the sign of Mars, such an abuse of the strong hand was bound to scandalize peaceable people, and old Parisians looked back with regret to the days when a few pickets of mounted police were enough to keep onlookers in order while Guimard's coach drove along the Grand Avenue of the Champs-Élysées, with a louis d'or emblazoned on it, and the porcelain chariot of the Beaupré went past, with a prince of the blood for equerry.

CHAPTER XIV

PROMENADES AND PLEASURES
OF PARIS

THE newspapers of 1806 tell of a certain Calixte Vilcot,
an old man of 102 years, who had just walked from
Valenciennes to the Tuileries to beg a small pension
of Napoleon, and had returned home the same way.[1]

Although not all such great walkers, the Parisians of that
day used their legs far more than we do. As we have seen,
the dearth of carriages often forced them to do so, but they
did not complain too bitterly, for however muddy and mal-
odorous it might be, the capital offered unrivalled pleasures
of the eye to those exploring it. Everybody was agreed on this
at the time. No provincial entering Paris for the first time but
was captivated on the spot, like M. Musard, one of the few
lively characters in Picard's boring plays. He had hardly been
set lose in our streets before he had forgotten his business,
his lawsuits, his daughter's marriage, his wife's objurgations,
to give himself up to the joys of this new paradise.

Old Parisians themselves could never resist the pleasure of
strolling about, to which they devoted an enormous part of
their daily routine, and the women indulged in it as well as
the men, in spite of their light shoes, the gutters and the
clumsy paving-stones. 'Walking is in fashion, these first fine
days,' says the *Journal de Paris* in 1808, 'even for fair ladies
not accustomed to showing themselves. From noon to four
o'clock they may be seen inspecting the novelties displayed
on the boulevards, seated near the Théâtre des Panoramas,
or resting after a walk at the entrance to the Bois de

---

[1] He obtained a pension of 600 francs a year. But an annuity granted to a
centenarian can never be a very ruinous present.

Boulogne.' To get an idea of the society of that day, therefore, we must take a look at its usual meeting-places, and we may begin with the boulevards just referred to.

They had changed little in appearance since the old regime, having preserved their double row of elms and their side-walks of beaten earth. The Consulate had, however, replaced the ditches that bordered them by wooden barriers to protect pedestrians from the traffic, and the Emperor had the whole expanse between the Madeleine and the Pavillon de Hanovre levelled and repaved. In this area the world of fashion frequented only the Petit Coblentz, a few yards from the Boulevard des Italiens, in the immediate neighbourhood of the Chaussée d'Antin. It was there that the *émigrés* of 1791 had come to take leave of their friends before going to join the army of the Princes, and Coblentz, whose name had survived their unfortunate escapade, was still the place where it was good to be seen.

'People have been going there for the last twelve years,' says a chronicler. 'For twelve whole years I've seen the same chairs there, the same Papas, the same daughters. Between nine and ten o'clock is the time to go there, to rest from the burden of the day and take the air, or rather, to be suffocated with heat in a narrow pathway furnished with four rows of chairs, in the midst of the crowd of visitors jostling one another, cheek by jowl, squeezed together and moving forward at the rate of about an inch a minute. When you enter the walk you feel as though you were entering a stove; you can't breathe till you are out of it again. After this delightful half-hour you go and eat ices at Frascati or the Jardin Turc, and talk your fill about the pretty women you've just seen at Coblentz and the good jokes you've heard there.'

The fame of the Jardin Turc, a big café with shady terraces that were the delight of family parties, takes us to the other side of Paris, towards the popular Boulevard du Temple, the home not only of the theatres but of the tight-rope walkers and tumblers, where ever since the eighteenth century a sort of perpetual fair had been carried on.

You could never have read a *Guide to Paris*, or an account of the travels of an English or German tourist, if you were unaware of the marvels to be met with in those quarters, from the *Jongleurs Indiens* – great sword-swallowers – to the *Espagnol incombustible*, who drank boiling oil and walked barefoot on red-hot iron.

De Jouy, Prudhomme and Kotzebue all delight in giving us details of the exploits of the *Petite Tourneuse*, who spun round like a top for half an hour at a time, and the boy that turned cart-wheels between two candle-ends. They stopped to look at the dwarfs, at the five-legged sheep, the two-headed calves, the she-monkey with her tits painted pink 'for the information of connoisseurs', and the girl with a beard as long as a capuchin monk's. 'No trickery there', declares Kotzebue, 'I examined it very closely.' And we know how meticulous was our German.

They were equally dumbfounded by *Jacques de Falaise*, the eater of frogs, by *Munito*, the wise dog that told fortunes by cards, by the duels between flies, armed with pins for swords, and by the liliputian chariot races with fleas for horses.[1]

But these popular attractions were as nothing to the sensational turns that ensured the vogue of the *Cirque* and one or two other establishments near by. No real connoisseur would bother with street players when at the distance of a stone's throw they could go and admire the cavalcades of the Franconis, or the tight-rope feats of *Forioso*, *Ravel* and the unforgettable Mme Saqui.

Miracles of aerial balance, flights between heaven and earth, these were what the public of the First Empire doted upon, this was the ideal spectacle for a nation whose very fame and fortune may be said to have walked the tight-rope for fifteen years.

* * *

Paris had three large public gardens – the Tuileries, which attracted the fashionable world and soon benefited by the proximity of the new Rue de Rivoli; the Luxembourg, refuge

---

[1] The sport was more than a century old. In 1673 Mme de Sévigné wrote to her daughter: 'M. le Dauphin was told the other day that there was a man in Paris who had made a masterpiece of a little chariot drawn by fleas. He said to M. le prince de Conti, ' "My cousin, who made the harness?" "Some spider in the neighbourhood," said the Prince.'

of quiet folk,[1] and the Jardin des Plantes, so named because it was devoted to animals. But it also had a fourth, which, in spite of its small size, was visited by the clientèle of all the other three: the garden of the Palais-Royal. There, on the stroke of noon, old gentlemen might be seen taking out their watches as they waited for the report of the little legendary gun, while for the rest of the time every variety of human fauna was to be seen there, including a species of poultry much in favour with the local naturalists.

But we may leave these light creatures on their perches for the moment, since a later chapter will be devoted to them. In any case we are now engaged only on a tour of reconnaissance.

With the first spring of the nineteenth century Philippe-Égalité's old garden renewed its youth. Its lawns were restored, and eight rows of lime-trees were planted, mingled with thuyas. But how small these were! In a vaudeville performed at Mme de Montansier's theatre, the librettist assures us that

> 'The trees, ten years hence,
> May give shade to the strollers . . .'

The Parisians cannot have been afraid of sunstroke, for the Palais-Royal, shadeless though it was, had never enjoyed such popularity. Lawns and arcades were crowded from morning to night. All the amenities and facilities of life were to be found there. Around this enchanted garden stood fifteen restaurants, twenty-nine cafés, seventeen billiard-saloons, the shops of twenty-four jewellers, six booksellers, eight watchmakers, six wigmakers, six provision-merchants, one dentist-pedicure, shoeblacks, a reading-room, a manufacturer of pictures in hair and a cutter-out of silhouettes. And we are purposely leaving out the gambling-houses, lending-houses and plain 'houses', to be dealt with elsewhere.

There was a similar muddle of shops, especially milliners' shops, in the wooden arcades known as the Camp des Tartares, until they were replaced by the Galerie d'Orléans.

'One might be shut up for life in the Palais-Royal,' it was

[1] The Consulate enlarged it by the addition of the former close of the Carthusians, which later became the nursery gardens (1803).

said, 'and so long as one had money one would want for nothing.' Did you need a pair of boots? You would find 'seamless' ones at Colman's, No. 8 in the Galeries de Pierre, for the trifling sum of 600 francs. Did you want a hair-cut? You would be trimmed in the height of fashion at Carron's or Sainte-Foix's. Did you need a suit? You could go to the *Véloci-Tailleur*, who would take your measurements, lend you the *Journal des Débats*, and almost before you had had time to run through Geoffroy's article, the suit would be ready, even to the gaiters!

If it had been possible to die of thirst anywhere, it could not have been in the arcades of the Tribunate, for at every step you would have seen the sign of some famous café. Café de Foy, frequented by officers, Café de Chartres, the rendezvous of stockbrokers, Café de Valois, where chess tournaments were held, Café de la Rotonde, with its summerhouse in the garden, Café Borel, whose ventriloquist played such amusing tricks, Café des Mille-Colonnes, famous for its ices and its fair waitress, Café Corazza, Café Lemblin and many others.

Past the doors of these cafés the crowd of sightseers and gossips jostled one another all the afternoon. And day after day they were seized with hilarity at the sight of an odd procession: the devotees of Cambacérès escorting the Arch-Chancellor, covered with decorations, promenading the arcades in his embroidered coat, his three-cornered hat and his wig in the fashion of 1780. There was the fat d'Aigre-feuille, his head shining like a pumpkin; there was his exact opposite, the thin, melancholy Villevieille; the secretary Lavollée, his cousin Duvidal, Noël the notary, Collin the bookseller. All these solemn personages, surrounded by footmen, went through the Camp des Tartares, stopping in front of the shops, talking little, and regulating their pace by the slow steps of the great man.

The onlookers roared with laughter. They lined up in advance, they climbed on chairs; and when the procession arrived it was greeted with cheers and cat-calls.

The jest became so preposterous that after a time Bonaparte was worried. 'You must see to this', he said one day to Josephine; 'only a woman can tell a man he is making himself ridiculous.' But no doubt the undertaking proved too difficult after all, for the fertile imagination of the Minister of Police was eventually called upon. Fouché at once thought of an expedient. The following week he organized a procession exactly like that of Cambacérès, and while the latter was going his daily rounds, he saw, coming towards him, a portly man dressed like himself, decorated with all the Orders of Europe and followed by a whole troop of supers and servants.

Alas! Fouché had counted without the imperturbable calm of the Arch-Chancellor of the Empire. He merely pouted. 'Is it carnival time?' he said to d'Aigreville, and continued his tour at the same solemn pace.

* * * *

A combination of *al fresco* pleasures with those of dancing and music, iced drinks and dazzling fireworks was the programme offered by the Paris Pleasure Gardens, or Amusement Parks as we should call them today – allurements accounting for their enormous success on fine evenings under the Consulate and the Empire.

Like many other institutions, this was no novelty. People had danced madly by starlight during the Directory, and the following generation continued to do so, though with a little more restraint. A poster announcing a ball at Tivoli set the tone. 'The quiet behaviour and extreme decency reigning in such a numerous assembly will allow mothers to bring their daughters here, since they will run no risk of enjoying themselves at the expense of morality.' A text to be strongly recommended to the lessees of our modern dance halls.

Tivoli, the first of the name, founded by the Ruggieri brothers, occupied at that time the extensive gardens of the former Hôtel Boutin, in the Rue Saint-Lazare, opposite the present Avenue du Coq. Opinions were much divided as to the interest of the amusements it provided. Redhead Yorke laughs at the French for daring to compare Tivoli to London's Vauxhall. 'They might as well compare a candle to the sun!' He thought the lighting of the garden very poor, the fireworks lacking in brilliance, the acrobats very inferior to Flockton's English troupe; and he was surprised to see so few dancers pirouetting round the orchestra. As for the lake, it was only twenty yards long by three wide, though it was there that 'the Parisians display their knowledge of navigation!'

About the same time, Sir John Carr declared on the contrary that Tivoli had been created 'by the wand of an enchanter'. He admired the gravel walks bordered with orange-trees and the arbours of roses and honeysuckle. He saw a lot of spectators eating ices under the trees and applauding the feats of the performers, and he counted nearly 300 people dancing the waltz, imported from Germany, in graceful attitudes. Everything found favour with him, even the little sheet of water on which couples were amusing themselves by canoeing.

It is strange to read two such different accounts from the pen of two compatriots. Ought not families to agree among themselves?

Up to the day when Tivoli removed its illuminations, its balloon ascents and parachute descents – triumphs of the Garnerin family – to the slopes of the Rue de Clichy, Frascati had bid fair to become the most fashionable resort, thanks to its specially favourable situation above the boulevard, at the corner of the Rue de la Loi. A dance hall with room for 1,000 couples, gambling arcades in which supper was served, a small garden crowded with rustic bridges, temples and mills in painted wood, with miniature rocks and cascades – here was enough to attract the world of fashion. It responded, it even flocked there to excess on the evening when Juliette Récamier was nearly suffocated by her admirers, 'paying dear for the pleasure of being beautiful.'

Not all the like establishments that our city had to show at the beginning of the century enjoyed such a lasting popularity. The Jardin des Capucines, which offered 'shades favourable to the sweet effusions of love, the confidences of friendship and the artifices of coquetry', disappeared from between the Place Vendôme and the boulevards when the Rue de la Paix was driven through; and the *bals musettes* – popular dance halls with accordion bands – with their rustic restaurants, which had opened at Bagatelle and Mousseaux, did not survive the resumption of possession of these two estates by the Imperial Crown.

As for the Hameau de Chantilly, which made the fame of the Élysée-Bourbon for a few years, it was turned out of there by Murat, the new owner of the Palace. Of its ephemeral fame only one document exists: the poster in which the manager of the place, Velloni, invited the public to come and dine under the thatched roofs of the Hamlet, play at see-saw and shuttlecock, and dance on the Grand Terrace.

'The price of admission', he announced, 'will be one franc per day, of which sixty-five centimes will be taken in refreshments of some kind.'

So that admission to the Élysée, round about 1800, actually cost only five sous. It must be admitted that this was dirt cheap.

❊   ❊   ❊   ❊

The attractiveness of a town is much less dependent on the ingenuity of its amusement purveyors than on the permanent spectacle it presents to itself: the animation of its streets, the beauty of its vistas, everything in fact that gives it a personal, lively charm.

Paris possessed more attractions of this kind than any other capital, but they were not to be found in its new quarters, which were to remain encumbered with public works until the end of the Empire.

Dare one confess that the talent of the Sovereign as a builder of towns appears somewhat questionable? Of the two Napoleons, the better urbanist was the one with no genius. The other, the Great Man, did not always see things in the right light.[1] When by good luck his plans had real beauty about them, they were so ambitious that it would take ten years and more to carry them out.[2] For his contemporaries this meant enormous undertakings being embarked in all over Paris, and a gigantic pile of building materials on the public thoroughfares.

[1] One day he thought of erecting a church of Saint-Napoleon on the Place du Carrousel; another day, a column to Charlemagne on the Place des Victoires; a cemetery for Generals on the esplanade of the Invalides; a temple of Janus on the Pont-Neuf. Later on he talked of rebuilding Saint-Cloud, repairing Versailles as a Home for old soldiers, moving the Jardin des Plantes to the Parc Monceau, and so on.

[2] This was the case with the Madeleine, the Bourse, the Arc de Triomphe. As for the Palace of the King of Rome, he stopped short at the foundations.

For a long time the Carrousel, the Place des Victoires and certain parts of the boulevards were thus turned into depositories of freestone, through which carriages and pedestrians would have the greatest difficulty in passing. For a long time the Rue de Rivoli and the Rue de Castiglione, hardly paved, hardly built, would remain fringed by waste ground, and at the least gust of wind the riverside dwellers would complain of being blinded by the dust.

The state of some localities became so shocking during the last years of the Empire, especially those of the Madeleine, the Étoile and the slopes of Chaillot, that foreigners could not conceal their surprise. When Napoleon, showing the fat King of Wurtemberg round the capital, asked him what he thought of it, the other answered, not without irony, 'I think it's very fine ... for a town that the architects have taken by assault.'

Fortunately the stroller encountered fewer hindrances in the central quarters. These had even become more accessible than before along the banks of the Seine, the scenery of which had been singularly beautified since the beginning of the reign. Four bridges built;[1] 3,000 yards of new embankments – all the result of ten years of effort. Works really worthy, in this case, of the Napoleonic idea.

Now the houses no longer stood with their foundations in the mud of the river bank; the lower streets were no longer in danger of being turned into Venetian canals, as they had been during the horrible winter of 1801–02; the small arm of the Monnaie ran less risk of drying up, as it had done a year later.[2] Along the river, in future, traffic would circulate almost without interruption from the Quai d'Orsay to the Quai Montebello, from the Barrière des Bonshommes to the Place de Grève. And what a marvellous journey! Nowhere in the world could anything like it be found.

The Parisians were well aware of this. They never tired of the changing spectacle of their river with its boats, its timber-

[1] The bridge of the Louvre, or the Arts, was opened in 1803, and so was the future Pont-Saint-Louis, between the island of that name and the Cité. The bridge to be known later as of Austerlitz was not opened till 1906, the future Pont d'Iéna in 1812.

[2] In September 1803 the little arm was literally dry. The poor went hunting for old sous in the sand.

floats, its barges laden with merchandise, its water-coach coming from Boulogne. A pleasant, convenient observation post had been at their disposal since the spring of 1804: the Pont des Arts, or rather, of the Louvre.

Of this light foot-bridge, which was to have a long life, it was at first attempted to make a sort of hanging garden. Boxes of flowers and shrubs, removed at night to a little conservatory in the middle of the bridge, decorated both sides of it. 'By this means', said a poet-journalist, 'the air is gently cooled by that of the river, and scented with all the perfumes of the heliotrope, the rose, the mignonette, the jasmine and the orange flower. Two lines of charming women complete the embellishment of this truly picturesque passage, which in every way resembles that of a happy life – it is too short.'

The beauty of the scenery could not, however, blind one to certain eyesores still disfiguring the Seine: on the banks, too many floating mills and laundry boats. There was also an aspect of the scene that scandalized the moralists. The youth of the First Empire was rightly fond of cold baths, but erred by its ignorance of the use of bathing-drawers, which led strollers on the embankments to fancy they had been transported to the shores of the St. Lawrence or the Potomac, among some savage tribe. 'Yesterday evening', complains a censor, 'I saw a mother and daughter gazing from the top of the Pont des Arts at seven or eight completely naked bathers, who, having climbed on to some coal barges, were flinging themselves, one after another, into the Seine. The mother was making the most ridiculous remarks on the danger these divers were running, with no thought of the danger incurred by her own daughter.'

But perhaps the picture was a little on the black side. A Parisian of the eighteenth century would have been more indulgent towards these bathing enthusiasts and the simplicity of their attire. Witness the tale of Duclos, swimming one day near the Pont-Neuf and retrieving the bonnet of an unknown lady, which a gust had blown into the water. Restoring it to her *in naturalibus*, 'Excuse me, Madame,' he said, 'for having no gloves.'

CHAPTER XV

MARRIAGE

Short-term marriage – A melancholy divorce – Decadal wed-dings – The Church reassumes its rights – Spouses unknown to each other – Napoleon and the family – Marrying Prefects – Personal Columns – A matrimonial agency

AFTER the Revolutionary experiment a slump of a peculiar kind made itself felt throughout society – a slump in marriage. It seems to have been due to two causes, the social upheaval and, to no lesser degree, the law concerning divorce. By authorizing it in its most expeditious form, divorce by mutual consent, the deputies of 1792 intended to declare their respect for individual liberty; but perhaps they could not have foreseen that, in the case of many marriages, the system of the open door would greatly increase the number of draughts.

The Frenchmen and Frenchwomen of the Directory took it upon themselves to prove this. Turning conjugal duty into a short-term obligation, they ceased to treat seriously a link that could be fastened and unfastened with such ease, and the lives of many couples consisted simply of a series of honeymoons, shining every time in a different sky.

For those with a taste for fresh pleasures these rapid exchanges must have had their advantages, but legal union under this guise was hardly distinguishable from free love, nor passion from a passing fancy, and serious people must have asked themselves what, in this adventure, or rather these adventures, was to become of the love of home, respect for one's name, the education of children and other outworn ideas, still worthy of respect after all, in which the France of yesterday had believed.

Long before Brumaire there had been protests in the Council of the Five Hundred against the abuse of divorce. 'What could be more immoral', exclaimed Regnaut de l'Orme, 'than to allow a man to change his wife like a coat, and a woman to change her husband like a hat? Is this not an assault on the dignity of marriage? Does it not turn it into a succession of concubinages?'

And a few days later, at the Council of the Elders, Philippe Delville had spoken to the same purpose. 'We must put an end to this traffic in human flesh that the abuse of divorce has introduced into society.'

Alas, the traffic in human flesh was destined to last longer than either of these Assemblies. Long after the end of the regime, short-term marriages persisted and divorces remained as frequent. More often than not the rupture was accomplished without pain, because it was desired by both parties. Sometimes, however, when some affection was still alive in the heart of husband or wife, the separation became more distressing, as with the Talmas, when after eleven years of wedded life the tragedian decided to leave his delightful Julie Carreau. She adored him, as everybody knew, and it is easy to imagine how she suffered when she allowed herself to be driven to the Divorce Office, once she was convinced that she had lost the game.

Few pages can be more touching than her account of the last actions of the two spouses, soon to be two strangers.

'We went to the town hall in the same carriage,' wrote Julie to one of her intimate friends. 'We talked the whole way about indifferent things, like people going into the country. My husband helped me out of the carriage; we seated ourselves beside each other, and we signed our names as if it were some ordinary contract we were entering into. Before we separated, he went with me as far as my carriage. "I hope," I said to him, "you will not deprive me altogether of your company, it would be too cruel. . . . You will come and see me sometimes won't, you?" "Certainly," he said, with an air of embarrassment, "always with great pleasure." I was pale, my voice shook in spite of all my efforts to control myself. At last I reached home and was able to give myself up entirely to my grief. Pity me, for I am very unhappy.'

While many divorces were thus surrounded by melancholy, matrimonial ceremonies, on the contrary, assumed an operettish aspect, much in harmony with the psychology of some of the partners.

They had to be celebrated in the decadal temples – in the

churches, that is to say, that had been turned into public
Assembly Halls, with an altar to the Fatherland, symbolic
decorations and so forth. Magistrates read passages from the
law to the bride and bridegroom, and delivered an address,
while an orchestra played suitable music.

As marriages were usually dispatched in batches, the procession of couples often presented a rather ridiculous sight,
which the onlookers were not slow to make fun of. Woe to the
couples showing too great a difference in age! The wags
showered jokes on them worthy of the scurrilous works of
Vadé, and the orchestra, joining in, chose items from its
repertory to underline the comicality of the situation.

Was a Negro marrying a White? He was treated to the aria
from *Azéma*:

> Ivory with ebony
> makes pretty jewels . . .

Did an old lady appear on the arm of a twenty-five-year-
old groom? They were given the refrain from the *Prisonnier*:

> Old wife, young husband,
> Will never agree . . .

And the crowd would take up the chorus, enjoying themselves as they would at the theatre.

People living in the Faubourg Saint-Germain today and
attending the church of Saint-Thomas d'Aquin will no doubt
have some difficulty in believing that masquerades such as
these were taking place in their parish church in the year
VIII. There is, however, a detailed account in the report of
an official of the Directory who had just attended the Negro's
wedding, and thought it his duty to describe the incident to
his chief, the Minister of Interior.

'Citizen Minister,
'I denounce the public to you: it behaved yesterday with
the utmost indecency.

'At the Temple de la Paix,[1] in the Xth arrondissement,
during the marriage celebrations, there was such a hubbub
going on that no reading or speech addressed to the congregation was any use. The orchestra in particular added

[1] Saint-Thomas d'Aquin.

to the disorder by choosing tunes intended to provoke laughter.'

Here followed the two instances refered to above, and in conclusion,

'This abuse, Citizen Minister, if it is not stopped, might well reduce the number of marriages. At any rate, some young women affirmed in my presence that they would rather remain single all their lives than provide amusement for the public in this way, at the risk of being hooted at.'

* * * *

Thanks to the policy of religious tolerance initiated by the Consulate, weddings soon reassumed a more decent form. People were given leave to celebrate them on any day of the week, thus avoiding the publicity of collective ceremonies.

The decadal cult tried in vain to preserve its matrimonial monopoly. The festival of the *Bons Ménages*, which it organized in the year IX, in the Temple de la Victoire, was not very successful: it served chiefly to demonstrate the spaciousness of the church of Saint-Sulpice and the insufficiency of happy couples to fill it. On the other hand, the Catholic priests, who had enjoyed relative freedom since the start of conversations with Rome, were beginning to bless a number of unions on the quiet.

To avoid offending public opinion these religious weddings took place at first without any show, and very early in the morning. The engaged couple arrived at the church towards seven or eight o'clock, and went on to the town hall afterwards. When the reverse order was prescribed after the signing of the Concordat, the church service was postponed to the end of the morning in the case of many weddings in the Faubourg Saint-Germain, while the official world mostly adopted the fashion for nocturnal ceremonies.

It was at midnight that Junot, then already Town Mayor of Paris, led pretty Mlle Permon to the altar; at midnight that the Third Consul married the daughter of Barbé-Marbois, and at midnight, too, that the daughter of Champagny, Minister of Foreign Affairs, was married in the same church of Saint-Thomas d'Aquin, where ten years earlier the negro's wedding had provoked such uncontrollable peals of laughter.

As a proof of the change wrought in manners since that time we may quote a letter in which one of Champagny's nieces describes her cousin's wedding:

'On Wednesday I had a most amiable note from my aunt, begging us to attend the wedding, which was to take place at night. . . . We had a carriage for M. Balzac and ourselves, which took us to the town hall at half-past eight. The Mayor made a rather odd speech, in which, among other things, addressing Mademoiselle, he urged her to assume *paternal* feelings; he said that their union would be a happy one because it was the fruit of the wishes of their parents and of a *long-standing affection* (they have known each other for ten days!) In spite of the solemnity of the ceremony, everybody found it difficult to keep a straight face.'

The company left the town hall to go and take supper; then, at midnight, they went to the church, which they found completely lighted up.

'The chancel was full, for we were nine carriage-loads. M. le curé of Saint-Thomas d'Antin made a long address, but even if it had been longer one would not have tired of listening. I was really edified by the way people behaved in church: the two fathers and the two grandmothers on their knees all through the address and the mass. The two mothers looked like angels. On coming out of the church Zéphyrine and her husband got into Mme Martroy's carriage, and M. and Mme de Champagny drove away alone. We did not get home till two o'clock.'

In this pleasing account one detail gives us pause: the couple had known each other for barely ten days. This was precisely the usual defect of First Empire marriages. Arranged in a hurry, during an army leave, they were rushed through, as a rule, after a meeting at a ball, or because an old aunt with money to bequeath wanted her nephew to settle down. There was no engagement in the ordinary sense: the two families came to an understanding, sometimes almost without consulting the interested parties; money matters were settled, then everything was carried through at the speed of a cavalry charge.

K

The bridegroom sent his presents: dresses, shawls, jewellery, miniatures, packed in the traditional *corbeille* in the shape of an egg or a conch-shell, or representing an altar of love. He did not forget the gloves, the lace, the bottles of Eau de Ninon and the complexion creams to be enclosed in the *Sultan*, a sort of *corbeille* No. 2. The contract was signed in the presence of a small gathering of intimate friends, and the wedding was celebrated according to the nocturnal ceremonial just described.

More often than not the honeymoon would be even shorter than the engagement. Instead of a wedding trip, the husband, if an officer, would soon be on his way back to the front. On his return, if he did return, he might be surprised to learn that he was a father; but there was also a chance that the young wife, on catching sight of him, might ask herself, 'Who is this handsome soldier walking in without knocking?'

Another rock on which marriages under the Empire might founder was the enormous difference in age between husband and wife. Many distinguished soldiers, who had not had an opportunity of marrying in their youth, thought of it late in life, and offered their name, titles and fortune to attractive young persons who might have been their daughters. This was the fate of Augereau, Oudinot and many others. General Mouton, twenty years older than his wife, begged his aides-de-camp 'to think of her as a statue in black marble'. General Legrand, at the age of fifty-odd, married a young lady of seventeen. And it was not only the brass hats that went in for these experiments. Many a former officer, many a veteran soldier, once home for good, cherished the thought of seeing some fresh young creature at his side. They had faced so many dangers that one more risk did not alarm them, and these heroes of the Old Guard hoped to become the heroes of the New.

There is nothing surprising, therefore, in the confidence imparted one day to Stendhal and entered, piping hot, in his diary. 'The Abbé Hélie, who has confessed and studied mankind at first hand, tells me that out of a hundred marriages there are twenty-five good ones, between people in love with each other, and fifty in which people get on together – even love each other – although the husband is often deceived.'

The Abbé's assertions may have been somewhat fanciful, but more official statistics confirm his poor opinion of the morals of his time. For one thing, there were far fewer married people than formerly. In the department of the Seine they numbered hardly one-fifth more than the unmarried. According to another, no less significant figure, the total number of illegitimate children registered in Paris, in certain years, was almost equal to a third of the legitimate births.

In the environs of the capital the proportion must have been greater still, for the local youth was said to be pleasure-loving. When a little maidservant of the Chateaubriands was confined one morning at the Vallée-aux-Loups, with no clear idea of where the infant came from, the good people of the neighbourhood thought nothing of the incident. 'For a long time now', wrote Mme de Chateaubriand in her *Souvenirs*, 'nobody in Châtenay expected a girl to *be* a girl on her wedding day.'

And what happened at Châtenay must have been the order or the day elsewhere, for the morals of Paris had reached the provinces, the small towns and even the countryside. We have only to read what Bishop Le Coz says of his Breton flock, the prefect Dupin of the people under his jurisdiction in the Bocage, and Henri Beyle of the unmarried couples of Toulon. All that generation grew up at a time when morals had little importance, and the France of the Empire, daughter of the France of the Directory, could not become a school of virtue from one day to another.

It was Bonaparte's ambition to make the family the pivot of society once more. It took him only a few months to have it expressed in the *Code Civil*, but it would take a long time for the principles to find their way into conduct, and for the marriage tie to recover its former strength.

It must be admitted that in the Master's entourage, especially his own family, the good example was hardly set. With the exception of Louis, who had become a valetudinarian early in life, all his brothers had mistresses; Joseph made a collection of them. Lucien, all the time he was Minister of Interior, treated the fair petitioners and the actresses of the theatres as a Pasha does his favourites. And the Corsican blood was no less ardent on the female side: Élisa's quasi-official liaison with Fontanes constituted her, so to speak, Grand Mistress of the University; Caroline consoled herself for Murat's infidelities by falling into the arms of Junot. As for the too sensual Pauline, she was preparing to embody Canova's Venuses by infatuating all the handsome men she met on the way.

The Imperial pair themselves had not always been a model couple. Josephine's fancies, in the early days of her marriage, are only too well known. And a few years later, only the ingenuousness of a provincial ecclesiastic can have allowed him to welcome Bonaparte's sobered spouse on the threshold of his church with the words, 'One of the great days for the curé of Le Havre and for his clergy is that on which it is permitted them to offer the tribute of their admiration to your *virtues* ...'

Bonaparte himself had had many love affairs, but they would always occupy only a secondary place in his life, for he had a domestic soul. He was born to be a husband – and was to prove it more than once. Hence his relative severity with regard to the irregular situations of other people.

He could tolerate the idea of discreet liaisons being formed at a Court like his own, where the men sought to shine and the women to attract. He was well aware, for instance, that Louis de Narbonne was living with the former Vicomtesse de Laval; that Caulaincourt was Mme de Colbert's lover; that Berthier, even after his marriage, was still faithful to Mme de Visconti. He was the first to smile at these old romances. He only began to frown when the affair appeared to be turning into a scandal; when Chaptal was seen everywhere in public with Mlle Bourgoin, or when Talleyrand made his English mistress preside at his official dinners. Then he did not spare his thrusts: he led his Minister of Interior to believe, rather cruelly, that the actress had granted favours to himself.[1] He ordered Talleyrand to marry Mme Grand; but the matter

[1] One evening when he was working with Chaptal, Bonaparte sent for Mlle Bourgoin. She arrived, and was openly announced. Chaptal, in a furious temper put his papers away and left. When he got home he sent in his resignation.

was not so simple as all that. For one thing, Talleyrand, as a former Bishop of Autun, might be considered as still belonging to the priesthood, besides which, his mistress was already married. The drawing-rooms buzzed with discussions of this doubly litigious problem.

In a letter to Benjamin Constant, Julie Talma sums up the affair after her own manner. 'The pure priests', she says, 'are greatly scandalized by the marriage of the Foreign Minister. But since the Pope has released him from the priesthood, what are they fussing about? Either one is a Pope or one isn't: what one has done one can undo. They say too that the woman hasn't been able to get a divorce from her husband. These are all miserable quibbles. What if one did have two husbands? If it's a misfortune to have none, it can't be so bad to have two!'

How difficult it was to speak seriously of marriage in this country, on the eve of the *Code Civil*! One had to be a Napoleon, to attempt to endue the French of 1802 with respect for institutions.

Imagine the astonishment of a young civil servant, Maine de Biran, sub-prefect of Bergerac, on finding one day in his mail a note from the prefect of Dordogne enjoining him to draw up *a table of the young ladies of the arrondissement of the age of fourteen years and over, belonging to distinguished families,* that is to say, to rich ones. The order came from the Minister of Interior, and had been received by all the prefects of France, with printed tables prepared for the purpose. There was a column for the names, another for the probable dowries, another for future inheritance, etc.

Only families with an income of at least 50,000 livres were to be listed. But the Government, laying claim to good taste, wished to devote some attention to the prepossessing appearance and good education of the girls it was inventorying. In a final column reserved for the purpose there must also be entered 'the physical attractions or defects, the talents, behaviour and religious principles of each of the young ladies'. Was she as fresh as the dawn or pitted with smallpox? Did she thrum the harp? Or the pianoforte? Did she paint in watercolours? And what of her Easter devotions? The Duc de Rovigo, Minister of Interior, was anxious to be informed on these various points. It was a wonder he didn't ask to have a lock of her hair included in the dossier.

Once the central power had all these lists in its hands, it could make use of them to marry the candidates of its choice to rich provincial heiresses and therewith strengthen the regime. It was not a bad idea.

Perhaps Napoleon was also hoping that this matrimonial propaganda would provide the country with a higher birth-rate. Nothing interested him more – witness his conversation with Mme Fabre de l'Aude, already mother of twenty-four children.

'And when will you have the twenty-fifth?'

'Sire, whenever Your Majesty likes.'

Why not ask her to bring a whole regiment into the world?

* * * *

The Government was not the only matchmaker. The press took a hand in it too, and its Personal Columns had long been open to the enemies of celibacy. Kotzebue made a note of the following insertions in the newspapers of 1804: 'A young lady aged thirty, well-born, with one thousand six hundred francs and some nice furniture, wishes to enter into a legal union with a man of good morals, having a situation in an office or something to look forward to.'

Let us hasten to put the young lady with the nice furniture in touch with the author of the following: 'A widower with one thousand four hundred francs per annum, resident for the last ten years in a pleasant apartment near the Tuileries, seeks a lady of suitable age, good-tempered, with some means of her own, to offer her suggestions that may suit her, or listen to her own.'

A less serious offer, no doubt, is that of the sly old fox who leaves the lady the choice between his right hand and his left:

'A man of sixty-three, in good health, widowed, without children, would like to meet a lady possessing all the qualities usually desired, for the purpose of perhaps offering her his hand on better acquaintance, or, if she prefers, of combining their interests without other tie than that of friendship, to which, for his own part, he promises to be entirely faithful.'

For those to whom this sort of thing did not sound convincing, there was another means of finding a sister soul, which was to go to the Agence Universelle, No. 46 Rue Neuve-Saint-Eustache, and lay their case before M. Vuillaume, manager of the establishment. This extraordinary man, who fondly believed he had seen brilliant service in the armies, had, like Napoleon, a passion for marrying off his fellow creatures. He had only to see in the papers that General X or Colonel Z had just been killed in battle, to rush to the domicile of the glorious deceased, to find out if he had left a wife, and whether the marriage had been a happy one or not. If the widow appeared inconsolable, he left her three weeks to weep. If her grief did not seem so great, he behaved more expeditiously, organized a grand dinner-party to which a substitute-candidate would be invited as if by chance, and unmasked his batteries at dessert.

The schemes of the Agence Universelle did not always succeed, of course. Richard Lenoir, for instance, refused to give his daughter to the Marquis de Maubreuil, who had been suggested to him as a son-in-law. But for one failure, how many brilliant successes! M. Vuillaume was a past master in the art of contriving matches and making a comfortable income for himself.

But after a time, sad to say, he became exhausted by all this diplomacy; his nerves gave way, and in 1814 he ended up where many of his clients ought to have begun: in the asylum at Charenton. Yet another victim of marriage!

CHAPTER XVI

AN OLD MARRIED COUPLE

*A home on the Quai Malaquais – Family celebrations and
domestic quarrels – The hypochondriac – Too facile tears – The
servant problem – Romance of a tender-hearted girl – An an-
cestress of Mme Montaudoin*

FEW middle-class people of the First Empire thought of
writing their memoirs. Historians of everyday life owe
all the greater debt of gratitude, therefore, to a charitable person who took the trouble to write down, evening
after evening, every trifling detail of her day. Let us open
Mme Moitte's notebook: there could be no description more
minute, nor at times more comical, of a modest Parisian home
round about 1805.

Although a pencil portrait by David gives him the air of a
provincial churchwarden, Moitte was far from being a non-
entity. A *Grand Prix de Rome*, a member of the Institute, he
occupies an honourable place among the sculptors of his
generation. But neither his Mausoleum for Desaix nor his
statue of General Custine seems to have brought him wealth.
A few official commissions, often paid for in driblets, a few
insignificant honorariums – a job at the Musée Napoleon, the
vouchers of the Academy, the pension of the Legion of
Honour – these were the whole of the artist's income. The
couple made ends meet, however; they even managed to
save, thanks to the estimable Mme Moitte, who was a para-
gon of domestic virtues.

Married for a quarter of a century, the couple, now nearing
the sixties, lived near the Institute, at No. 30 Quai Malaquais,
the former home of the Maréchal de Saxe, the pink and white
façade of which still stands today, a few yards from the Rue
de Seine.

The second floor, on which they lived, was undoubtedly
less imposing than the first-floor apartment occupied by the
painter Vien. But not everybody is a Senator of the Empire.
And for their fifteen hundred francs rent the couple enjoyed

a good deal of space. The two principal rooms, drawing-room and bedroom, overlooked the embankment. At the rear were two other bedrooms, a kitchen and two ante-rooms, one of which could be used as a dining-room. On the floor above there were two more small rooms, not to mention the 'amenities', which would have deserved the name better if they could have been reached without going through the kitchen and climbing a staircase as steep as an Alpine pathway.

Where did they wash? Probably in some dark cubby-hole. The French of those days were not much spoilt in that respect, and the Moittes could consider themselves lucky in possessing – for use on grand occasions – a bath tub shaped like a sabot; a near relation, that is, of the one in which Marat was murdered.

There was not much to be said of the furniture, for to the eye the chief luxury was displayed on the walls. His fellow artists had presented Moitte with a number of fine works of art, including a picture by David, paintings by Carle van Loo, and drawings by Vincent Norblin, Bouchardon and Fragonard, all of which must have been worth a great deal more than the mahogany bookcase, the chest of drawers with griffin feet, the Tronchin table and even the marriage bed with its curtains of blue taffetas. A number of little painted wooden beds, made up here and there in the other rooms, owed their existence to the fact that Mme Moitte augmented her resources by taking in boarders, little girls of the neighbourhood whose education she superintended.

She herself had had no children; their place had been taken by Louise, a sweet-natured creature they had taken charge of long ago, and who had grown up in the house. She played a double role there. Paid monthly for her services – doing needlework, looking after the little boarders, giving lessons in sol-fa – she was treated so much as a daughter of the house that she addressed her adoptive mother with 'thee' and 'thou', and lived in exactly the same way as her hosts. When the Moittes went out to dinner, they not only took Louise along with them, but she was generally asked to bring her music case with her, for she had a pretty voice and played the piano agreeably.

There were many occasions of the sort in this little circle

of artists, in which hospitality was practised with as much simplicity as charm. People entertained one another without ceremony, for the pleasure of spending a few hours together, venturing twenty sous in a game of *As courant*, or playing parlour games that amused even the most serious among the guests. Houdon, for instance, the great Houdon, was seen one day playing spillikins with Mme Moitte's young boarders. And one Sunday Louis David and his wife invited the whole family, including the schoolgirls, to come to supper, and dance till two in the morning, in their grand house in the Rue de Seine.

The regular gatherings at the Quai Malaquais, which took place every Friday, were of course far less pretentious. Consisting of a mere handful of intimate friends – the Viscontis, the Van Loos, the Taunays, sometimes the Viens or Berthélemy the historical painter, they were mere gossip parties round a few glasses of syrup. But the menu was more substantial when there was a birthday or some other happy date to be celebrated. On November 10, 1806, for instance, two anniversaries coinciding – the Moitte's wedding day and the sculptor's birthday – provided a splendid opportunity for our hostess to put a leaf in her table and give herself an enormous amount of trouble.

Early in the morning we see her starting out to buy provisions in her little grey dress spotted with brown. She runs to the butcher, ransacks the fruit shop, returns laden with victuals, puts the pot on the fire, runs off again to the pastrycook and the confectioner, and after working like mad, discovers she has only just time to make herself presentable.

Now the little grey dress is exchanged for a handsome red one *à la turque*, with a taffeta skirt and a lace tucker. The table is laid, and Mme Moitte awaits her guests, a little feverishly, as befits the occasion. Will no one be late? Will the dinner be cooked to a turn?

By good luck all the guests were punctual, and the feast could proceed without a hitch. The menu, given in detail in the diary, allows us to appraise the digestive capacities of middle-class circles. 'Meat soup, radishes, butter, gherkins, boiled beef, two chickens, little pasties, cutlets, fowl with truffles, two partridges, salad, cauliflowers, charlotte, sponge cakes, tartlets, cheese, jams, coffee and liqueurs, meringues, macaroons, sponge fingers, sweets and peach preserves.'

After this one was justified in considering that the wedding anniversary – the 're-marriage' as it was called – had been celebrated in due form. But the most touching family festivals are not enough to restore harmony to an old partnership when things are not as they should be. And it is now time to confess that this was the case with the Moittes.

* * * *

Though they were really very fond of each other, husband and wife quarrelled all day long. It was the eternal little drama of associates who have seen too much of each other, who know each other's defects too well and can no longer put up with them. Everything becomes a subject of disagreement between them: a meal served too late, too long a walk, a badly chosen menu, a pot of mustard that can't be found, or worse still, an Academician who snores, tosses about in bed and prevents his wife from sleeping! We must pity these two martyrs to life in common, though, selfishly, we cannot regret their quarrels, since without them the famous diary would lose much of its flavour.

If old Moitte had always been in a good temper, we should have lost the picturesque vocabulary that his wife invented to picture his ups and downs. If he tries to be funny, she says he's playing the *nana*, the *sottasse*. If he grumbles more than usual, he's *mioumiou, quinquin* or *grimaudin*. And when she talks of *patauderie* [loutishness] the Moitte barometer is decidedly pointing to a storm.

This happened only too frequently, as often as not for some purely futile reason. Nor was the fault entirely on one side. Moitte was certainly a difficult man, but why accuse him, without the slightest justification, of running after the women of the Palais-Royal like his friend Barthélemy? Why, he wanted to know, was his wife in such a fluster? Why was the room in a mess, with piles of old papers all over the sofa? Why cook the stew on the bedroom fire?

Madame Moitte retaliates by reproaching her husband, in bitter terms, for leaving his overcoat lying on the bed, on the side where she herself would be sleeping. Upon which he retorts, 'My overcoat hasn't got the itch!' A delightful existence, as may be seen.

The most serious of all Mme Moitte's grievances was Monsieur's craze for always imagining he was ill. 'I had to get up at six because of one of Moitte's *patauderies*. He never considers me, and was insufferably insulting about it. His inflammation, which was nothing, has kept him in bed at an awkward time, and now he's got stomach trouble! That makes nineteen days on whey, and he won't touch it now. On top of all that, the piles! He declares I'm the cause of all his troubles!'

A few weeks later he has influenza. 'Moitte coughs a lot. As usual, he behaves under this indisposition with the greatest cowardice I've ever seen. I've written to M. Portal against my wish, but if he had the whole Faculty to see him he wouldn't be satisfied. I shudder to see him growing old with such bad grace. Is he expecting his youth to start all over again?'

And finally, pains in his legs. 'Moitte is still very tiresome, with his leg that's supposed to be wasting away. He treated me to his moans and groans yesterday, before going to sleep, and I slept badly. . . . He complains of pains he hardly feels, if at all, for he eats and sleeps extremely well. . . . What a man! What a man!'

Actually, Mme Moitte was in far worse health than her husband, as the doctors were soon to realize, and much of her neurasthenia may be attributed to this cause. The neurasthenia was undeniable, it could even be termed chronic, for our heroine's lamentations represent a large part of her daily confidences. Floods of tears at every moment, and why, if you please? Because she had just been reading *Atala*, because she had mislaid a handkerchief or lost a game of cards; because Louise had said something unkind, had put on her 'pompous airs', or, when sent to buy provisions, had not brought back the right kind of meat.

The poor girl was the first to suffer under these jeremiads, which only too often proved infectious. 'I had a scene with Louise because I'd pointed out to her that she wasn't very attentive. She cried enough to give an angel a swollen face.'

Another day: 'I had an altercation with Louise about her

harsh words to me when I remarked that none of the young ladies left any milk for the cats. She took such offence that I shed floods of tears.' If all the riverside dwellers of the Quai Malaquais were afflicted with the same sensibility, it is not to be wondered at that the Seine was sometimes seriously flooded.

Mme Moitte's irritability did not prevent the two women from loving each other most tenderly. Sudden fits of temper were only to be expected in such a large household, with Madame determined to do everything herself, without neglecting the education of the four little pupils. Up to 1806 she had managed without a maidservant. A man of the name of Laurent Bringuier, keeper of the Desaix monument, came to polish the floors, brush his master's clothes and do the rough work of the apartment for the sum of twenty-four francs a month. But the poor man died, and the family was obliged to look for other help.

The tradesmen had at first nothing very promising to suggest. 'The butcher's wife was full of the depravity of maidservants', writes Mme Moitte sadly. A few days later, however, the fruiterer suggested a 'treasure' of the name of Ursule, who was engaged – but soon returned her apron because she considered it inadmissable that she should be accompanied on her errands. No doubt her profits on the marketing were to be made on the quiet.

Another candidate presented herself. Opinions were reserved. 'Catherine is not at all good-looking and seems very stupid. I hardly think her capable of understanding anything.' She took the situation, however, but chose to consider the wine nasty and her apron too small. She broke the crockery, forgot to say 'Madame' when speaking to her employer, and had an exaggerated fondness for the pleasures of the Carnival.

On Shrove Tuesday the wine merchant who had his shop on the ground floor of the house got up a little dance. Catherine was given permission to go to it, with strict orders to return at midnight. 'We two Moittes went to bed. Louise stayed up till one in the morning to fetch Catherine, who wouldn't come up and made an awful scene because she wanted to stay on at the dance. We had to get the doorkeeper.

Moitte got up, to make her go to bed or else to turn her out. At last she went to bed, and Louise locked her in and went to bed herself soon after. It made us all ill.'

Having had enough of young maids, Mme Moitte now engaged a person of mature age answering to the name of Mme Carré. She was treated with consideration, and even allowed to bring her caged canary with her, for she adored birds. As ill luck would have it, she also loved wine. 'When Louise came into our room in the morning she told us Mme Carré had got drunk last night. We were much surprised and upset.' A further discovery, no less unpleasant, revealed that she was a fly-by-night; she was found one night, hugging the walls of the Rue de Seine, with a candlestick in her hand, burning her employers' candles at both ends.

Evidently the maids of the First Empire were no better than ours of today, so this domestic question, the housewife's eternal nightmare, supposed to date only from yesterday, probably goes back to the suppression of slavery.

❊   ❊   ❊   ❊

As though all these worries were not enough, the Moittes were soon to be faced with troubles of another kind. An intrigue was about to be enacted under their roof, of which Louise would be the victim. A case of breach of promise.

No mention has been made so far of a friend of the family, Taunay junior, who collaborated in Moitte's work, and was a cousin of his wife's. Between the latter and the young sculptor somewhat tender relations had probably existed in the past. The Diary is understandably silent on this point, but certain sketches in the margins – a vase with the last remains of incense burning in it, guarded by two faithful dogs; a sentence let fall by Taunay: 'You are the first woman I loved', and finally when one day Mme Moitte fell seriously ill, the need she felt to confess her sins to the curé of Saint-Séverin and to describe them with 'all the details of the crime', all give reason to suppose that some fifteen years earlier one cousin, still pretty, and the other, still a tyro, may have carried the family spirit beyond fitting limits.

All this, of course, had ceased to be anything but ancient history. Mme Moitte was now fifty-nine, Taunay thirty-seven, and as the men of his generation were less indulgent than we are towards the autumn of a woman's life, her former gallant looked upon her as a dowager. As a pupil of her husband, however, he had remained an intimate of the household. He not only dined at the Quai Malaquais nearly every day, but he soon took up his abode there, in a little room specially done up for his use.

He might have wished for greater independence; he may have considered that his employer made him do a lot of work and paid him badly for it, and that his cousin was going too far in keeping back the little money he earned, under pretext of settling his tailor's bills and preventing him from making a fool of himself. When he wanted to redeem his watch from the pawnbroker's he was obliged to ask for an advance of twenty-four francs, which hardly suggests opulence. If he stayed out after eleven at night he was spied on like a school-boy. Drawbacks of family life, which in spite of all its good sides has always something of a cloistral regime about it. But Taunay had good reasons for putting up with it: he had an intrigue at home, this time, with Louise.

What with their games of lotto in the winter, and of battle-dore and shuttlecock in the summer, on the lawns of the Ranelagh, the two young people had formed a liking for each other. One evening when they had all gone to dine at the little house at Passy that the family had taken for the season, Mme Moitte suggested a walk round the garden, and took the arm of her former admirer. 'Louise was the subject of our conversation; it turned out that he is in love with her.'

The poor lady's reactions are fairly easy to imagine: sur-prise, a little chagrin, but at the same time a certain pleasure. Though it may not be pleasant to find oneself promoted to the rank of mother-in-law when one has known better things, it is nevertheless a means of survival in the sentimental sphere, a sort of honorary membership of the heart. Many of our novelists have made a study of this particular case. We may therefore believe that Mme Moitte would willingly have agreed to the marriage if she had been sure that it would make the girl happy. But she thought exactly the opposite. One could not be acquainted with this strange young man and not realize that he had an abominable character.

You might shower attentions on him, embroider waistcoats for him, buy him purses and cravats, work his monogram in hair, nothing would prevent him from being himself; that is to say sulky, capricious, making scenes on the slightest excuse — because Louise had chatted with one of Moitte's pupils, because she had been to see Croemer, her piano teacher, because their opinions differed regarding such and such a writer. One day, for instance, when Mme Moitte took it into her head to read some passages from Rollin's work aloud, our hedgehog rolled himself up in a ball. 'Taunay *opposed* the reading from M. Rollin. I tried to go on. He sulked! He played draughts with Moitte and went away without saying good night to his beloved.' Quarrelling about Rollin; wasn't that the last straw!

*   *   *

Other, more serious, disagreements came about. At first the fiancé had been all impatience, now he began to withdraw, appealing to the state of his finances, the difference between his age and Louise's — multiplying the ifs and buts. And when plied with questions he ended by confessing that he had a mistress, a cruel creature, 'with whom he was ashamed to be living, but whom he could not leave, because she would betray the secret of a friend'.

We need not try to penetrate the mystery, nor take this liaison tragically. Taunay was not long in liquidating it. At the cost of certain 'sacrifices' he was soon 'relieved of his burden', as he expressed it, and the two women were the happier for it: Louise, thinking of the future, and Mme Moitte, thinking of the past. For there is no age limit to jealousy.

Henceforth, so it would seem, there could be no obstacle to the marriage. The young man promised to behave seriously, to be circumspect in his relations and to leave off going to the café. But why was his temper still so whimsical? Why couldn't he make up his mind? Weeks passed, they quarrelled, they made it up, and M. le Maire was still waiting.

For the Moittes the Taunay affair was becoming a sort of nightmare. One morning the lady of the house, determined to discover the truth, asked her cousin to come down to her room. 'He came in with his face all distorted, and wet with tears, and made as if to embrace me. I repulsed him and sent him into the drawing-room. I called Louise, who started to have it out with him. I went in soon after. He confessed himself vanquished, but went on resorting to commonplaces about his age, and being afraid of not being loved. All sorts of rubbish. How long is this to go on?

At this game the nerves of the whole family were bound to give way. Louise was the first to fall ill, then Mme Moitte, and finally Taunay himself. Upstairs and down, they nursed one another, exchanging cups of *tisane*, comforting one another, begging one another's pardon. A regular madhouse.

The year 1806 was nearly at an end, and the situation was still just as confused. At last, on December 31 there came a thunder-clap. Moitte returned from the studio earlier than usual. 'He shocked us both by saying in a shaking voice that Taunay was a rogue, and then he handed us a letter from him, addressed to me, in which he tells me that I am really quite right; he is not fit to undertake the responsibilities of marriage, and he feels he should not be seen in this house any more; in view of which he begs me to have his belongings ready to be handed over to the porter who will come to fetch them.'

If these explanations appear a little vague, we have only to wait another twenty-four hours to see what a handsome New Year present Mme Moitte was to receive on the morning of January 1. 'When I got home I found the key of the studio and another letter from Taunay which upset me and gave me the greatest pain. In this letter he confesses to '*a malady hardly suitable to the marriage tie*', and says that it was on this account that he felt he ought not to enter into a union unworthy of a young lady in radiant health; that not daring to make such a painful confession, although, he says, he has not incurred it by licentious living, he had preferred to show the difficult side of his character, to which he now appealed, for the sake of dragging out an unhappy life that could not last much longer, far away from us.'

Thus ended the Taunay romance, begun in the style of the troubadours and ending in a hospital report. But suppose its hero was having recourse to this hindrance to get out of the venture without loss? We may well suspect this when we

L

learn that, two or three days later, a doctor he had gone to consult prescribed ... drinking Bordeaux! His case cannot have been very serious.

What was far more so was to have betrayed a young affection, disturbed the peace of a household of which he was the guest, and gone on for months repeating promises, indulging in fits of tears and scenes of jealousy, only to hoax everybody in the end and play the *Malade imaginaire* for fear of a *Mariage forcé*.

*   *   *   *

We have not many more pages of Mme Moitte's Diary to turn over, for the poor woman's health, already failing, became suddenly worse, and it was not long before she was forced to lay down her pen. What was the nature of her disease? The doctors attending her – and God knows there were enough of them – seem to have been at a loss. One shook his head, affirming that 'the abdomen was full of air, and after the air comes the water'. Another prescribed 'soapy pills'. A third advised laying 'an omelet fried in oil and sprinkled with fennel' on the swollen part of her body. Alas, they might break as many eggs as they liked, the result of this cookery was nil.

As the attacks grew more frequent, Moitte, used as he was to bemoaning his own sufferings, became really anxious. He forgot his old selfishness, and even consented to sleep in another room so as not to disturb the patient. 'At last', she sighs, 'we have arranged for him to sleep on the other side of the house tonight, of which I am very glad.' A sad twilight of conjugal life, in which the prospect of sleeping in peace is greeted as deliverance!

But the two old people were still really attached to each other, and Mme Moitte was to prove this a few weeks before her death. She disclosed to her husband that she possessed a 'woollen stocking' – 25,000 francs saved sou by sou, day after day, out of the household expenses, after the fashion of one of Labiche's heroines, the estimable Mme de Montaudoin. Thanks to this small fortune – for such it was at that day – old Moitte would be able to end his days in peace.

'He was so taken aback by this windfall', writes our heroine, 'that he began to weep for emotion. I hope it will give him the courage to go on working, if I live; and if I die he will bless me, for after all, though it's an asset he could have done without, he will find it very pleasant.'

In these last lines the poor woman, who was to die a few days later, reveals her whole self. She had her faults: too quick a temper, too frequent fits if grizzling, but a heart of gold nevertheless. And her husband knew it, for he was not a bad fellow himself.

We should not laugh at the old couple; they represent two perfect types of middle-class Parisians of the first half of the century, a race that was by no means contemptible after all.

Writers and artists, not long after, entertained us at their expense by showing us only their absurdities. We cannot help smiling at Henri Monnier's dowagers and Daumier's old men. But we should not forget that the stringed bonnets of the former and the rabbit-skin hats of the latter often sheltered very good people. Such as we see them, with their little ambitions, their harmless crazes, their unconscious absurdity, they are related to the Moitte couple, and can be considered the ancestors of our middle class of today.

As to the merits of the latter, opinions are greatly divided. All the same, it is permissible to suggest that if its qualities and defeats were weighed one against the other, the good would outweigh the bad.

And could not the same be said of M. and Mme Moitte?

CHAPTER XVII

PUBLIC MORALS AS AN INVESTMENT

Three worlds well-known to the Police: prostitutes, thieves, gamblers – The Panorama Moral *– The nymphs of the Palais-Royal – A badly-lighted parlour – A paying préfecture – Adventures with pickpockets – Cheating the Customs – Gambling and gamblers*

NAPOLEON, running that morning through the daily report from his Prefect of Police, must have realized at once that Dubois was approaching a particularly serious subject. A personal letter accompanying the document and bearing the motto of the Freemasons' Lodge, *Amour et Vérité*, opened in these terms:

'Sire, I have to speak to you about the streets of Paris. Corruption is rife there.... Let me explain: You have probably never heard of the *Panorama Moral*, an ironical name for the most immoral thing in the world. In the Rue de la Loi, behind a gated entrance, opposite Beauvilliers the caterer, at Mme Saint-Amand's, a – practically public – entertainment has been established ...'

What was the attraction? We can hardly describe it as crudely as the Prefect. Suffice to say that the panorama bore no resemblance to its namesakes of the boulevard, those enormous optical illusions so skilfully depicted by the painter Prévot, representing the wonders of Paris, Naples and Amsterdam. The wonders here consisted of natural beauties of a more intimate character, which those with a taste for scenes from real life came to contemplate on the quiet. They were shown into little parlours furnished in their honour, the walls of which resembled those of Nero's palace in *Britannicus*:

'Even these walls, my Lord, may have eyes.'

They had eyes in the Rue de la Loi, and the hostess made a decent profit out of them. Mme de Saint-Amand herself might have adopted the motto *Amour et Vérité*.

But the Chief of Police was not given to joking in his official reports. He went on to enlarge upon his subject, addressing the Emperor in pathetic terms. 'Sire, you may well have a great task to fulfil, that of making us more virtuous; we should then be really worthy of loving you. Nothing, says Plato, is more disagreeable to the gods than the offerings of the impure.'

Probably Napoleon considered that Plato had nothing to do with the *Panorama Moral*, and that Dubois, on the other hand, was little qualified to play the moralist. More than one unkind story was told of him and his wife, formerly Mlle Rosalie, but he did at least take his duties seriously, and the Emperor believed him to be one of those cunning poachers who can, in case of need, make excellent gamekeepers. Hadn't he every sort of reason for knowing the more or less shady *milieux* of the capital? The prostitutes because he made a profit out of them, the gambling houses because they paid him a tax, the thieves because he himself was to some extent in that line.

And now that we are clear as to the morals of the man, we may explore the pretty world that formed his clientèle.

* * * *

When a foreigner came to Paris in Napoleon's day, the first things he wanted to see were the reviews on the Carrousel, with the Emperor and his bodyguard, and the prostitutes of the Palais-Royal. In all the records of their travels left us by tourists from across the Channel and the Rhine this double leit-motif is obligatory, and the second often plays a more important part than the first. The most serious-minded people, family men among them, could hardly wait to get out of their carriages before rushing to 'this horrible scene of debauch situated in the midst of the great city, which has corrupted and rotted the whole of society.'[1]

The *fête galante* held there differed little from that of the preceding century. Under the arcades, so Yorke tells us, 'the gaming houses alternate with hovels in which seductive young women follow the avowable profession of selling you garters, thread, lavender water, toothbrushes and sealing-wax.

[1] Yorke.

You enter, and the most you perceive in the shop is a few packets of toothpowder mingled with balls of thread. These places are to the neighbouring seraglios what cook-shops are to restaurants. In the former you are served in a twinkling of the eye: the dish you have ordered is brought at once to your table.'

It was towards the close of day that the Palais-Royal assumed its true character. Then beauties of all ages and colours – for there were even negresses among them – nymphs whose transparent tunics began very low at the top and ended very high at the bottom, came to seek their fortunes under the arcades. 'They are so shameless that a well-bred woman cannot walk past them without feeling shocked and even offended.'[1]

But the masculine element felt otherwise. To be convinced of this we have only to study the painting in which Boilly shows a corner of the arcades, with stout gentlemen in kersey-mere trousers surrounded by fair promenaders, who can scarcely be taken for their daughters.

Between these inquisitive creatures and their patrons brief romances sprang up such as the shade of Restif de la Bretonne would not have disowned. The surroundings of the Palais afforded them favourable refuges in abundance, some of them, it is said, hired out by Mme Montansier in the annexes of her theatre. There were others to suit all purses, from the mezzanine floors of the arcades, usually inhabited by the most elegant of these ladies (the imperial bearing of one of them led her to be nicknamed Josephine, which worried the authorities), to the more or less wretched lodgings in which certain matrons sheltered the small fry of the battalion of Cytherea.

These charitable persons, who played an important part in the life of the Palais-Royal, were always ready to help a shop-girl out of work who wanted a new dress, or a little nursemaid tired of leading her charges round the shady walks near by. How could the poor girls withstand the lure of such easy money? But these adventures ended badly at times.

During the summer of 1803, for instance, the frequenters of the gardens, having heard howls coming from a neighbouring house decided to go up to the second floor, where they

[1] Sir John Dean Paul.

found a crowd of miserable youngsters on the landing, left there by their nursemaids, who were engaged in less childish occupations in the apartment opposite. The police, called in on the spot, arrested the nursemaids, took charge of the children, summoned their parents and gave them a thorough dressing-down. 'The Commissioner', says Prudhomme, who recounts the anecdote, 'had the double satisfaction of saving the children from the dangers that threatened them and giving a lesson at the same time to all mothers, who, in the situation in life to which nature has confined them, should never cease to watch over the upbringing of their children.'

*　*　*　*

Although the trade of gallantry was more flourishing at the Palais-Royal than anywhere else, it was rife in many other quarters of Paris. In the side streets off the boulevards, at the doors of the theatres, in the windings of the Butte des Moulins, in the little streets of the Carrousel, strange loiterers everywhere offered their services to the passers-by. Some dragged them off to the rear of the poulterers' sheds in the market-place of La Vallée, others into the deserted halls of the former Abbey of Saint-Germain, as far as the pavement of the cloisters.

Kotzebue, who had known Paris before the Revolution, thought the prostitutes had increased in number when he returned in 1804, but they seemed to him rather less brazen, attacking pedestrians only in dark places. In the lamplight 'they merely showed themselves'.

One evening, at the junction of the Rue Vivienne and the Rue des Petits-Champs, he counted no less than fourteen of these ladies. 'Out of the fourteen, only one dared to hang for a moment on my arm and beg me to take her under my pelisse, because she was very cold, which I could well believe; but she let go as soon as I replied curtly, "No, mademoiselle!" All they venture to do in such a case is to retort with a mocking air, "Ah, you are cruel!"'

We need not admire his virtue, for he adds a little farther on that 'out of a hundred of these women I hardly saw two that were pretty.' From which we may deduce that the young woman of the pelisse was hideously ugly.

Although he had breathed the air of the capital, the German dramatist could not flatter himself that he was acquainted with all its mysteries. What would he have said if he had visited the strange house described in a police report, which might well have been called the 'black market of love'?

At number 102 Rue de Vaugirard, every Thursday from eight to midnight, men and women of all classes of society met together in a darkened drawing-room. They were admitted only by introduction and on payment of twelve francs, a very moderate fare for an excursion to the seventh heaven. But they must not attempt to find out who their fellow passengers were. Love, reputedly blind, is even more so when the lamps are extinguished. When the session was over, they went their several ways, the ladies leaving a quarter of an hour earlier to avoid being followed.

This ingenious anonymity lasted until the day when the Commissioner of the district knocked at the door, gave orders for the drawing-rooms to be lighted up, and discovered – in what attire! – a certain number of honourable Parisian personages: three marquises, a banker, a head clerk of the council of State, a barrister, an advocate at the Court of Cassation, enough to compromise both nobilities, that of the sword and that of the robe. To limit the scandal, these gentlemen were allowed to go free, and only their blushing accomplices were arrested; a difference in treatment that was perhaps not very equitable, but it is a commonplace that men always stand by one another.

The police had many exploits of this kind to their credit. One day they raided a house in the Rue Campagne-Première, where the former curé Bonjour, having founded a religion and ensured its adepts the privilege of *impeccability*, was organizing strange ceremonies, degenerating into Saturnalias. Another day they interrupted the performance of an obscene play, *Messaline*, acted by young adepts before a masked audience. Another time, by way of a change, they gave chase to a maniacal vitriol-thrower, who had burnt some poor prostitutes in the Rue Croix-des-Petits-Champs; or they seized a collection of smutty books in Barba's bookshop – which would not be lost to everybody, since the Prefect was in the habit of showing these curiosities to the friends he asked to dinner.

Or again, they turned their attention to a special type of persons now infesting places of amusement: unpleasant individuals who based their morals on those of Greece and imitated Socrates in every respect, though without going the length, unfortunately, of drinking hemlock.[1]

These instances, out of a number of others, prove that Dubois was not mistaken in saying of the capital 'Corruption is rife there.' In this respect the Paris of the Empire, though perhaps a little better than that of the Directory, did not differ from it very sensibly. It might have been supposed to have sown its wild oats in Barras's time, but the follies of youth sometimes endure a long while, and behind a façade of middle-class respectability the morals of the city had actually remained exceedingly doubtful.

One of the chief headaches of the authorities was the ever-increasing number of prostitutes. In 1806 an English newspaper reckoned it generously at 75,000, but even if the figure was exaggerated, the actual total cannot have been much less than that of the population of an average prefecture. What could the police do against such an army? Fouché tried at first to carry out mass arrests, but the prison of the Petite-Force could not have held so many inmates. And after all, did they want to set 'all the bachelors of Paris' against them?

Wisely therefore, acting on the advice of Dubois, they contented themselves with supervising these ladies more strictly, submitting them, above all, to more regular medical examination. This turned out to be anything but useless, since out of 300 prostitutes examined during the month of Messidor, year VIII, they found twenty-eight syphillitics and ninety-three suffering from scabies. Idylls of the streets of Paris, how much you lost of your poesy!

Any measure taken to safeguard public health is always to be welcomed, but unfortunately Dubois's best ideas were too often tainted by his fondness for perquisites. Every time they

[1] They could claim a notorious sponsorship, for Cambacérès's 'little failing' was no secret. It was to him that the Emperor said one day, when he was complaining of having been delayed by a fair visitor, 'Next time, my friend, you will have the goodness to say to this lady, "Take your hat and stick and buzz off!" '

were examined, the clients of his dispensary had to pay a tax, part of which the ingenious Prefect slipped into the drawer of his desk.

It may be said in his favour that he generously devoted this revenue, every month, to his mother-in-law's dress expenses, and as the lady was reputed to have had a very adventurous youth, her good son-in-law may have considered that he was performing an act of restitution.

*　　*　　*　　*

With a Prefect of Police of this mentality, how could those under his jurisdiction be expected to behave like little saints? In fairness to the population of Paris, it must be said that it was mostly honest; but it included, nevertheless, a certain number of rogues, and tales of robbery loom large in the chronicles of the time.

Coat-snatchers provided the greater number of these incidents. These ancestors of our pickpockets knew all the tricks of the trade even then; they operated for preference in narrow streets in which people jostled one another, in the Passage du Perron, for instance, between the Rue Vivienne and the garden of the Palais du Tribunat. An editor of the *Journal de Paris* tells us that strolling through there, the day before, he had been robbed by some philanthropic sharpers:

'These gentlemen, thinking no doubt that my handkerchief was in my way, purloined it with a dexterity worthy of admiration. Thinking that tobacco might do me harm, they relieved me of my snuffbox with the same skill. Fearing they might be tempted a third time by my watch and purse, I vowed I would never go through that narrow passage again, and I shall continue to make the detour until the Government has had it widened."

Adventures of this kind were the terror of provincials who had lost their way in the capital. When Junot's old father came up from his native Burgundy to see a parade by the First Consul, and got entangled in the mob on the Carrousel with his wife and daughter-in-law, he was terribly worried. 'Take care, my daughter-in-law! You should pin your shawl together. . . . A cashmere worth two thousand francs! *I'm* keeping my hand on my watch, so I can laugh at the rascals!'

But the little Parisian, who was soon to become Duchess of
Abrantès, knew the ropes – she would not lose her shawl.
Whereas the poor old man soon found he had been robbed of
his watch, and saw his womenfolk burst out laughing as they
reminded him of his good advice. We may be sure that on his
return to Montbard he declared all Parisians to be thieves.

Though he may have been wrong, it must be confessed
that some members of the guild had very inventive minds.

An incident in which David the painter played an involuntary part is narrated by the press of 1807. Posing as David's
servant, and purporting to have been sent by him, a 'well-
wrapped-up individual' went into a money-changer's shop in
the Passage Feydeau. David, he said, asked for 18,000 francs
in coin to be taken to his studio at the Louvre, in exchange for
the same sum in notes, which he had there. A clerk slipped
900 louis into a bag, accompanied the pretended servant to
the Louvre, went upstairs with him, along passages, and
knocked at the door of the room in which the artist was supposed to be working. Upon which the unfortunate man was
knocked on the head with a hammer, and the thief ran off as
fast as he could go. Needless to say, the author of the *Rape
of the Sabines* and that of the rape of the bag had never met.

❋   ❋   ❋   ❋

The murderous tricks of swindlers belong to all time, but
a form of robbery that assumed unusual importance during
the first years of the nineteenth century was that perpetrated
by the defrauders of the Customs. Never, in all the history of
Paris, had they operated with such an abundance of means.
The inadequacy of the city wall, which in 1800 was hardly
more than a moral barrier, the low standard of the inspecting
personnel, who often allowed themelves to be hoaxed, and
sometimes bribed, the fact that the system of taxation had
been declared defective and reorganized four times in twelve
years, all helped to facilitate fraud. Moreover the constant
increase in import duties made it more and more lucrative.
A man could earn his day's wages now by smuggling a few
pints of alcohol. If he was able to substitute barrels for bottles
at regular intervals, he would soon have made his fortune.

Such was the ambition of a number of dare-devils who

combined to defraud the town dues, as one might form a company for the exploitation of a mine. In these gangs, often
organized in regular brigades, there were unemployed workmen, vagabonds driven out of the countryside, military
deserters, officers cashiered from the army. In 1809, there was
actually a bona-fide lieutenant-colonel in their ranks, an aide-
de-camp of the Governor-general of Saint-Cloud.

These men used all kinds of devices to deceive the Excise:
faked carriages with bodies containing up to 300 litres of
brandy, bottles with false bottoms, the upper part of which
was filled with hydrochloric acid, hollow logs capable of holding all the cognac of Charentes and all the marc brandy of
Burgundy. They also made use of hoisting apparatus at times,
set up at night close to the city wall, which allowed them to
transfer enormous bales of contraband.

But it was by underground channels that their trade was
carried on to an even greater extent. Between a number of
cellars situated on either side of the barrier, mysterious con-
duits had been contrived, which made lucrative springs gush
in the back shops of certain wily traffickers. The principle of
the pipe-line, in fact, applied more than a century in advance
to supply Paris with alcohol.

Not a month went by without a police report of the discovery of one or more of these systems of pipes, which increased in number under the very nose of the authorities. In
the course of the year IX alone, seventeen of them had to be
filled in. One of them started from the bottom of Belleville
and ended at the Faubourg du Temple. In another, which
debouched near the Barrière des Vertus, a train of sixty-
three 'fiddles' of spirits of wine was seized. But the longest
of all was undoubtedly the gallery, 300 yards in length, which
started at Passy, under the house of Citizen Lanchère, to end
up at Chaillot, under the Convent of the Filles-Sainte-Marie.
What must the good nuns have felt like when they heard
what their cellar had been used for?

When the smugglers were tired of this war of moles, they
came up above ground and had regular battles with the
Customs' employees. Dubois affirms that there were 'nearly
10,000 of them, all armed, courageous, commanded by fear-
less enterprising leaders'. He adds that, according to his in-

formers, several of them intended to disguise themselves as
infantrymen, to accompany suspicious convoys. If they were
not allowed to pass they would shoot.

And in pursuance of this scheme we find them taking the
Porte de Fontarabie by assault, shooting an unfortunate
policeman at the Barrière de Neuilly with a blunderbuss and
killing two others on the Pont de la Liberté, who were attempting to stop one of their carriages. We might be reading
of an army of gangsters, in the happy days of dry America.

With a reinforced Police Corps these incidents became of
course less and less frequent. But the smugglers' activities
never ceased entirely, even after the establishment of the
Empire. They went on digging out their subterranean channels, and the only means that could be found to hinder them
was to destroy all the buildings situated outside the walls in
the immediate neighbourhood of the barriers.

This was the origin of the famous zone, so long familiar to
us, with its bare grass plots and its dilapidated shanties. Many
Parisians have thought it more recent, contemporary, that is,
with the fortifications of yesterday. But the decree of *non
aedificandi* within a perimeter of a hundred yards really dates
from January 11, 1808, and had no other object at the time
than to assist the supervision of the Customs. Let us render
unto Caesar the things that are Caesar's, and not attribute to
M. Thiers a decree of Napoleon's.

* * * *

The sharks of the Barrier were no greater rascals than the
sharks of the gambling dens, but whereas defrauding the
Customs meant a loss of money to the Treasury, the gaming
houses brought some in to it. It was therefore fairly natural,
if not very moral, that the police should be less severe towards
one form of robbery than the other, and should even treat
with some consideration certain clever people whose kitty
represented an inexhaustible milch cow for the Government.

The lease of the gaming tables might change hands, its
holder might be called Perrin or Davelouis, but the contracts
forced upon him always demanded larger and larger royal-
ties. From 1,800,000 francs at the beginning, they amount to
3,500,000 in 1806, with an estimate of 5,000,000 when a

general peace should have been signed. These official payments were augmented by various clandestine bribes for the benefit of Fouché and that of the honest Dubois. In return for which, Parisians had the right to spend their nights in fourteen licensed gambling-dens and blow their brains out if luck went against them.

As may be imagined, it was at the Palais-Royal that the best-known gaming-houses were to be found. Readers of *La Peau de Chagrin* will remember Balzac's description of the famous 113, where such high stakes were played for round the roulette tables, while the unlucky gamesters went to recover their breath in an adjoining room, called the room of the wounded.

Several establishments of the sort opened into the arcades. At No. 9, a den where the tricksters played a little game at three francs, while fashionable vamps brought punters with them from a neighbouring dance-hall – the *Pince-cœur moral et sentimental* – capable of breaking a bank of fifty louis. A little farther on, at No. 150, a gaming-house doing equally good business was affiliated to a money-lending establishment that furnished beggared customers with the means of trying their luck once more, at an interest of six per cent *per month*. But the most complete organization was that of No. 64, where tables for trente-et-quarante, passe-dix and biribi adjoined a gunsmith's shop displaying a selection of fine pistols. The house was also inhabited by a former priest of most obliging character. With everything thus at hand, the customers could, in the space of a few hours, be ruined, commit suicide, and pass to a better world with the help of religion.

Apart from the Palais-Royal, the gambling world frequented a number of private houses such as that of the Duc de Luynes in the Faubourg Saint-Germain, and certain saloons with even more widely open doors, that were not unlike the gambling-hells of today. Of these, the Club des Princes and the Club des Étrangers, founded in the Rue de la Loi by MM. Castellane and Livry, were by far the most popular. Masked ridottos were given there, and suppers enlivened by the presence of a number of pretty women, while people gambled recklessly.

Many were the foreigners that came to be fleeced there, like the Englishman, Dawn, who allowed himself to be robbed, one evening, of all the money he had on him, plus 40,000 francs on his bond.

Such glaring differences in the functioning of the law ended inevitably by disturbing public opinion. But though the Government was the first to realize the immorality of gambling, it was also the last to wish to suppress it, since it made such a profit out of it. There was a time, however, when it seemed about to take heroic measures, all the same.

On June 24, 1806, a decree of the Emperor's was published in these terms: 'Houses in which games of chance are played are prohibited over the whole extent of our territory . . .' But a certain Article 4 added the following: 'Our Minister of Police will draw up special regulations in this respect for places where mineral waters are found . . . and for the city of Paris.' A formula which amounted to saying that the prefects of the Departments in which Spa, Aix-le-Chapelle, Plombières, Luxeuil, Aix-les-Bains . . . and Paris were situated, were respectively entrusted with the *non-execution* of the present decree.

But what need was there to go into details? The official drafting of the bill, safeguarded morality and the gaming-houses at the same time. With the result that for many years to come one would still see, round the green tables, madmen trying their luck, foolish old women selling their jewels and piles of louis disappearing under the nimble rakes of the croupiers.

CHAPTER XVIII

THE OTHER SIDE OF THE EPIC

*The misfits of glory – Recalcitrants and deserters – The Army
as seen by Paris – Mars on the spree – When an officer wants
to read the paper – Junot and the picket – A man who knew
how to address the ladies*

A CHARMING picture by Boilly, to be seen at the Musée
Carnavalet, shows the Paris conscripts of 1807 marching past the Porte Saint-Denis.

With cockades stuck on their hats they march gaily along,
under the leadership of a handsome fellow with a theatrical
carriage, who might be twin brother to Elleviou.[1] Carriages
and riders have drawn up to let the little company pass; sightseers line the way, with street-urchins pushing through to the
front; women smile to the departing youths, and the latter
display such high spirits that it would take little more to
make the crowd follow them. Was the prospect of donning a
uniform to go and risk their lives on the banks of the Niemen
or the Vistula so attractive as all that?

A popular song-writer of the day seems to have doubted it.
He says:

> 'The gaiety of this regiment
> Is worthy of censure.
> Conscripts leaving gaily
> Is quite against nature.'

We shall see that the rhymester was right, and that in
reality the Imperial recruits pulled very different faces when
it came to shouldering their knapsacks.

In the ranks of the Napoleonic army the number of
hardened fighters was legion; you could find thousands of
grenadiers like Coignet, fusiliers like Fricasse, sergeants like
Bourgogne, hussars like Bangofsky, cavalrymen like Parquin,
trumpeters like Chevillet, all more or less related to the illustrious Flambeau whom Edmond Rostand placed at their

[1] Tradition has it that the famous singer sat for this figure.

11   Departure of the conscripts, 1807

12   A Grand Parade in the courtyard of the Tuileries

head. But alongside these heroes who rushed into battle as if to a festival, it must be confessed that there existed a crowd of less brilliant soldiers, not to mention many poor devils who had never had but one ambition: not to be soldiers at all.

These rebellious victims of conscription had been heard of ever since the Consulate. In Paris, in 1802, the town hall of the sixth arrondissement was the scene of a regular riot while the drawing of lots was proceeding. Some of the youths fought the dragoons, who made use of their arms. About fifty wounded and twenty dead were left on the field, among them mere onlookers, old men and children. One poor youngster of twelve got a sword-thrust in the belly, 'in spite of the protests of the spectators', as the Minister of Justice so gracefully expresses it.

A number of violent incidents were also reported from the provinces. In the little town of Montereau-Faut-Yonne the troops had to go into action. At Chartres, a little later, three gendarmes were butchered. At Brussac, in the Ariège, several individuals armed themselves with stones and knives to come to the assistance of the conscripts. Not to mention the departments of the Ouest, Morbihan, Finisterre, Les Sables, where the rebels formed themselves into gangs and attacked the mounted police. To escape recruitment, many a poor devil mutilated himself, cutting off one of his fingers, or ruining one of his eyes with a poisonous powder sold by a certain Taissière, student of medicine. Wily fellows managed to procure false certificates of discharge by bribing some military surgeon. But many of them followed a simpler procedure: they did not answer the call-up. Out of two hundred and forty-four conscripts due to assemble on the Place des Vosges on the 25th Prairial, year XI, only fifty-eight put in an appearance, and that the proportion should have been so small does not seem to have greatly surprised the authorities.

One way or another, however, the recruitment was completed, and the young soldiers started off to join their corps. But how many of them would disappear at the first turning? It was reckoned that about a tenth of the recruits escaped in this way. The gendarmerie had all the more difficulty in recapturing them in that the population, more often than not, lent them assistance; for at that time desertion was considered

M

only a venial sin. The poor wretches were pitied for being brought on to the strength against their will; they were hidden at their request, and rescued by force if need be.

A state of mind that offends our ideas of today, and was perhaps at first merely a survival of the old regime, for conscription was of recent invention.[1] But it was soon detested on its own account, as its exactions increased.

For at first the armies that accomplished such great things were not very large. It is even difficult to believe the modest figures to which the system of exemption and buying out reduced the proportion of the mobilized troops. In 1806 there were only 14,300 Parisians serving under the flag, out of a population of 547,000: one man in thirty-eight was a soldier — and this in the year of Jena.

But the day was near when the war would become far greedier, when the total mobilization would greatly exceed a million, and Napoleon, recalling young men who had been exempted or bought out, and calling up the classes in advance, would seek recruits even in the schools.

Then, as the blood tax became really onerous, desertions and refusals to serve increased to an alarming degree. In 1810 it was admitted that 16,000 recalcitrants had been personally convicted, and their families obliged to pay 170 millions in fines. By the end of another two years the countryside was teeming with absentees. Flying columns pursued them and captured 60,000, who were sent to the main army; but they had hardly been taken on before they began escaping again. De Ségur estimated the number of deserters at more than a thousand a day; Thiers declared that 150,000 men had already left their corps, one month after the crossing of the Niemen; and Albert Sorel reckoned that henceforth 'it would take almost an army to recruit another one'.

It is easy to imagine the little dramas being enacted at that time in an untold number of villages: the officers of the Consulate on half-pay, the disaffected soldiers of yesterday and the day before, who had begun trailing their dirty uniforms and down-at-heels boots along the roads, plying more or less

[1] It was established by the law of Fructidor, Year II, voted on the report by Jourdan. Bonaparte was to make better use of this tool, forged by the Revolution, than anybody else.

avowable trades, were now joined by the mass of deserters. The farmer's son went to ground in the barn, the miller's son in the mill; they were fed in secret, since they did not dare show their noses out of doors; always on the look-out for the gendarme, for the sound of a trotting horse along the road, fleeing from the terrible brigades beating the woods and thickets and running after them like a pack of hounds.

We look in vain for this aspect of the great epic in Raffet's lithographs, and we are far indeed from the joyous conscripts of 1807, marching along the boulevards with tricolour streamers on their coats and a flower between their teeth!

* * * *

Had the painters agreed among themselves to show us the everyday life of the First Empire under false colours?

Two drawings by Norblain de la Gourdaine, also in the collection of the Musée Carnavalet, depict the most attractive scenes. Under the chestnut-trees of the Tuileries, young women in light dresses are seated near the ornamental lake. They have no eyes for anything but an officer bending his enormous plume towards them, apparently delighted with the effect he is producing. Confronted by such a charming idyll, one is led to suppose that the Paris of those days doted upon these valiant soldiers, so attentive to the fair sex, as heroical and gallant as could be desired. Yet the contemporary memoirs and newspapers, and still more the police bulletins, seem bent on proving to us that relations between the military and the people of Paris were, on the contrary, very strained.

In spite of a flattering legend, the evidence against the Napoleonic troopers accumulates; admirable under fire, they too often appear, when on furlough, mere vulgar swash-bucklers, drunkards, scroungers and ravishers. Exchanging blows, forcing their way into shops, drinking, and settling their bills by insults, harrying women, insulting and even beating them up on occasion, such were their most usual peccadilloes. Made for the life of the camp rather than for that of the barracks, treating the street like a conquered country, they had a moral law of their own that was the complete negation of morality: they thought they were above the law – that having bravely allowed their own heads to be punched, they had the right to punch other people's, and because they had thrashed the enemy it was lawful to thrash the bourgeois.

Delightful principles, which they applied conscientiously, but which were naturally not to the taste of peaceable people. The handsome soldiers were applauded when they paraded on the Carrousel, but for the rest of the time they were the terror of Paris.

As all well-ordered charity begins at home, they started by fighting one another. Between man and man, regiment and regiment, any quarrel arising was settled by a duel. One day when the Minister of Police was walking in the Bois de Boulogne, he witnessed a tournament in the grand manner between the 12th Hussars and the 15th Light Infantry. 'Four men from each corps were fighting one another, while the main body occupied the walks to prevent the combatants from being separated.'

As he was not fond of blows, and happened to be in civilian dress, Fouché did not attempt to intervene. He contented himself with drawing up a report. But how many times would he and Dubois have to record similar affrays! Hardly a month, hardly a week would go by without soldiers of all arms, guides, artillerymen, dragoons, members of the Consular Guard, drawing swords in the pleasure gardens of Vaugirard or at the Barrière du Maine, behind the Jansenist mill.

Rivalries between corps, questions of service, affairs of prostitutes, anything was sufficient excuse for a quarrel. The finest duel of all was undoubtedly the one fought in the middle of the Champs-Élysées by two horsemen of the Guard, naked to the waist, before an attentive audience of strollers of both sexes. A session well calculated to demonstrate the bravery of the military and the curiosity of the ladies.

That bullies should cleave each other in two might be permissible at a pinch, but their brutality became intolerable when they attacked perfectly inoffensive citizens. If a passer-by brushed against them, however lightly, or bumped into them by accident, they would accept no apology, but fell

upon the unfortunate man. The son of the proprietor of the
Café de Valois had his skull cleft in this way; a young man
was cut to pieces by an infantry sergeant outside the door of
the Senate; at the Barrière de Charonne soldiers killed a
civilian; in the plain of Montrouge three soldiers disem-
bowelled a stranger, under the pretext that he had 'looked at
them in an insulting manner'. Sometimes our gay dogs operated in numbers: a party of mamelukes pillaged the shop of a
caterer in the Rue d'Argenteuil and drank up his bottles of
anisette cordial, forgetting that the law of the Prophet for-
bids alcohol; a unit of the 20th Light Infantry cleared out a
cabaret in the Rue de Vaugirard; gendarmes of a picked corps
went to beat up conscripts in an inn at Saint-Cloud; infantrymen of the 18th fought a regular battle in a wine-shop in
Montmartre and broke twenty-three window-panes. There
was no end to the exploits of these heroes on the spree, for
whom the sword was a dangerous companion.

French soldiers have always prided themselves on courting
the ladies. Under the Empire, unfortunately, they did not
select them too well. Their conquests usually consisted of
loiterers of the worst type, those that the police kept their
eyes on, round the Place de Grève and the evil haunts of the
Palais-Royal. Sometimes they constituted themselves their
champions and prevented the guard from arresting them, at
others they had disputes of a sentimental order with them
and gave them the sort of punishment that marks an epoch
in a woman's life.

Far worse was it when they attacked respectable girls,
forced the door of some woman's shop, hustled a woman dis-
tributing handbills on the Pont-Neuf, or took advantage of
an unknown woman, six of them together, on the embankment of the Port-au-Blé, and then threw her in the river, for
the sole purpose of making her forget this good, or bad,
quarter of an hour.

Lest the picture seem too gloomy, however, we must admit
that the troopers' amusements were not always so macabre;
often they merely gave vent to their native joviality. They
went in for delicate jokes, in the streets and in public resorts,
which would have the greatest success when recounted at
night in the barrack-room. One incident, which occurred at

the Palais-Royal, and is narrated in a police bulletin, will serve as an example.

'Yesterday evening a soldier was amusing himself by making water through the grating on the tables and the guests in the underground café of the *Caveau*. The café waiter came up in haste to reproach the soldier with the indecency of his behaviour, whereupon the soldier set about him with a stick and seriously injured him.'

If ever the old French gaiety were to be at an ebb, it is plain that the army would take upon itself to restore their sense of humour to the Parisians.

*   *   *   *

In officer circles the tone was of course somewhat different, but they showed many of the same defects.

To begin with, the habit of fighting one another for more or less absurd reasons. Men who, on the field of battle, would assist each other at the peril of their own lives, would agree to meet, nobody knows why, in a clearing of the Bois de Boulogne or an avenue at Mousseaux, and next morning Commandant Duchâtel would wound Capitaine Sibuet, Major de Sainte-Croix put paid to Lieutenant-Colonel Sicaud de Mariole, and General Grenier kill General Destaing in cold blood.

Sometimes the seconds caught the infection of the duel. Thus a certain Capitaine Millet, after exchanging insults with the representative of the opposite party, put a bullet through his head and ran off as fast as his legs would carry him. They called this settling an affair of honour.

Towards civilians the arrogance of the officers knew no bounds. When they went into a café to have a look at the *Moniteur* or the *Débats*, they tore the paper out of the hands of the bourgeois reading it, without a word of apology, and the man took care not to protest if he valued his ears. It was the custom now to let these gentlemen do as they liked.

The most elementary rules of everyday life, such as those governing the traffic, were not made for them, in their opinion. They could be seen galloping hard through the streets, at the risk of knocking people down. One of Berthier's aides-de-camps overturned a greengrocer's barrow; his friend

Edmond de Périgord injured a street porter; another smashed in the window of a grocer's shop.

These young madmen were only following the example of their superior officers, who would not allow themselves to be held up by anybody, quarrelled with the Customs officers when they were travelling, like General Thiébault, or refused to pay dues on entering Paris, like the Colonel of the Empress's dragoons, who attacked the official in charge of the Barrière de l'École, tore his rifle out of his hands and broke his leg.

Perhaps the most typical case, however, was that of Junot, who thought it unconscionable that he should observe the regulations he had signed himself. One day when, dressed in mufti, he was galloping along one of the lateral avenues of the Boulevard des Invalides, a man on picket duty challenged him and told him that riders must keep to the middle of the high road. Seeing Junot shrug his shoulders, the man seized the horse's bridle and they went off to have it out at the police station. There the sergeant displayed the instructions bearing the stamped signature of the Town Mayor, which ordered sentries to allow none but pedestrians along the sides of the Boulevard.

'I am the Town Mayor!' shouted Junot in a rage.

'That's not possible,' retorted the other, 'for you would then be at variance with yourself.'

'And anyhow,' added a fusilier, 'we don't recognize the Town Mayor in civvies.'

All of which was perfectly logical and could have been settled in a trice. But the Great Chief was beside himself. He dragged the unfortunate sergeant – who really deserved to be congratulated – to the Invalides, had him locked up at the Abbey for twenty-four hours, and cashiered the fusilier, guilty of recognizing generals only in uniform.

Other exploits of Junot's might be cited, which give no better account of his sense of proportion: a ridiculous scene at Garchi's ice-cream shop, and more outrageous still, a game of billiards with café waiters in an establishment in the Champs-Élysées, which ended in a frightful quarrel and a battle with cues.

But people were surely very narrow-minded to take offence

at these freaks? Were not the officers of the Empire free to amuse themselves as they chose? They might, for instance, do a moonlight flit and have their furniture removed by armed infantrymen under their landlord's nose; disturb the sleep of the inhabitants of the Boulevard du Temple and beat up the watch when they interfered; enjoy a choice supper in a café of the Palais du Tribunat and cudgel the proprietor instead of paying him; they could even go to an enclosed nunnery in the same quarter, force their way in, smash everything up and wound a woman with a sabre cut.

Did they perhaps show a little more consideration when their amorous enterprises were undertaken in other circles? It would hardly seem so, in the light of this dialogue between a superior staff officer and a good shopkeeper's wife, whose daughter he had just accosted in very gross terms: 'Monsieur, my daughter is an honest girl!' 'So much the better, that's how I like them.' And the same cynicism is apparent in an incident that Dubois considers worth relating at length:

Having just lunched with some friends at a draper's house in the Rue des Petits-Champs, a certain Aubry, a major in the 12th Infantry, caught sight of an attractive young lady in the window of a house opposite, and determined to go up to her apartment, accompanied by a lieutenant of his corps.

At the first words addressed to her she waxed indignant, tried to throw the men out, called her aunt who was living with her, the doorkeeper and another tenant of the house. As the two officers persisted, and made to beset the 'pretty hussy', she retaliated by slapping their faces. Not to be outdone, Aubry then slapped her face in return and broke his cane on her head so that a piece of it shot into the street. A Homeric struggle was needed to get rid of the boors, and when the prefecture had completed its investigation, it was found that their victim was a Mlle Decrès, that she belonged to one of the best Brussels families, and had come to Paris to obtain a post at Court, in the service of the Empress. She would be able to give Josephine an idea of the upbringing of some of her husband's officers.

While manners such as these were current, the life of the

civilian population could not always be rose-coloured; but the days of warfare in lace ruffles was over, and it was not altogether surprising that a certain number of cads should penetrate the ranks of the epic heroes. The finest tapestries have a strange appearance when looked at on the wrong side.

CHAPTER XIX

EVERYDAY LIFE AND PUBLIC
HOLIDAYS

*Parisian Military Festivals – Wet flags – August 15, under the
Empire – Enthusiasm after Tilsit – A maker of barometers
turned poet – Hymen and pork-butchery – The awakening of
Angeline*

I N THE daily life of a city like Paris, public festivals are
not only necessary interludes but a valuable means of
propaganda, which governments make use of for the
benefit of their policy. There had never been so many great
days of rejoicing in the streets as there were during the Revolution, and neither the Directory nor the Consulate allowed
them to fall into abeyance. For reasons easily understood,
the Empire merely set to work to alter their character by
devoting them in most cases to the celebration of the fame
of our arms.

This became apparent from 1804 onwards, when, three
days after the Coronation, a grand military ceremony took
place on the Champ de Mars: the Distribution of the Eagles.
On that occasion, unfortunately, the civilian population cold-
shouldered Napoleon. Gusts of melted snow swept down on
the crowd, to the great detriment of the gold-laced uniforms
and the ladies' dresses. While the troops marched past in a
sea of mud, the spectators in the stands soon found they had
had enough of it, and Josephine herself quitted the scene,
leaving Caroline Murat, with her bare shoulders, to be the
last to hold out. Here and there on the flooded plain a few
enthusiasts hung on, but the Day of Flags, so brilliant in the
picture at Versailles, had really been mostly the Day of
Umbrellas.

This was the case with only too many of the military fêtes
in Paris. There were few interludes in the war during the
summer season; it was nearly always in bad weather that
rejoicings were organized in honour of the crack troops passing through the capital. When the Imperial Guard did so in

November 1807, it was treated, oddly enough to a banquet in the Champs-Élysées – a meal that a deluge of rain turned into an aquatic entertainment.

For August 15, however, which from the beginning of the Consulate had been the great annual holiday, one was usually sure of fine weather. Its main defect was lack of originality. Gunfire and maroons in the morning, jousts on the Seine in the afternoon, with the famous Forioso announcing, on occasion, that he was going to cross the river on a tight-rope, and making himself scarce at the last moment; open-air theatres in Marigny Square, pantomimes, acrobats, tumblers; or tourneys between knights picking up rings with the tips of their lances; then in the evening the inevitable fireworks, the ascension of a luminous balloon, and a grand ball at Tivoli – enough to amuse the sightseers and allow the newspapers to declare next day that the festival of August 15 had never been so brilliant.

There was also a certain monotony – and a great deal of exaggeration – in the accounts of the rejoicings called forth by our victories. Of course a glorious bulletin from the Army leaves nobody unmoved, and Mme de Rémusat was unfair when she declared that 'the feeling of French vanity is not very common among the Parisians'. Still, great events did not always provoke the delirious enthusiasm among the crowd that the press and the police reports took such pains to describe. History, as seen from the street, no longer looked the same on the eve of Austerlitz as it did on the morrow of Marengo.

That year, 1805, the country was going through an alarming financial crisis. Récamier's bank had stopped payment, several bankruptcies resulted, and a number of industries were at a standstill. At the beginning of the autumn, therefore, people were none too pleased to see our armies taking the field again.

When on November 26 an early morning gun announced the taking of Vienna, the horizon brightened for a time. There was a rush for the gazettes, and people spent a fortune in candles for the fairy lamps. But this flash of rejoicing did not last long. Next day everybody reverted to 'their unsatisfactory personal affairs, the scarcity of money, the excessive interest demanded for it, and the slackness in commercial operations'. And a fortnight later the great news of Austerlitz – which some papers spelt Osterlitz, because we have never been good at geography – was welcomed by official demonstrations rather than by the raptures of the population. This was particularly noticeable on January 1, when the Tribunate went with great solemnity to hand over to the Senate the flags taken from the enemy. On that day Cambacérès allowed himself to be deluded by the plaudits, without inquiring where they came from. But a more acute observer, Fiévée, wrote to Napoleon: 'A proportion of the people had so evidently been paid, that public decency was affronted.'

Certainly, now that *Te Deums* had become almost a daily form of entertainment, Paris seemed to be more and more difficult to stir up. War having started again, this time with Prussia, when the double victory of Jena and Auerstedt was announced, the capital was pleased, at it had been pleased by Austerlitz, that is to say without over-excitement, like a well-behaved child.

Its attitude of reserve was actually so marked that the authorities were surprised. In a confidential note the Foreign Minister, Champagny, exhorted the prefect of the Seine to stimulate public opinion, to do whatever he thought appropriate to 'facilitate the explosion of its enthusiasm'. And dotting his *is*, he asked Frochot 'to give *some encouragement* to the dance resorts ordinarily frequented by the people of a Sunday, the *bastringues*, that is, to make them more attractive, better attended, gayer, more animated. . . .'

The Imperial Government reduced to subsidizing the accordion dance-halls and shilling hops, and the purveyors of triple time, to make the French realize the importance of such an event as the collapse, in five weeks, of the powerful army forged by the great Frederick, was that not a sign of the times?

Frochot's 'encouragements' would be more useful still the following year, during our struggle with the Russians, and particularly after Eylau, a bloody butchery that sent a host of frankly pessimistic rumours circulating through the city. The police spent their time inspecting the cafés, 'where the spirit of the *habitués* did not conform to the wishes of true Frenchmen'. It needed the victory of Friedland, the interview between the two emperors, and above all, the Peace of Tilsit, to steady the general morale and let loose a wave of gladness, which this time would be spontaneous.

When Napoleon re-entered Saint-Cloud, he was overwhelmed with evidences of the love everybody bore him, including these lines penned by a poor madwoman before throwing herself out of window: 'I am not sorry to die. But I would have liked to see the return of the Emperor. His arrival will restore people's happiness!'

The August 15th that followed Tilsit was undoubtedly the most brilliant ever seen, or to be seen by the Empire. Never had there been so much gaiety in the streets; never, on the houses, so many yards of calico covered with allegories and dithyrambic phrases. To celebrate the great man who had just given them peace, even the vendors of thermometers turned poets, and this quatrain was to be seen on the shop of Chevallier the engineer:

> 'I know not what genius will venture
> To sing a hero guided by victory.
> For my part, I could not make a thermometer
> Capable of marking the degree of his fame!'

*   *   *   *

When would the people of Paris return to this happy mood? Not, of a certainty, during the two years to follow, for hostilities were soon to be renewed almost everywhere, like a chronic pestilence, and after the Spanish affair, after the new campaign in Austria, even after the costly victory of Wagram and the Treaty of Vienna that followed, many people were convinced that unlimited conquests must burden the county with endless wars.

Hence a general disquiet, an increasing coolness on the part of the public, which even the finest spectacles could not dispel. Not even Bonaparte's marriage to the daughter of an emperor, not even Marie-Louise's entry into her new capital.

Seated beside her husband in the gilded Coronation coach in which Josephine had preceded her, when Paris saw her

pass under the scaffolding round the Arc de l'Étoile, decorated with painted canvas, drive down the Champs-Élysées,
slowly across the Place de la Concorde – a spot that must
have recalled many sad family memories to the great-niece
of Marie-Antoinette – to reach the Tuileries with her escort
of pages, grand dignitaries and Highnesses; when Paris witnessed all this, the Paris that Napoleon believed to be so
responsive and impressionable, it showed deference, curiosity, but according to an eye-witness, 'neither enthusiasm nor
gladness'.

To wake it up a bit, it would have to be given its usual
diversions: bands, theatres, greasy poles, tilting at the ring,
break-neck sports, seesaws. Above all, it must be gorged with
victuals: 4,800 pasties, 1,200 tongues, 1,040 legs of mutton,
1,000 shoulders of mutton, 240 turkeys, 360 capons, 360 fowls
and 3,000 sausages. These were the prizes of a tombola to be
distributed to twelve buffets along the Seine, where fountains
of wine would spout. So that for the lower classes the marriage of Marie-Louise would long be a synonym of a formidable attack of indigestion.

What impression had the young sovereign made as she
passed by? She was not considered very pretty, firstly because she wasn't, and secondly because people rather regretted Josephine, who knew how to dress and had made
herself really popular. The populace always prefers marriages
that have come about of their own accord to unions arranged
by the notaries . . . or the diplomats.

So Marie-Louise's face had appeared insignificant, though,
as Dubois wrote complaisantly: 'Her manner was considered
noble and gracious, her figure handsome and of good augury
for the hopes of the nation, which sees in her the mother of
the heirs of the throne of Napoleon.' In short, a good mould
for emperors. And the blond, rosy Austrian was to justify
these prognostics, for less than a year after the marriage the
guns of the Invalides would announce the birth of the King
of Rome.

For the crowd counting the detonations that day – twenty
were to signify a princess, twenty-two a little prince – this
was doubtless the finest, most moving chapter of history seen
from the street.

Several accounts, including those of the Comtesse de Boigne and the Duchesse Decazes, depict the scene in almost the same terms: pedestrians stopping suddenly in the squares and gardens, anxious faces leaning out of the windows, and suddenly, when they had taken it in, an immense shout of joy 'going off like a discharge'. But of all the contemporaries it was Stendhal, as usual, who gave his reportage the most picturesque turn.

'I was in bed with Angeline. The cannon woke her at ten o'clock. It was the third report. At our nineteenth, which was the twenty-second for the public, we heard clapping in the streets. In the most solitary places, such as the Jardin des Augustins, everybody applauded the twenty-second gun. My wigmaker told me that in the Rue Saint-Honoré people applauded as they do at the appearance of a favourite actor. It's a great and happy event.'

And all the French thought the same. Whatever their sex, age or condition, whatever their political leanings, they were glad to see the future of the Empire assured, even if they were not too fond of the Emperor . . . and even if they had just woken up beside the charming Angeline.

CHAPTER XX

IN THE PROVINCES

'The smell of the Provinces' – Evening parties in Marseilles – A ball at Moulins – The Chariots of Thespis – In love with the First Consul – The great Prefects – A country gentleman – Exemplary little girls – English Exiles in Verdun – Mme de Staël and the Prefect

A SMALL town?' says a character in one of Picard's plays. 'Oh, yes, twice a year, a select company, a game of bouillotte at thirty sous. . . . A few very ugly, very dried-up old ladies, a few old squireens seriously discussing the excellence of their tobacco; a few very starched young men, a handful of very silly young women; two candles on the mantelpiece, a couple of tallow dips on each card-table; a little dog under one, a big cat under another; there's nothing so elegant as a party in the provinces.'

If a contemporary is to be believed, this picture was inspired by life as it was lived at Castelnaudary in 1801. In France at that date, sad to say, there were hundreds of Castelnaudarys. Most of the large towns of today were then only small. Except for Paris and Lyons, not one had a population of 100,000. Only our two ports of Marseilles and Nantes came near to that number.[1] But at Lille and Strasbourg, at Amiens and Limoges, Grenoble and Nancy, Nîmes and Toulouse, statistics vary between 20,000 and 50,000. Toulon had scarcely 12,000, and many prefectures were hardly as populated as one of our country towns.

If these little centres had at least been able to communicate easily with one another! But the bad state of the roads, already mentioned, and the cost and scarcity of means of transport, kept them apart and forced their inhabitants to live as it were inside a retort. Goods, news, fashions, all that contributed to the liveliness of existence, reached them only in slow motion, at the rate of travel of the canal-boats, that

[1] Whereas Paris had 630,000 inhabitants at the end of the Empire, Lyons had 115,000, Marseilles 96,000 and Nantes 77,000.

13 Marriage Procession of Napoleon and Marie-Louise, 1810 (Painting by Garnier at Versailles)

14 Rural interior

Bourgeois interior

took a fortnight to get from Orleans to Indret, or of the carts that took twelve days on the journey from Lyons to Paris.

In the departments at a distance from Paris one might have been at the end of the world, the 'public news-sheets' being obtainable only after a delay of one or two weeks, while letters took almost as long as in the century of Mme de Sévigné. If we add that out of 37,000 communes, 36,000 were without a post-office of any sort until the end of the Empire, it will be easy to see why certain victims of the provinces speak of them with bitterness.

The man with the greatest grudge against them was undoubtedly Stendhal. He had a comprehensive horror of all the towns he had passed through. Dijon, for him, was nothing but 'a mess of a town'. Rouen, of which he ignored the cathedral, the Palais de Justice and the Gros-Horloge, was merely 'an execrable hole, inferior even to Grenoble; the opposite of grandiose in every respect.' When he turned towards his native mountains he discovered 'an air of boredom and acrimony' in Gap. At Sisteron 'the smell of the provinces is doubly strong'. 'I'm in for it this time', he sighs. 'Bored expression of the townsfolk settled outside the cafés, stupid expression on everybody's face. I still find the sight of a small town painful to endure. *Transeat a me calix iste!*'

Even the port of Toulon could not disarm him. 'Ugly streets, like those of Grenoble' (this native of the Dauphiné evidently had his knife in his home country!) 'even uglier, perhaps, paved with little pointed stones. What a come-down after the Rue Saint-Ferréol in Marseilles!'

For Beyle was more indulgent towards Marseilles, where he had lived for some time, carrying on a few love affairs, and going to respectable parties for little girls, which amused him. The only time he was really bored there was at the balls given by a certain Mme Félip, which elicited this note in his Diary. 'A few women of thirty-five who looked ridiculous when they danced. I watched General Cervoni for a time, playing bouillotte: he did nothing but yawn. As a rule it's only about once in a quarter of an hour that you hear anything mentioned not concerned with bouillotte. After an hour of this the General took his departure. A fine evening for a

N

man whose position has become important, who is envied, and who doubtless considers himself fortunate!'

Was better entertainment to be found elsewhere? A letter of Julie Talma's from Moulins in 1805 would suggest the contrary. By way of welcoming the officers of a regiment on its way to Lyons, the authorities of Allier organized a party to which Julie was invited. 'Would you believe it?' she says, 'I spent two hours at the ball. There was a fearful crowd. The people in these parts would put up with anything for the sake of a ball. They filled their pockets with all the sweets and fruit off the buffets. I don't think you'd find such a senseless rabble anywhere but here.'

She does, however, record a sensational turn: a dancing display by some mamelukes, who didn't do at all badly, their only fault being that their faces were 'insufficiently washed'.

* * * *

The theatre was undoubtedly still the favourite pastime of the provincial towns. According to Salgues, there were 128 regular theatres in the departments in 1813. There were two each in Lyons and Rouen, three in Marseilles and Brussels, and in Bordeaux, where fashionable society was fairly extensive, there were four.

Attracted by good fees, the stars of Paris came to act there fairly often. Mlle Contat asked 5000 francs a night. In the last year of the Empire Mlle Duchesnois was paid 700 francs in Lyons. During the summer of 1804 Talma acted in several tragedies before the audiences of Bordeaux, who wanted to keep him till the end of the autumn. 'And even then they will only let him go under protest, and on condition that Mlle Mézeray is sent to console them. Brunet saw the time coming when they would keep him by force . . . and on his return he gave such a good report of their politeness and friendliness that the entire Volange family started off to pay them a visit on their own. It seems that when the Bordelais decide to treat people well they don't do it by halves.'

But many towns had too slender a budget to afford such prodigality. They had to be content with the little local company, or entertain touring troupes, mostly recruited in Paris from the Café Touchard, an establishment in the Rue de

l'Arbre-Sec, that went trailing primitive scenery, soiled cos-
tumes and very modest talent from one end of France to the
other.

In 1803 a woman, half-adventuress, half-artist, given to
impulsive action and used to gunfire, who later signed her
memoirs Ida de Saint-Elme, met with one of these companies at Aix-en-Provence. Being rather hard up, and having
recognized some old friends among them, she suggested joining them. The impresario engaged her, after telling her in
confidence that he was going to give a performance at Digne,
but they were not travelling like princes.

'Madame is no doubt aware that the ancients made use of
chariots?' he said.

'Well, what of it?'

'Well, we are going to follow their example, in a country
full of their monuments.'

'Meaning that we're going to Digne in a cart?'

'How quick you are at guessing!'

The young beauty gaily assumed her role in this novel
roman comique. Eleven persons settled themselves as best
they could in the straw at the bottom of a cart protected by
a tattered canvas hood. And this total did not include the
ingénue's Persian cat, nor the *soubrette*'s parakeet, nor the
leading actor's pug-dog. 'We were the most comical party in
the world, and the journey was enough to make anybody
laugh that had the sense not to take life too seriously. At last,
between a tirade from *Sémiramis* and a grand aria from
Barbe-Bleue, we arrived safe and sound, having only been
upset once.'

It is to be hoped that the performance given to the audience at Digne was not spoilt by any further *débâcle*.

*   *   *   *

Far more sumptuous were the tours organized by the Consular Government for its own benefit when it visited the
departments.

After rescuing from anarchy towns and villages where
people had been tearing one another to pieces for the last ten
years, Bonaparte not only brought them back towards French
unity, but he laboured to enrich them, to give their lives

more amplitude and security. From the very first, he endowed them with an administrative framework so strong that those to come after him would hardly dare to alter it, in spite of changes in the Government. With the prefects of the Consulate, who were soon to be those of the Empire, and often carried on as those of Louis XVIII, a new era may be said to have begun for the provinces, a regime of which the working and peasant population and the middle classes soon felt the benefit. So that even more than in Paris, perhaps, everybody was eager to acclaim the Pacifier.

The excursions he made in almost every direction, once his power was established, often aroused indescribable enthusiasm. Each of them resembled a honeymoon, in which France and her idol exchanged their first effusions of love.

Illuminations, fireworks, banquets, gala performances at the theatre – enough to excite the provinces for weeks on end, to set Normandy rejoicing next to the Lyonnais, Reims next to Lille and Amiens. Everywhere the flower of the city's youth formed a guard of honour, offering flowers and gifts to Josephine; the great man was greeted with addresses, often a bit flat, with verses, often a bit foolish, but expressing genuine adoration. At the Théâtre des Arts in Rouen there was such a throng that people were literally nearly crushed. At Amiens, while Bonaparte was visiting a factory, a young girl belonging to one of the first families in the district fell on her knees at his feet, murmuring, 'Ah, I swear that I love you!'

She had no petition to make. 'She was', said the newspapers, 'simply in love.' Touched by such an unexpected scene, the First Consul addressed this young lady with great kindness. That evening Madame Bonaparte sent her, in a box, a very fine medallion decorated with a portrait of her husband, painted on enamel by Isabey and enriched with fine pearls. We might almost be reading the Queen's words in the last scene of *Carmosine*: 'Give that kiss, my child . . . I am not jealous!' And who knows whether, later on, Musset did not light on this tale of the girl of Amiens?

But the Consular travels did not only produce sentimental incidents suited to a young lady's album. Wherever he went, Bonaparte gave orders for useful undertakings and entrusted the prefects with their execution. He left behind him these representatives of the central power, to become the moving spirits of each region.

They were splendid workers, these *missi dominici*, whose enormous role has been so well described by Louis Madelin: Beugnot, who succeeded in developing Normandy; Rambuteau, who designed the road over the Simplon Pass; Jeanbon de Saint-André, to whom we owe that of the Rhine — men belonging to every party, but recognizing only one, that of France, from the moment they were singled out by Bonaparte.

Following on the colourless administrators of the Directory, the prefects were not content merely to govern, they set themselves to build. Old towns reconstructed from their ruins, like Lyons, or modernized, like Cherbourg; new towns created out of nothing — sometimes in too great haste, like Napoleon-Vendée;[1] roads improved, canals dug, marshes drained, bridges thrown over the rivers, dykes built to keep out the sea — so much for the material effort.

But the presence of these high officials in our provinces was to have a further result. The prestige that surrounded them, the uniform they wore, and soon, the title of Count or Baron that would reward their labours, would make each of them a powerful personage, around whom social life would be organized. Where up to now there had only been a population, there would henceforth be a society, a little official world, with its ceremonial, its festivals, its receptions, which would give the provinces the illusion that they were becoming a little like Paris. No doubt their daily existence would remain only moderately gay, but it would nevertheless have improved a bit since the days of Picard's comedy and General Cervoni's games of bouillotte.

*   *   *   *

On the fringe of this new society, however, especially in the Midi, there would still be a France that was difficult to

---

[1] Napoléon-Vendée — La Roche-sur-Yon of today, intended for 60,000 inhabitants, had only 300 to begin with. The town was built of puddled clay, which dissolved in the first shower of rain. When the Emperor paid it a visit in 1808 he drove his sword into the wall of a barracks. 'You've made a town of mud!' he said. The engineer was discharged, but Napoléon-Vendée was none the better for that.

tame: that of the nobles whom the Revolution had more or
less ruined, but who, careful of their traditions, were making
the best of a dull existence on the small plot of land still
remaining to them. The memoirs of Léontine de Villeneuve,
Chateaubriand's enigmatic correspondent, whom he dubbed
the *Occitanienne*, afford a curious picture of one of these
pockets of resistance.

The girl's whole childhood had been spent with her father,
mother and sisters in the château of Hauterive, near Castres.
The house, which had been pillaged, had only the scantiest
furniture left out of its former grandeur. The drawing-room
had been refurbished as best it could with a white wallpaper
decorated with garlanded hearts, chintz curtains in the windows, no clock on the mantelpiece. Here and there, however,
a few remnants of the past, such as the armchairs upholstered
in *petit-point*, and in the dowager Marchioness's room an
enormous bed '*à la polonaise*', with its four tufts of feathers
'not too badly worm-eaten'.

The other bedrooms were much simpler, with 'angel beds'
to sleep on, rush-seated chairs and bare brick floors.

The estate, still extensive, was managed by M. de Villeneuve himself. In the saddle at dawn, he woke his servants,
allotting them their tasks, and then rode all round his
property; lived, in short, the life of a big farmer whom people
would refer to as Monsieur le Marquis. It was not till dinner-
time that he changed his clothes, became a gentleman again
and presented himself in the drawing-room.

There he found his mother and his wife, usually surrounded
by a few friends; for in spite of their modest way of life, they
entertained a good deal. In this society of small fortunes,
hospitality was the one remaining luxury. The extreme cheap-
ness of foodstuffs and the insignificant wages demanded by
domestics made these liberal habits possible. There was no
butler, but there was still a cook, and places were always laid
for country neighbours, inviting themselves without ceremony, and cadets from Tarbes or Toulouse arriving on horseback, often followed by their portmanteau. Some of these
might stay at the château for weeks at a time. They were
given a warm welcome if they were pleasant people, a civil
one even if they were not; but if the visitor was an

émigré, this gave him every privilege, 'even that of being a bore'.

So that round the table at Hauterive there were always a few odd characters, worthy of a place in Balzac's gallery, from the old Abbé, brother to the Marquis, lost in meditation, to the hare-brained Vicomte, twice or thrice ruined, married no one quite knew to whom, deserted by his wife and deprived of all his possessions except an enormous nose, a taste for popular songs and an impulsive temperament.

At dessert there was much talk of politics, and this sort of conversation cannot have been very entertaining for the little girl, but her upbringing had taught her patience.

Neither she nor her sisters were spoilt children. 'We slept in big bedrooms where no fire was ever lighted', she wrote later. 'Our winter dresses were mere cotton sheaths; a fairly thick shawl and good heavy shoes were all we were given, with which to brave snow, fog and icy winds. When we came in shivering, we were forbidden to go near the fire, except for a moment, to restore circulation to our hands.'

During meals, the young people were trained to be silent. Nobody cared to know whether the fare was to their liking. In the matter of tit-bits it was a family joke that 'Léontine had a right to sugar because she was born before the Continental System'. But rare fruits, such as the luscious pears of Saint-Pons, were reserved for the grown-ups, and the lower form thought it quite natural to expect only the scraps.

By way of amusement the child was allowed to read *Robinson Crusoe*, and Royaumont's Bible, to play in the courtyard of the château in summer, taking care not to trespass beyond a certain boundary mark, and in the autumn to go and roast chestnuts in the kitchen. At bedtime she went up to her room with her governess, the guileless Mlle Lefranc, who made her 'say the *Pater* twice over, the second time in Latin, under the impression that it was a different prayer'.

This was how little girls were brought up, towards 1810, by the old nobility of the Languedoc.

*   *   *   *

In addition to these gentry, digging themselves in so obstinately in their châteaux, there were involuntary exiles in many parts of the Empire, provincials against their will. First the Englishmen interned by Bonaparte after the rupture of the Treaty of Amiens; then, a little later, those Frenchmen whom his police had politely requested to take up their residence at a distance of forty leagues from Paris. So many unexpected guests who ended by turning certain towns into a sort of secret tribunal for unruly schoolboys. And this was not one of the least curious aspects of the provinces at that time.

Imagine the feelings of a British tourist, swigging champagne at Hardy's or Corazza's when, on the 3rd Prairial, year IX, an orderly came to tell him he was a prisoner of war and must present himself next day to the Paris Government, to be told where he was to be interned. This measure was adopted as a reprisal for the seizure of our ships by our neighbours; but for the 7,000 islanders who thought themselves quite safe with us this sensational counter-stroke must have appeared harsh, all the same. Some were sent to Fontainebleau, to Orleans or Valenciennes, others to Châlons or Nancy, the unluckiest to the fort of Bitche, and the majority to Verdun.

We get many details of the English colony's sojourn in Verdun from the Diary of James Henry Lawrence[1] and the *Letters* of his learned compatriot James Forbes.[2] It must obviously be unpleasant for people who had set out to amuse themelves in Paris, to find themselves treated as hostages and kept away from their homes for months and years in a subprefecture of the Meuse. But apart from this, there is no need to exaggerate the severity of an exile which, according to the evidence of the victims themselves, would seem to have been very bearable. Thanks to the goodwill of the local authorities, especially General Wirion, their internment looked from the first more like a country holiday.

Forbes rented a handsome apartment at the cost of a guinea a week. His board for the same period amounted to two louis, including champagne and other choice wines, and he may be said to have put a good stomach on his misfortunes. Miss Forbes took dancing lessons from the best dan-

[1] James Henry Lawrence, *A Picture of Verdun*, 2 vols. 1810.
[2] James Forbes, *Letters from France in the years 1803–1804*. London, 1806.

cing master in the town, at ten sous a time, music lessons
at twenty-five sous, drawing lessons at thirty sous. In fact
the family 'enjoyed every pleasure for one louis a day', con-
cludes the captive, 'except those of the mind and of sweet
liberty'.

Even sweet liberty seems not to have been entirely denied
to the English colony. In summer they were allowed to organ-
ize excursions into the surrounding country, with rustic meals
at the inns, and in winter, wolf and wild boar hunts. Drawing-
rooms were thrown open for their benefit, too, and subscrip-
tion balls given there to the delight of the young English
ladies. The men got up races, with Lord Yarborough and the
Honourable Tufton [sic] as stewards, at which thorough-
breds were run at an entrance fee of fifty louis. There was the
theatre, too, which gave performances in English. One evening the internees acted *Douglas* and *The Revenge*, and a
London newspaper, *The Argus*,[1] has this to say of the performance:

'The theatre was full. Everybody of importance in Verdun,
from the point of view of rank and elegance, had flocked
there. We may mention Lord Yarmouth, Colonels Abercromby and Scott of the land forces, Captains Gower and
Brenton of the Navy, and all the officers detained at Verdun
as well as the civilians acting as hostages; the ladies shone
with special lustre, having donned their gala dresses, and so
did the gentlemen, who were wearing opera hats with black
cockades. In a word, it was a very English spectacle and a
curiosity in its way – an English play and an English farce,
acted in France by prisoners of war before an audience composed of their like.'

*   *   *   *

Since this was not a unique example, since the English in
Nancy, better treated even than those in Verdun, took part
in masked balls and the festivals of the Carnival, and were
entertained in the homes of the best families of Lorraine,
there was probably no need to pity the fate of the internees.
If the French prisoners who were soon to people the hulks of
Portsmouth and Chatham had had the benefit of the same

[1] A Napoleonic propaganda newspaper printed in London.

treatment, they would doubtless not have retained such terrible memories of their captivity.

✷   ✷   ✷   ✷

From 1805 onwards the Departments had a further clientèle, that of the political enemies of whom the Emperor wished to rid himself. He who, as a rule, was so fond of centralization, employed an exactly opposite method with the Opposition, decentralizing it as fast as he could, and thus becoming the chief purveyor of the provinces.

If the presence of Barras was detected in Paris, or that of General Lecourbe in the outskirts, the former was immediately invited to retire to the Dauphiné, the latter to the Midi. No less categorical orders were given to Léon de Rohan-Chabot, to the Tourzel family, and to Mme de Béthune-Charost. The first received his passport to Brussels, the others to Dijon and Geneva.

Hundreds of expulsions followed – those of M. de Narbonne, of Mme de Balbi and many others. On each occasion there were brief memorandums or furious notes addressed to Fouché: 'If M. Chénier dares to make the least remark, inform him that I shall give orders for him to be sent to the isles of Sainte-Marguerite. The day of jokes is past. Let him keep quiet, it's all he has a right to. Don't let that huzzy Mme de Staël come within reach of Paris; I know she's not far off it.'

Another time, on the subject of the same person: 'That woman is still plying her trade of intriguer. She has approached Paris in spite of my orders. She's a regular pest . . . I shall have to have her removed by the gendarmerie.'

It must be admitted that the Châtelaine of Coppet was the most incorrigible of rebels and mischief-makers. When she was supposed to be in Switzerland she was actually at Lyons, appearing in a box at the theatre during a performance by Talma – apparently for her sole benefit. Or she would start off for Auxerre, complain that she could not sleep there, take the road to Blois, via Briare, hit on the idea of driving round the capital within a radius of forty leagues, and write to her friends, declaring that she could be really comfortable only on the cushions of a post-chaise or in Paris.

But she surpassed herself one evening at Buissonrond,

where she had gone to dine, in defiance of orders, with her friends the de Boignes. Sitting opposite to her at table was M. Finot, the Prefect of Savoy, who must have been feeling rather embarrassed, since he was bound theoretically to keep watch on her movements. As he was a man of the world the conversation was none the less enjoyable, until Mme de Staël asked him for news of an official she had known earlier as a sub-prefect.

'He is now a prefect and thought very highly of', replied M. Finot.

'Really! I'm glad to hear it; he's a charming young man. As a matter of fact,' she added carelessly, 'I've usually found that class of *employees* very pleasant.'

The Prefect reddened, the guests turned pale; only the culprit seemed not to have realized that she had committed an impertinence. But we may let Mme de Boigne tell the end of the story. 'We had reached the second course. A very urgent letter was brought to M. Finot; he read it and put it in his pocket. After dinner he showed it to me; it was an order to have Mme de Staël taken back to Coppet by the gendarmerie, from detachment to detachment, the moment he received the letter. I begged him not to give her such a disagreeable shock in my house; he assured me he had no intention of doing so – adding with a certain bitterness, "I don't want her to change her opinion of employees of my class." I took it upon myself to let her know it was time to return to Coppet, and he contented himself with giving injunctions to the postmasters to furnish horses only for the direct route. She had a fancy for a trip to Milan.'

Really, Corinne had some odd ideas about life in the provinces!

CHAPTER XXI

A BATTLE EXTRAORDINARY

*The two bread crises: 1801 and 1811 – The bakers' grievances
– Paris does not like black bread – The Reserves are thrown
in – Disquieting rise in prices – Robespierre's maximum – Flour
goes into hiding – Tardy solution of the crisis*

1811 – the year of the King of Rome, of the comet and of a famous wine – was greeted by the people of that day as a period of relative peace.

Napoleon had not taken the field himself since Wagram. He left his lieutenants to fight, and only too often to be beaten, on the other side of the Pyrenees, but for the last twenty months he had remained almost entirely in the neighbourhood of the Tuileries, Saint-Cloud, Fontainebleau and Compiègne, spending his time between the cares of politics and the joys of recent paternity.

But during this sort of breathing-space that the god of war allowed himself, he was suddenly forced, after all, to fight a battle. Although history hardly mentions it, it was nevertheless a pretty fierce one, and there may be some interest in reviving the memory of it after the trials of the same nature that our own generation has just gone through. This battle of 1811–12, which bears no name in the textbooks, might be called the 'Battle of the Bread'.

Up to the middle of summer the harvests had promised to be very good. But towards the end of July thunderstorms had broken out, devastating Beauce and Brie. In the Midi torrid heat had roasted the crops where they stood, and it was clear that the cereal product would be less than mediocre everywhere. Now a lack of corn in a country where so much bread is eaten as in France must always be a serious matter. Having been through the Revolution, the Emperor knew this better than anybody: he did not forget that most popular uprisings of the past have begun in front of empty bakeries. Hence his policy in the matter of victualling. 'Is it wise to let corn be sold dear when nature provides it in abundance?' was one of his favourite sayings, and he certainly thought that when she remained ungenerous, corn should still remain cheap.

It was with this idea that, from the beginning of the Consulate, he had regulated the trade, reducing the number of bakers so as to keep a better hold over them, building up substantial reserves of flour and throwing them on the market when supplies began to dwindle, fighting obstinately, in short, against the threats of famine that had always been his nightmare.

An early crisis, in the year X, had come near to being very serious. With a good third of the usual production lacking, the price of bread had suddenly gone up. The four-pound loaf, which usually cost from twelve to thirteen sous, was already selling at eighteen by the beginning of the autumn of 1801. A cartload of bread was pillaged in the open street, Rue Saint-Honoré, and in working-class quarters people were not afraid of declaring that the bakers deserved to be guillotined.

There was the same unrest in the provinces: trouble had broken out in Amiens that cost an officer his life. It was said that the people of Rouen had murdered their Mayor and burnt down the market hall at Darnétal. Other affrays took place in the Oise, the Aisne and Seine-et-Marne, where the people of Provins had held up a boat loaded with flour.

To restore order, at any rate in Paris, the Consular authorities had commissioned a private society, the Compagnie Bendecker, behind which the inevitable Ouvrard was probably manœuvring, to purchase considerable quantities of corn in Belgium and the Vendée, to be sold to the trade at a loss. In this way the ovens had been kept going, but at what a price! The operation, once over, was found to have cost more than fifteen and a half millions.

There followed, fortunately, a whole series of fat years. In spite of the rupture of the Treaty of Amiens, the four-pound loaf had gone down to twelve sous again in 1803, then to eleven, and even to the incredible price of nine, in 1804, the rise occurring afterwards remaining very slight. Seven years later the loaf still cost from thirteen to fourteen sous, and the public had become so accustomed to this price that the idea of a change did not occur to it.

Consternation was all the greater, therefore, when towards the middle of summer, 1811, it was known that flour was about to become scarce again. Victims of the drought already mentioned, the Departments of the Midi had drawn heavily on the region of Paris, and the 1,300 sacks per day required for the provisioning of the capital could not be found.

* * * *

All governments are alike. When a problem perplexes them, they set up a commission with instructions to study it. Napoleon, for all his genius, could not do otherwise. An Administrative Council was created, known as the *Conseil des Subsistances*, and under the presidency of Montalivet, and later of Comte de Sussy, Minister of Commerce, certain high officials such as Maret, Director of Supplies, Pasquier, the new Prefect of Police, Dubois, his predecessor, and Réal, Councillor of State, met to palaver every week. What came of their deliberations? To start with, a bulk purchase of 6,000 quintals of Flemish corn, which allowed the reserves to be built up again to some extent, but had the drawback of sending up the market price. Since flour was costing more and more, the bakers were not long in asking permission to raise the price of bread a little. It was then that the battle started. On one side were the shopkeepers trying to avoid ruin, on the other a Government anxious to prevent a rise, the unpopularity of which it could foresee.

Intervening in person, the Emperor first thought of a system of subsidies. The State was to pay five francs per sack to every baker buying flour. A credit set aside for this purpose was consumed in a few weeks, and it was patent that it had done nothing to improve the situation in the trade.

Early every morning the bakers' shops were invaded and rapidly cleared out. It was all the more difficult for them to satisfy their usual customers, because people from the suburbs, attracted by the difference in price, had formed the habit of coming to buy their bread in Paris. 'For some days now', writes the Prefect of Police, 'the bakers have noticed people they had never seen before, buying four or five loaves at a time; people from the country have asked for as many as eight four-pound loaves at the same shop. It is thought that some are being exported to Versailles, Arpajon, Long-jumeaux, Poissy and elsewhere, and even to Mantes.'

The same thing was happening on a grand scale with regard to the sale of flour. The stocks of Chartres and Étampes were going off to the Ouest, those of Picardy up to Artois and those of Brie down to Lyons and Marseilles, so that a circle of dearth was growing round the capital.

In the city itself certain symptoms, familiar to old Parisians, already portended the crisis: the run on dried vegetables, at no matter what price, and the barrels of boiled potatoes that housewives were fighting for in the open street, around the Cornmarket – or rather, the Market without Corn.

Aware of the turn things were taking, Savary, Minister of Police, thought it advisable to inform the Emperor, now on his way back from Holland via the Rhine Provinces; but at first he only drew from him a somewhat contemptuous reply: 'I have received your letter of October 30. You in Paris are like children; you lose your heads from fright. What will it be like when bread is at eighteen sous and the bakers have used up their stocks? You must take precautions but not lose your head. Never be frightened. Fear never does any good. All you have to do is to await my orders for five or six days.'

In spite of his apparent phlegm, Napoleon must have taken the subject seriously, for on his return to Saint-Cloud he hastened to authorize the increase in price that he had always forbidden up to then. Bread went up by one sou.

But to spare the poorer population the extra expense, he tried to put in practice an idea he had cherished for a long time, which was to persuade certain classes to accept a bread less white, but more nourishing, than usual, and costing less to make – the coarse black bread the little Corsican of yore had munched with so much relish.

An initial experiment attempted in 1801 had unfortunately produced very disappointing results. The Parisians of the year X had shown that they clung above all else to their white bread, appetizing and tender under its beautiful golden crust. The second attempt was even more negative, and Malivet summoned up courage to confess to the Sovereign that 'the loaves of inferior quality found no buyers, even at the price of eleven and twelve sols'.

With more circumlocution, Pasquier announced the same
fiasco. 'This exclusive taste for fine bread shown by the
people of Paris is unfortunate when times are difficult. A
striking instance of this has occurred lately, for more than
half the necessitous population give four sous to their baker
to change the four-pound loaf given them by the charitable
committees, which, although inferior, is really excellent.'

* * * *

When an engagement took a bad turn, the Emperor used
to send the Guards into action. In the Battle of the Bread he
thought the moment had come to throw in the Reserves.

These were the stocks of flour built up by the State and
warehoused in various depots in Paris and the outskirts. To
begin with, it was decided to sell 300 sacks a day to the
bakers, at the rate of seventy-three francs the sack – a very
moderate price, adopted in the hope of checking the rise in
the wholesale price. But they were reckoning, alas, without
the speculators.

Before ten days had gone by, market prices had, on the
contrary, gone up to twenty-four francs, so that the retail
dealers made an immediate profit by selling with one hand
what they had bought with the other. Besides which, the
wholesale flour merchants, forsaking the Paris market, where
they were hindered by the competition of the Reserve, sent
all their goods henceforth to Normandy, leaving nearly all
the provisioning of the capital to the care of the State.

Soon it was no longer 300, but 600, 700 or 800 sacks that
had to be drawn daily from the public warehouses. To refill
them, ever larger sums would be required. The total advances
deducted from the Sinking Fund was to reach ten millions by
the spring of 1812.

If only these sacrifices had succeeded in saving the poor
from having to pay more for their bread! But this was not so:
the price of the four-pound loaf went up from fifteen to sixteen sous, and then to seventeen. And in spite of this, honest
bakers were unable to cover their expenses. Some had already
shut up shop; others were pawning their clothes at the Mont-
de-Piété.

After lavishing fine words on them, Pasquier himself realized that these unfortunates were at the end of their tether, and that fresh assistance was imperative. 'For one thing, their services are indispensable,' he wrote to Savary, 'besides which, they have an enormous influence on public opinion. They are of the people themselves. There are 640 of them. Add their wives, their journeymen, their relations, and you can see what a number of plaintiff mouths there are, vociferating, sowing bad news and alarm in every way.'

Arguments such as these never fail to interest the public Powers. A maximum price of eighteen sous for bread was authorized, therefore, and supplies from the Reserve were increased to 1,300 sacks a day, representing pretty nearly the total *intra muros* consumption. What more could people demand?

Thanks to these measures the bakers ceased complaining for a few days, but the intervention of the State proved a two-edged sword. While it maintained prices in Paris by artificial means, those of the provinces, left to themselves, merely went up the more rapidly. Soon, in certain regions, panic broke out, causing regular riots. On March 2 people fought in Caen. A regiment of Guards had to be stationed there, and eight looters, among them two women, were shot without mercy after appearing at a court-martial.

Disturbances were less serious in the proximity of the capital, but every day large quantities of bread continued to pass the barrier. The operation had become so profitable that everybody had a hand in it now, from the market-gardeners who came back from the Halles with enormous stocks of loaves to the well-to-do bourgeois who filled their carriages in the same way.

And the infernal price race went on. The sack of flour, which had cost ninety-three francs at the beginning of February, was worth 115 on April 6, and in the first days of May the bakers of Rouen were selling their bread at thirty-six sous – four times dearer than in 1803!

This time it was too much. In the words of Pasquier, 'Anxiety was turning to terror.' Abandoning his optimism, Napoleon, who was preparing to go and rejoin the main army, and did not want to leave public opinion behind him at boiling point, decided that a strong hand was called for, and

o

a few days later he issued two decrees that must have reminded many people of the Revolution.

The first made it obligatory for the producers of corn to declare their harvests, and subjected them to requisition if necessary. It also forbade all subjects of the State to buy grain or flour 'for the purpose of hoarding them, warehousing them or making them an object of speculation'. A double attack, some thought, on the right of property and the freedom of commerce.

The second decree, which fixed a maximum market price of thirty-three francs the hectolitre for all corn sold in the markets of the Île de France, had little to distinguish it from the Maximum of Robespierre.

*   *   *   *

'You'll be all right in a fortnight', said the Sovereign to his high officials on leaving for Dresden. He was sadly mistaken. The same causes always producing the same effects, what happened in 1794 happened again in 1812: as it could no longer be sold freely, corn went into hiding.

At the beginning of June Réal reported to the Council of Foodstuffs 'a considerable decrease in milling dues in the neighbourhood of Paris, and their almost complete cessation in a few places'. The Imperial decree permitted grain to be requisitioned at the farms, but the effect of such an operation was to be feared at a time when wholesale departures of conscripts had already had a powerfully disturbing effect on the countryside. Production remained free, therefore, and sales under the counter became the rule almost everywhere. A month later, the failure of the tax was universally recognized; it had had no result beyond that of still further depleting the Reserve, and bringing on to the market types of flour mixed with beans, horse-beans and haricots.

Panic began to spread among the public. Every morning there were unruly queues in front of the bakers' shops, and the rumour spread that 'the people of Paris were to be reduced to half a pound of bread'. Such a measure would have been bearable (as we have discovered in our own day), but at that time it sounded terrible, and the Council of Foodstuffs did not dare contemplate it, any more than they had seriously attempted to requisition flour. Its members contented themselves with repeating that the end of July was approaching and a good harvest would put everything right.

Unhappily, they were once more mistaken. Though the harvests of 1812 were not bad, the market had been too thoroughly upset to recover its balance for many a long month. Flour made only a timid appearance; the price dropped a point or two, then went up again steeply. This was particularly noticeable when, on November 11, Saint Martin's Day, a date that usually coincided with the lowest prices of the year, corn increased two francs in price – an event unprecedented in market history.

This was the situation when winter began. It threatened to be a very severe one, and this brought interminable queues of poor people to the doors of the bakeries. From one week to another it became necessary to increase the supplies of the Reserves by a thousand sacks, and they could not be found. In the meantime the Emperor had returned from Russia – in what state of mind may be imagined. Was the great military tragedy to be doubled by a year of famine in France?

At this point the luck changed. Just when hope seemed lost, a considerable drop in price was announced on December 28 in the market at Montlhéry, and soon spread throughout the country; the miracle that had failed in July was accomplished six months later. Nature was still the kindly sorceress she had always been, but like a coy mistress she had demanded to be implored.

Seen from a distance, this long crisis of 1811–12 has more than one lesson to give us. Its effect on the public mind was mainly due, no doubt, to its occurrence after a period of great prosperity, but it might also have been prevented, or at any rate attenuated, by a different policy.

No help was to be expected from the requisition of flour, or the resurrection of the Maximum, the danger of which had been demonstrated by the Jacobin experiment. On the other hand a restriction of consumption might have been attempted, applying certain measures with which we are now familiar, and which the good sense of the people makes them willing to accept when circumstances demand it.

If the First Empire avoided having recourse to them, it was

because it wanted above all to keep on the right side of public opinion. It had committed every sort of audacity, it had held its own against Europe; but by a singular contrast this Government, which has remained the type of authoritarian regimes in our history, feared nothing so much as the re-actions of the man in the street.

And that is why bread tickets did not see the light in 1812.

CHAPTER XXII

THE GREAT COLLAPSE

*The Empire packs up – Entry of the Allies into Paris – Opinion
in the Midi – The little war and the great one – Vive le Roi –
A Bonapartist schoolboy – During the Hundred Days – An
Archbishop's vacillations – The invisible hand*

HISTORY, as we see it happening day by day, might be
summed up as a series of more or less sensational news
items. It was an item of the first magnitude for the
Parisians of 1814 when on the morning of March 29 they
noticed a long line of vehicles drawn up at the doors of the
Tuileries: ten travelling berlines, a number of wagons and
an enormous coach covered in grey dust sheets. The Empire
was packing up; they were waiting for Marie-Louise's departure.

The berlines were intended for the Regent and her suite;
the wagons for the chests of the Treasury. As for the coach,
already crammed with saddles, cavalry saddlecloths, boots
and harness, it was the Coronation equipage, the one that
had carried the first Imperial couple to Notre-Dame and the
second along the Champs-Élysées. A double family relic!

For some hours the lower servants were seen loading bales
of valuable objects; then at last Marie-Louise appeared, her
features discomposed, with her ladies-in-waiting and Mme de
Montesquieu carrying the little King of Rome. Up to the last
minute he had fought and screamed, 'I don't want to go
away! I don't want to leave my house! As Papa isn't here, I'm
the master!' They soothed him as best they could, and towards midday the procession started off in the direction of
Rambouillet, preceded by a detachment of cavalry and followed by a crowd of domestics on mounts of every size.

The decision taken by Napoleon's wife to leave the
Tuileries, the ill-fated Palace that Louis XVI and Marie-
Antoinette had attempted to escape from before her, and
from which, in the new century, three kings, a queen and a
last empress would escape after her, had been forced upon

her by the arrival of the allied armies at the gates of the capital. All next day the fate of Paris hung in the balance. To follow the engagements going on in the neighbourhood of Belleville and La Villette, the strollers in the Jardin des Plantes converged on the Labyrinth, whence they could see the infantry fire in the distance, above the top of the great cedar. 'The little world of swans and banana-trees to which our power had promised eternal peace was disturbed', sighs Chateaubriand. But the centre of the town was much more so!

Here were wounded men dragging themselves along towards the hospitals, poor lamed soldiers of the line, handsome cuirassiers, unrecognizable in their great white capes spattered with mud. There, led by their mistresses, were the little pupils of the Montmartre boarding-schools, disguised as boys for crossing the danger zone. In the suburbs of Saint-Martin and Saint-Denis, all along the boulevards especially, the people driven in from the country 'marched pell-mell with their cows, their sheep, their scanty baggage', seeking shelter at the entrances to the courtyards and sharing their last possessions – great loaves of black bread they had baked themselves, almost under the fire of the guns.

One more day was to go by, and over the roadway of these same boulevards, strewn with greenery – by whose hands it were best not to inquire – would pass the army of the victors. A sad episode in the life of Paris, a new sight for a city that, for centuries, had never seen 'the smoke of the enemy's camps', and was now obliged to watch them marching past, as if on parade – the imposing Prussian cavalry and the Russian infantry in strange uniforms, aligned in ranks of thirty men abreast.

In the words of an eye-witness, 'It was like a merciless, dark tide of green uniforms and bright plumes, the last waves of which were still submerging the barrier of La Villette while its mounting, ever-swelling flood beat against the chestnut-trees of the Tuileries and the railings of the Invalides.'

The crowd's reception was varied. In the suburbs men spoke to one another in low voices, with an occasional shrug of the shoulders. The true populace appeared aghast. But as one approached the Madeleine the public physiognomy changed. 'The enthusiasm of certain women increased with the aristocratic character of the quarter. In the Rue Montmartre they threw flowers; at the Chinese Baths they alighted from their carriages, they tried to mingle with the squadrons, they shook hands with the Cossacks. Which was as good as saying, as some were already venturing to do, 'Our friends the enemies.'

Politics played their part in this debatable enthusiasm. To the applause of the fine ladies, some young men were already sporting white cockades. But as the royalists themselves admitted, these formed only a small minority so far, and the cause of this veering of opinion must be looked for elsewhere.

The country was visibly exhausted. It was sick of the endless wars, the devastating levies of troops mowing down an entire generation, sick of the attempt at universal conquest, which it had thought inspired while it appeared to be successful, but declared to be mad now that it had failed. A state of mind that had nothing heroic about it, but for which the terrible sacrifices of the last two years provided some excuse. There were too many empty places in the home, too many widows' veils in the streets. But above all, nobody believed any longer in Napoleon's star.

Born after the retreat from Russia, this discouragement had increased after Leipzig. From 1813 onwards a thousand little incidents had shown how greatly the Emperor's popularity was on the wane. At the Variétés a play had been given, called *La Manie des Campagnes*, and in another people had dared to applaud this couplet dedicated to a Don Juan grown old – or to a tired soldier:

'You were what you no longer are,
    You were not then what you are now,
And you had the means of making conquests,
    And you had what you no longer have.'

The military miracles of the French campaigns had shown the scoffers to be wrong; but faced with the invasion of our soil and the risks of an unequal struggle, confidence weakened more and more. During that dismal month of February 1814, when the guns of the Invalides announced Champaubert and Montmirail, many people had sighed 'Alas, these are merely victories!' For what was wanted was peace, peace at any price.

And now that it was appearing hand in hand with defeat, they were both welcomed with a feeling of deliverance. Paris, finding itself spared, no longer panicked, no longer thought about anything, it merely breathed. While Europe in arms marched in procession before its eyes with white sleeve bands, it looked on as if at the theatre, listening to the strange music, admiring the fine uniforms – uniforms that the French, to borrow a quip of Albert Sorel's, 'had for the last twenty years hardly considered except from behind'.

*   *   *   *

Next to the reactions of the capital, what were those of the countryside? Three very different pieces of evidence will give us some idea. Let us first take a look at the royalist Midi. Let us return to the Château of Hauterive near Castres, where we saw the Villeneuve family leading a quite patriarchal life, collecting a little circle of dyed-in-grain gentlemen and bringing up their daughters like young heroines of Bouilly's tales.

The one we know best, Léontine, was now getting on for twelve. She was no longer the little wild creature amusing herself by roasting chestnuts in the kitchen stove. The conversations she overheard of an evening, round the fire, had given her to understand that not only was fighting going on near Champagne, but the English army had crossed the Pyrenees and was threatening her dear Languedoc.

To the peasants of the region war meant nothing but ruins and tears. As a rule they bothered their heads very little about the Empire, hardly more no doubt about the provinces higher up, but they agreed with these in cursing the severity of conscription. 'They will take all our children from us!' moaned the women. 'And I,' replied a man, 'sold my field to pay for a substitute for my son, and now they say they must go back and draw lots again.'

At the Château they heard little news, for the authorities of Castres were doing their best to conceal the situation. 'One is reduced to looking for the truth in the gazettes, through the darkness of lies or the light of a semi-confession.' Letters,

although censored, sometimes allowed themselves a few
words with double meanings. 'People met then to try and
understand, and turned every sentence over and over.'

Soon it was no longer possible to ignore the Battle of
Orthez, Soult's retreat and Wellington's march on Toulouse.
A great battle might be going to start a few leagues away
from Hauterive. A fine subject to stir the children's imagination! In the courtyard of the château, Léontine, her brother
and sisters played only one game now: War. They built a
redoubt, made pretence guns out of old gutter-pipes and
spent their nights dreaming of charges and volleys of musket
fire.

Meanwhile, between Castres and Toulouse, messages were
becoming more frequent; life seemed to hang on the arrival
of the post. On Easter Day, 1814, M. de Villeneuve, who
appeared to be listening to a distant sound, said to a peasant,
'One can hear it louder now, can't one?' 'What can one
hear?' asked the little girl. 'The guns: they've been fighting
before Toulouse ever since this morning.'

When the bell rang for High Mass all the family went to
church. At the moment of the benediction the curé pronounced these words, 'Let us pray for the living and the
dead', and a few sobs answered him. There were mothers in
mourning there, and others who had their sons in the armies.
The day went by without news. From time to time the inhabitants of Hauterive pressed their ears to the ground to
listen to the sound of the detonations. In the evening the
artillery fire died down at last; and without knowing which
side had won they said to one another, 'The game is finished.'

It was not until Easter Tuesday that an event occurred
which was to leave a deep mark on the child's memory. Sitting near a window, she was busy reading when the noise of
a horse galloping over the paved courtyard made her prick
up her ears. A man had just arrived, shouting, 'We've got
peace! We've got peace!' A few seconds later she saw her
father, her mother and all the family pressing round the
rider, exclaiming and gesticulating. He was an emissary sent
from Toulouse to announce the end of the war, the return of
the Bourbons and the accession of Louis XVIII.

The news was received with acclamation; it spread from

neighbour to neighbour, and soon, like a train of gunpowder, an immense shout of 'Vive le Roi!' ran from one end of the province to the other.

*　　*　　*　　*

The enthusiasm of the damsels of Castres would have been most displeasing to the schoolboys of Limoges, whose sentiments we can gather from a correspondence published by M. Edmond Pottier.

All, or nearly all, of them found it difficult to believe that Napoleon had fallen. The Army, with the exception of a few Field-Marshals, still worshipped its Head, and the schoolboys of that day were very like soldiers. In the twenty-six *lycées* of the Empire education was on military lines. The pupils were awakened by the sound of the drum; they wore uniforms and were grouped by companies, with adjutants, sergeants and corporals, and the Latin classes prided themselves on their drill and firing practice. When they went for a walk they were headed by a band composed of three flutes, two piccolos, a big drum, cymbals and a Chinese pavilion or 'Jingling Johnnie'.

Was it the effect of the uniform, or of the Jingling Johnnie? At any rate all these young men were fervent Bonapartists. The letters that one of them, Henri Philippon,[1] wrote to his father, a Paris official, show the emotion aroused in this small community by the events of 1814. First, the account of an abortive conspiracy.

'March 19, 1814. Last night, my dear Papa, we were in the greatest danger you can imagine. The Spanish prisoners in Limoges nearly set fire to the town. They were to run to the four principal magistrates and force them, at the pistol's mouth, to sign an order for the Cohort and the National Guard to lay down their arms. They were then to pillage everything in Limoges, burn it down like a conquered country and go on to join the English, who, as you know, have taken and passed through Bordeaux. But they were discovered, and every one of them shut up in the church of Saint-Pierre. You would think they were trying to force the

[1] An assumed name, the family possessing these letters wishing to remain anonymous.

doors, they are kicking it so hard. We can hear them talking
from our guardroom. The enemy is still advancing; there is
talk of evacuating . . .'

The Emperor's abdication was soon to make this measure
unnecessary, but the excitement among the college boys did
not die down – far from it. They went marching through the
streets, shouting, 'Down with Louis XVIII!' And their
fencing master, after slapping the face of a young royalist of
the town and challenging him to a duel, went off to have 'a
little binge with the officers'.

The mathematics professor, less bellicose, tried on the
contrary to ingratiate himself with the new regime by dedi-
cating to it some verses of his own composition:

> 'Live for ever, August Prince!
> Live for ever, Long live Louis!'

But this homage brought no luck to the august prince, the
sudden return of whose rival would soon force him to pack
up again. Young Philippon's missives would then be filled
with fresh enthusiasm:

'The shadow of the news of Napoleon's entry into Paris
had scarcely reached the school before all the pupils, by
common consent, had sold their lilies, and those that had
none gave money instead, to buy a tricolour flag. We wanted
to hoist it at once over the school, but the headmaster, M.
Payen, expressly forbade it until the post had confirmed the
news. In less than an hour we had made more than two hundred lovely transparencies. . . . The finest of all was done by
one of the pupils, the best at drawing; he did a portrait of
Napoleon and Marie-Louise, and above them, in the middle,
an eagle spreading its wings, with the motto *We never deserted it*. Now everything is nearly over in the school . . .
there's only one party, only one shout, only one voice: '*Vive
l'Empereur!*'

It would be heard for a hundred days; but after Waterloo
came a fresh thunderclap and another despairing letter:

'June 25, 1815. Yesterday when we came back from our
walk the newspapers had arrived. Our class masters told us
about it, and from joy we were plunged all at once into the
deepest dejection. Complete silence reigned in the courtyard;

we were just having our snack, and the bread dropped from our hands; everybody cried out, 'It's impossible! How could it happen?' The headmaster sent for the oldest among us, and after telling us the news, begged us not to shout anything that might compromise us, but to keep quiet ...'

Difficult advice to follow for young people with hot heads. On the following days, as they continued to go out with their eagles and their tricolour cockades, the royalists of Limoges prepared to beat them up, and the affray was only just averted. To defend themselves, fifty of the senior pupils had armed themselves 'in a formidable manner'. Some hid pistols in their shakos. Others pulled out the metal pegs on which they hung their coats in the dormitory, sharpened them on a stone seat, stuck a cork on the point and hid them in their breeches. 'Woe to anybody attempting to attack us in that state; we were prepared to answer them!' But the headmaster was informed, and prevented us from going out for a fortnight, not to punish us but to avoid the unpleasantness that our behaviour might have brought upon him in the town. For Limoges is up in arms against us.'

With Louis XVIII on the throne again, the town had certainly been seized with a fresh wave of fine royalist ardour. Thousands of white flags flew from the windows of the houses; the Corsican was everywhere referred to as the wild beast, the man-eater. Round his bust, in one of the squares, faggots were piled up, and Limoges burnt the effigy of Napoleon as Rouen had burnt Joan of Arc.

These great deeds were finally interrupted by a regiment of Lancers which, on its way through the region, stopped to put in its word. The mere sight of it calmed things down, since the brawlers knew they would have their ears cut off if they said a word against the ex-Emperor. For in the France now disowning him two sections of the population had remained faithful to him: the army that he had made so great and the young whom he had nourished with his fame.

*　　*　　*　　*

The same could not be said of the veteran dignitaries and officials, laden with honours for the last fifteen years. When the disaster came about most of them hastened to turn their gold-laced coats inside out; some of them even repeated this operation three times: after Fontainebleau, after Elba and after the Hundred Days. If it is true that a fool is a man that never changes his mind, never did France contain so many intelligent citizens as between 1814 and 1815.

A little book published at the beginning of the second Restoration, the *Dictionary of Weathercocks*, lists a few of the newly converted. There were *virtuosi* like Talleyrand and Fouché, traitors by nature as much as by interest; but there were also a number of inoffensive creatures, often quite honest men, who merely wanted to retain their functions, their titles or there prebends, and in order to do so they had gone from one camp to the other. In such troubled times the *volte-face* had become almost a necessity of daily life.

Unfortunately many of these fickle characters wielded too ready a pen. The advice given to criminals and lovers, 'Never write!' is equally valuable in politics, and certain personages of 1815 would have done well to follow it, to begin with Mgr Le Coz, Archbishop of Besançon.

His case is one of the most typical, for this prelate had for many years shown absolute devotion to the Napoleonic cause. Hailing from the Revolution – for he had been the Constitutional Bishop of Rennes – he resigned after the Concordat and was later regularly appointed to the archbishopric of the Jura. Politics apart, he was anything but a 'bad priest'. His pastoral visitations and his many acts of charity had made him popular throughout the cantons of the Dauphiné, where he was known as the father of the poor. In 1813 he published a pastoral letter on the subject of *Love for one's Native Country*, quivering with Bonapartism, and even surpassed this when greeting the regency of Marie-Louise:

Besançon, October 19, 1813
'For the last twenty years or so, Madame, it has been impossible for us not to see the hand of God directing the life – so extraordinary, so glorious – of our immortal Napoleon. . . . No, Madame, the history of the most famous of the Kings of Israel, destined from childhood to take the place of a *prince cursed by Heaven*, does not show us more clearly the leading finger of Divine Providence . . .'

'Physical and moral fogs' were, unfortunately, to darken the horizon of Besançon. The bad news that was spreading apace, the prospect of a siege to be sustained against the Austrian Army, shook the population of the town, who deserted the church in a body during the *Te Deum* celebrated on the anniversary of the Coronation. It was clear that 'the fire was going out'.

It was soon to go out at the Archbishop's Palace itself, or rather it was to be replaced by another flame, and from the prelate's inkpot two unexpected letters would issue in the following spring. The first was addressed to the Comte d'Artois:

April 28, 1814.

'The cherished name of Louis XVIII has been proclaimed in our twelve hundred parishes, proclaimed by every mouth, together with that of Your Royal Highness, but still more in every heart. Never have we ceased in this diocese, Monseigneur, to long for the return of our former masters. But what intensity was imparted each day to our longing by the *sceptre of iron* that has just been broken!

'At last the Day of the Lord has risen, for we do not doubt that this is a miraculous stroke of *the all-powerful hand of God ...*'

These protestations seem to have found little credence at the Tuileries, for when he passed through Besançon in October, 1814, the Comte d'Artois sent word to the Archbishop forbidding him to come and pay his respects. The precaution was even taken of posting gendarmes at his door, and a ceremony took place in the cathedral in honour of His Royal Highness, at which the head of the clergy was unable to appear. What an affront to Mgr Le Coz!

This only made it easier for him, however, to alter course again when Napoleon arrived from the Gulf of Juan, and we are the richer by a fresh masterpiece:

March 25, 1815

'To the Emperor,

'Sire, you really are a prodigious man. This is the cry of all these regions, and this cry, soon to be repeated throughout Europe, will go on through the centuries. In December 1813, in a Pastoral Letter on love for one's country, I demonstrated to my diocesans that by the choice of the French people and by the *sanction of Heaven* you were their true and lawful Sovereign. It is certain, Sire, that *an invisible hand* is leading your Imperial Majesty; it is certain that an angel of the Lord covers you with his immortal shield. Ah, may his spirit of wisdom never cease to inspire you!'

In this correspondence the worthy man has already drawn attention three times to the intervention of the divine hand. Would he see it a fourth time, driving Ney's cavalry towards the plateau of Mont-Saint-Jean and hurling the Empire into a certain historical lane? Fortunately for his memory, he was spared fresh flattery of the Bourbons: in the course of a pastoral visitation he had the sense to contract pneumonia and to die of it, which was really the only way to avoid changing his mind any more.

Let us refrain, in spite of all, from casting the stone at poor Le Coz. If his recantations appear somewhat comical, we must not forget that he was going through a difficult period, in which great soldiers, although bravery was their trade, showed the same weaknesses.

His mistake, and that of most of his contemporaries, was to have allowed himself to be dominated by events, to have yielded to the demands of everyday life. Long spoilt by fortune, believing the fine weather to be eternal, that generation collapsed suddenly under the storm. Having regard to recent examples, is it for our generation to judge it?

One man did so, the only one that had the right: 'There are vices and virtues of circumstances', asserts Napoleon in his *Memorial*. 'Our last trials were beyond all human strength! And then I was deserted rather than betrayed; there was more weakness than perfidy round me: it was the denial of Saint Peter.

'Repentance and tears may be at the gate.'

INDEX

Abercromby, Colonel, 201

Abrantès, Duchesse d' (Mme Junot), 22, 32, 50, 55, 126, 171

Aignan, dramatist, 107

Aigrefeuille, d', 93, 135, 136

Alfieri, Victor, 39

Amiens, Treaty of, 34–5, 205

Amphion, Mme, of Martinique, 95

Andigné, Fortuné d', 87

'Applications' in the theatre, 107–9

Armand, actor, 59

Armand, Mme, opera singer, 107

Arnaud, Baculard d', dramatist, 107, 117

Artois, Comte d', 222

Aubry, Major, 184

Aude, François de l', 49

Augereau, Marshal, 46, 53, 128, 146

Augier, Émile, playwright, 111

Austerlitz, victory of, 187–8

Balbi, Mme de, 202

Balzac, Honoré de, 145, 174, 199

Baptiste junior, actor, 58–9

Barante, Prefect of Carcassonne, 78

Barba, bookseller, 168

Barbé-Marbois, Marquis de, 41, 144

Barras, Vicomte de, 13, 26, 124, 169, 202

Beauharnais, Émilie de (Mme Lavalette), 75

Beauharnais, Eugène, 117

Beauharnais, Hortense (m. Louis Bonaparte), 56, 75, 84, 117

Beauharnais, Stéphanie de, 55

Beaulieu, actor, 115

Beaumarchais, Pierre-Augustin, 107n

Beaumont, Pauline de, her salon, 57

Beaupré, Mlle, 130

Beauvau, Princesse de, 52

Bellart, advocate, 116

Belloy, Cardinal, 45

Belmont, Mme, actress, 94

Bernier, Bishop of Orleans, 48

Bernis, Cardinal de, 119

Berthélemy, historical painter, 154–5

Berthelot, confectioner, 24–5

Berthier, Marshal, Prince of Wagram, 46, 53, 56, 74, 108–9, 125, 148; his aide-de-camp, 182

Bertin, Rose, court dressmaker, 125

Bessières, Marshal, Duke of Istria, 56

Béthune-Charost, Mme de, 202

Beugnot, Comte de, 41–2, 73–4, 197

Boigne, Comtesse de, 55–6, 191, 203

Boilly, Louis-Léopold, painter, 7, 77, 166, 176

Bonaparte, Caroline (Mme Murat), 35, 56–7, 84, 119, 148, 186

Bonaparte, Élisa, (Mme Bacciochi), 78, 84, 148

Bonaparte, Joseph, 38, 119, 147

Bonaparte, Joséphine, Empress, 25, 35, 38, 45, 52, 56, 74–5, 85, 92, 108, 124–7, 135, 184, 186, 189, 196

Bonaparte, Mme Laetitia, 22, 35, 75, 117

Bonaparte, Louis, 38, 84, 147

Bonaparte, Napoleon, Emperor, 7, 18, 21–2, 25; 'Saint', 29; 30–1, 33, 35; Coronation, 37–9; signs Concordat, 44–7, 52–3, 55–8; tries to reform public services, 66–8; 74–75, 79, 87–9, 91–4 and n; stern measures with actors, 102; 107; impending divorce, 108–9; 112, 117, 125, 131–2, 135; building plans, 138–9; draws up the *Code Civil*, marriage propaganda, 147–151; 164–5, 169n, 170, 173, 175, 178n, 186, 188; second marriage, 189–91; tours the country, 195–6; 197, 200, 202; fights the bread famine, 204–12; 213, 215; the Hundred Days and after, 218–23

Bonaparte, Pauline (Mme Leclerc), 22, 35, 56, 119, 148

Bonjour, Curé, 168

Bordier, engineer, 67

Bossu, Abbé, 43, 47

Bouchardon, sculptor, 153

Bouhot, Étienne, painter, 70

Bouilly, Jean-Nicolas, dramatist, 216

P